BEST of the BEST
from
TEXAS II

Selected Recipes from Texas'
FAVORITE COOKBOOKS

BEST
of the BEST
from
TEXAS II

Selected Recipes from Texas'
FAVORITE COOKBOOKS

EDITED BY
Gwen McKee
AND
Barbara Moseley

Illustrated by Tupper England

QUAIL RIDGE PRESS

Recipe Collection © 1996 Quail Ridge Press, Inc.

Typically Texas Cookbook © 1989, The Association of Texas Electric Cooperatives, Inc.; *Smoke & Spice* © 1994 Cheryl Alters Jamison and Bill Jamison; *Some Like It Hot* © 1992 Junior League of McAllen, Inc.; *South Texas Mexican Cook Book* © 1982 Lucy Garza; *Southwest Olé!* © 1993 and *Southwest Sizzler* © 1990 Barbara C. Jones; *The Star of Texas Cookbook* © 1983 The Junior League of Houston, Inc.; *Texas Accents* © 1990 The Cancer Research Foundation of North Texas; *Texas Barbecue* © 1994 Pig Out Publications; *Texas Border Cookbook* © 1992 by W. Park Kerr and Norma Kerr and Michael McLaughlin; *Texas Cookin' Lone Star Style* © 1991 Lone Star Chapter 22, Telephone Pioneers of America; *The Texas Experience* © 1982 Richardson Woman's Club, Inc.; *Texas Home Cooking* © 1993 Cheryl Alters Jamison and Bill Jamison; *Texas Sampler* © 1995 by Junior League of Richardson; *The 30-Minute Light Gourmet* © 1990 by Lulu Grace; *Top Chefs in Texas* © 1990 Sarah Jane English; *What's Cooking at the Cooper Clinic* © 1992 It's Cooking, Inc.; *Wild About Texas* © 1989 Cypress Woodlands Junior Forum; *The Wild Wild West* © 1991 The Junior League of Odessa, Inc.

Library of Congress Cataloging-in-Publication Data

Best of the best from Texas II: selected recipes from Texas' favorite
  cookbooks / edited by Gwen McKee and Barbara Moseley;
  illustrated by Tupper England.
    p. cm.
  Include index
  ISBN 0-937552-62-3 (paper)
  1. Cookery, American--Southwestern style. 2. Cookery--Texas.
1. McKee, Gwen. II. Moseley, Barbara
TX715.2.S69B47   1996
641.59764--dc20   96-7591
                                                         CIP

Manufactured in the United States of America
Designed by Barney and Gwen McKee
Chapter opening photos and cover photo courtesy of:

Larry Murphy, Austin Convention and Visitors Bureau,
Dallas Convention & Visitors Bureau, Pecos Chamber of Commerce, South
Padre Island Convention and Visitors Bureau, Bob Mengel, Waynell Harris,
Gwen McKee and Barbara Moseley

QUAIL RIDGE PRESS
P.O. Box 123 • Brandon, MS 39042
1-800-343-1583

Flags fly abundantly in Texas showing pride in state and country.

CONTENTS

PREFACE

In *Best of the Best from Texas II*, we are proud to present selected recipes from 99 leading cookbooks throughout the Lone Star state. The original *Best of the Best from Texas*, published in 1985, has been an incredibly popular cookbook, boasting favorite recipes from eighty of the leading cookbooks from all over the state. Since then, many wonderful new Texas cookbooks have been published and we were anxious to include them among the best. Hence, *Best of the Best from Texas II*.

Going back to Texas for a second helping has been a joy. We love the people, the countryside, the atmosphere, and certainly the food. The food in Texas has as much variety and diversity as the landscape. If peppers are grown near, well then the recipes are probably going to be spicy; look for good seafood recipes on the coast; and don't be surprised at the decided Cajun influence in eastern Texas, New Mexican influence in the western part of the state, and so it goes. Most people think of Texas cuisine as Tex-Mex; we feel it is more than that. It's spicy, it's lively, it's tasty, it's hearty, it's creative, it's Mexican, it's Southwestern... what it really *is* is "Tex-Mex Plus."

Chili is an important part of Texas' cuisine, and proud they are of it! President Lyndon Johnson, who served it at his ranch to dignitaries from all over the world, wanted chili to be the state dish of Texas; and it was so named in 1977. Its origins go back to San Antonio—not Mexico—so Texans certainly have every right to claim chili as their own. Chili cook-offs and festivals are common occurrences all over the state, with many prizes being brought back when Texans enter contests in other states!

Outdoor cooking stems from chuckwagon days, when that was the only way to cook. Today Texans fire up their grills and smokers as a matter of choice, and enjoy the good eatin' and camaraderie of an outdoor occasion. Throughout this incredible cookbook lies the food of the gods, including many recipes you'd expect to find: tortilla soups, sour cream enchilladas, chicken-fried steaks, chilis, salsas, etc. But whether you want to cook a bit fancy (like Shrimp in Champagne Sauce with Pasta), or dazzle with sizzle (Fiery Tex-Mex Rice), or dabble in ethnic fare (Angus McFarland's Scottish Shortbread), or indulge in a decadent dessert (Chocolate Velvet Mousse Cake), or impress your guests with something fun and delicious (Beer-in-the-Rear Chicken)...well, it's all here. And we can personally vouch for it being Texas at its best!

We wish to thank all the cooks who created these wonderful recipes, and all the authors, editors, chairpersons, and publishers for their cooperation in making this book possible. The Catalog of Contributing Cookbooks beginning on page 319 tells who they are and how you can obtain these wonderful cookbooks.

Thanks also to the food editors from newspapers across Texas who helped us with our research, as well as book and gift store managers, tourism and Chamber of Commerce personnel, and friends who gratiously called in to share their valuable input about Texas food and recipes and cookbooks. Special thanks to our Texas co-worker, Waynell Harris, for some dedicated legwork taking photos, and to our talented Tupper England for her always charming illustrations (that may just be a bit perkier since she is a happy newlywed).

We love Texas and her wonderful cuisine, and our hope is that the recipes herein will enrich your life with the joy of preparing and sharing some mighty good Texas food.

Gwen McKee and Barbara Moseley

CONTRIBUTING COOKBOOKS

Amazing Graces
The Authorized Texas Ranger Cookbook
Best of Friends
Best of Friends Two
The Blueberry Lover's Cookbook
Boardin' in the Thicket
Buffet on the Bayou
Canyon Echoes
A Casually Catered Affair
Celebrate San Antonio
Central Texas Style
Changing Thymes
Chuckwagon Recipes
Coastal Cuisine
Collectibles III
The College Cookbook For Students By Students
Cook 'Em Horns: The Quickbook
'Cross the Border
Cuisine Actuelle
Dallas Cowboys Wives' Family Cookbook
Dallas Cuisine
Decades of Mason County Cooking
Deep in the Heart
!Delicioso!
The Denton Woman's Club Cookbook
Diamonds in the Desert
Down-Home Texas Cooking
Duck Creek Collection
Eats: A Folk History of Texas Foods
Feast of Goodness
The First Texas Cook Book
Fort Worth is Cooking!
The Four Ingredient Cookbook

CONTRIBUTING COOKBOOKS

From Cajun Roots to Texas Boots
From Generation to Generation
The Gathering
Gathering of the Game
Gatherings
Gingerbread...And All the Trimmings
Gourmet Grains, Beans, and Rice
Great Flavors of Texas
Great Tastes of Texas
Homecoming
Houston Junior League Cookbook
I Cook You Clean
Jane Long's Brazoria Inn: An Early Texas Cookbook
Jubilee Cookbook
The Kimbell Cookbook
Lean Star Cuisine
The Lite Switch
A Little Taste of Texas
Lone Star Legacy
Lone Star Legacy II
Low-Cal Country
M. D. Anderson Volunteers Cooking for Fun
The Mansion on Turtle Creek Cookbook
Ma's in the Kitchen: You'll Know When It's Done
The Mexican Collection
More Calf Fries to Caviar
More of the Four Ingredient Cookbook
More of What's Cooking
More Tastes & Tales
Necessities and Temptations
New Tastes of Texas
The New Texas Cuisine
The New Texas Wild Game Cook Book

CONTRIBUTING COOKBOOKS

Not Just Bacon & Eggs
Pass it On...
The Peach Tree Family Cookbook
The Peach Tree Tea Room Cookbook
Perfectly Splendid
A Pinch of This and a Handful of That
Potluck on the Pedernales
Potluck on the Pedernales Second Helping
Raider Recipes
Raleigh House Cookbook
Raleigh House Cookbook II
San Antonio Cuisine
Seconds of a Pinch of This and a Handful of That
The Second Typically Texas Cookbook
Smoke & Spice
Some Like it Hot
South Texas Mexican Cook Book
Southwest Ole!
Southwest Sizzler
The Star of Texas Cookbook
The Taste of Herbs
Texas Accents
Texas Barbecue
Texas Border Cookbook
Texas Cookin' Lone Star Style
The Texas Experience
Texas Home Cooking
Texas Sampler
The 30-Minute Light Gourmet
Top Chefs in Texas
What's Cooking at the Cooper Clinic
Wild About Texas
The Wild Wild West

Appetizers

A popular movie setting near Big Bend National Park, this typical windmill
was a prop for the movie "Streets of Larado."

Almond Tea Punch

1 cup sugar
½ cup lemon juice
2 tablespoons almond extract
1 tablespoon vanilla extract
1 cup very strong tea

1 quart water
1 quart ginger ale
Mint sprigs
Lemon

Mix sugar, lemon juice, almond and vanilla extracts, and tea together. Then add water and ginger ale. Serve over lots of crushed ice. Garnish with mint sprigs and lemon.

The Second Typically Texas Cookbook

Texas Sunrise

4 cups cran-raspberry juice
2 cups pineapple juice
2 cups orange juice

2 cups club soda
1 lime
1 cup whole strawberries

Combine cran-raspberry, pineapple and orange juices in punch bowl or large pitcher. Add club soda. Cut lime into thin round slices, discarding ends. Float some or all of slices in punch. Stir in strawberries. Add ice, if desired, and serve. Makes approximately 10 cups.

Per ½-cup serving: Cal 62; Prot .361g; Carb 15.5g; Fat .1g; Chol 0mg; Sod 6.58mg.

Changing Thymes

The Perfect Pink Punch

1 (10-ounce) package frozen
  strawberries with syrup
1 (½-gallon) container
  pineapple sherbet

1 (2-liter) bottle cherry 7-UP,
  icy cold

Partially thaw berries, until slushy. Put in bowl and chunk the sherbet in also. Stir in 7-UP. Serve at once. Approximately 18 servings.

A Casually Catered Affair

Mama's Green Party Punch

3 cups water
3 cups sugar
4 teaspoons vanilla
4 teaspoons almond

1 (3-ounce) package
  lime-flavored gelatin
1 quart pineapple juice
1 (8-ounce) bottle lemon juice

Bring water and sugar to a boil, stirring until sugar dissolves. Pour into a 1-gallon jar or container, and add remaining ingredients. Finish filling gallon jar with water. Chill and serve. Yield: 50 servings.

Note: Use a sun tea jar for an easy 1-gallon container.

Homecoming

Christmas Eve Peppermint Punch

1 gallon peppermint ice cream
  in scoops
2 quarts eggnog
2 quarts ginger ale

2 cups heavy cream
1-1½ cups peppermint
  candy, crushed

Put first 3 ingredients in punch bowl. Top with cream, then candy, and serve. Yields 2 gallons that children love!

Great Flavors of Texas

Frozen Peach Margaritas

Margarita fans, you're going to love these! They are always a hit at summer parties. Make them ahead of time, keep them in the freezer, ready to serve to your guests as they arrive.

1 (6-ounce) can frozen
  limeade
6 ounces tequila
6 ounces Triple Sec

6 tablespoons lime juice
2 cups fresh peaches, peeled
  and sliced
4 cups ice cubes

Combine all ingredients except ice in blender. Blend well. Pour half of the mixture into a container. Then add 2 cups ice to mixture in the blender and blend well. Pour the blended margarita into a container for the freezer. Pour the remaining half of the mixture into the blender and add 2 cups ice to blend. Place in the freezer until ready to serve. Serves 6-8.

Note: Fresh peaches are a must. Put a supply of peaches in your freezer to enjoy throughout the year!

The Peach Tree Family Cookbook

Orange Frost

1½ cups orange sherbet
1 (6-ounce) can frozen orange
  juice concentrate, undiluted
4 ice cubes

1 cup ice water
3 (12-ounce) cans sugar-free
  lemon-lime soft drink

In a blender container, combine all the ingredients except soft drink. Cover; blend until smooth. Pour into 8 glasses. Pour soft drink into sides of glasses; stir gently. Yield: 8 servings.

Per serving (1 cup): Cal 93; Fat 1g; Prot 1g; Carb 21g; Chol 3mg; Sod 39mg; Dietary fiber 0g.

What's Cooking at the Cooper Clinic

Lake Austin Iced Tea

2 (6-ounce) cans frozen
   lemonade concentrate,
   undiluted
1 (6-ounce) can frozen orange
   juice concentrate, undiluted

1 cup sugar or to taste
6 cups water
2 cups strongly-brewed tea
1½ cups bourbon

Combine all ingredients in 1-gallon container. Blend well. Serve in tall glasses over crushed ice. Makes approximately 13 cups.

Per 1-cup serving: Cal 193; Prot .391g; Carb 32.9g; Fat .1g; Chol 0mg; Sod 6.24mg.

Changing Thymes

Richardson Woman's Club Coffee Punch

1 (2-ounce) jar instant coffee
2 quarts hot water
2 cups sugar
2 quarts half-and-half

1 quart ginger ale
1 pint heavy cream, whipped
½ gallon French vanilla ice
   cream

Dissolve instant coffee in hot water. Cool. Add sugar and half-and-half and mix well. At serving time, add ginger ale, heavy cream, and ice cream. Stir to mix. Makes 60 (4-ounce) servings.

The Texas Experience

Champurado
Original Mexican Cocoa

2 quarts milk
3 (2-inch) cinnamon sticks
½ cup cocoa
1 cup sugar

1 teaspoon vanilla
¼ cup corn meal
½ cup milk

In saucepan combine milk and cinnamon sticks. Heat until almost boiling. Combine cocoa, sugar, vanilla, corn meal, and ½ cup milk. Stir to make a thick sauce. Pour cocoa sauce into heated milk, stirring constantly with a wire whip or a rotary beater (5 minutes). Serve at once. Very delicious served with sopapillas or bunuelos. Serves 8-10.

South Texas Mexican Cook Book

Cream Cheese with Crab

1 tablespoon mayonnaise
1 tablespoon minced onion
1 teaspoon Worcestershire
  sauce
4 (3-ounce) packages cream
  cheese, softened

1 (12-ounce) bottle chili sauce
1 (6½-ounce) package
  frozen crab meat
Parsley

Add mayonnaise, minced onion, and Worcestershire sauce to softened cream cheese. Spread on a round flat plate; refrigerate until firm. Spread chili sauce over the cheese mixture, then shred drained crab meat over the chili sauce. Sprinkle parsley over top. Serve with crackers. Serves about 14. May be made the day before serving.

The Denton Woman's Club Cookbook

Spicy Hot Crab Dip

An elegant entrée when served over rice or in pastry shells.

1 (8-ounce) package cream
  cheese, softened
1 tablespoon milk
8 ounces fresh lump crab
  meat
2 tablespoons sherry
1 teaspoon Worcestershire
  sauce

¼ teaspoon garlic powder
1 teaspoon Tabasco sauce
Juice of ½ lemon
2 tablespoons grated onion
2 teaspoons prepared
  horseradish
¼ teaspoon salt
Dash cayenne pepper

Preheat oven to 375°. Combine cream cheese and milk. Blend thoroughly. Add remaining ingredients. Blend well. Spread mixture in a baking dish. Bake 15-20 minutes. Serve with assorted crackers. Serves 12-15.

Necessities and Temptations

Italian Shrimp Dip

2 (3-ounce) packages cream
  cheese
1 (0.7-ounce) package Italian
  dressing, dry

½ cup sour cream
1 tablespoon lemon juice
1 (4¼-ounce) can small
  shrimp

Mix all ingredients. Use as dip for potato chips or tortilla chips.
Yield: 1 cup.

Deep in the Heart

Clam Dip

*They say that you can't fight success, I'll not try! This recipe makes
clam lovers out of everyone—and will serve a crowd.*

2 (8-ounce) packages cream
  cheese
1 cup sour cream
2 cups clams, drained and
  minced
1 cup broiled mushrooms,
  chopped

Dash of salt
Dash of pepper
½ teaspoon soy sauce
2 tablespoons Worcestershire
  sauce
2 tablespoons fresh or frozen
  chives, chopped

Melt cream cheese slowly over a low heat. Stir and break up the
cakes as it melts.   Add sour cream, clams and mushrooms.
Season with the salt, pepper, soy sauce, Worcestershire sauce,
and chives. Stir well and keep hot over hot water, using your
finest chafing dish. Serve with crisp, rippled potato chips. This
is a prize!

A Casually Catered Affair

Great Guacamole

Try it! You won't believe it!

1 (10-ounce) package frozen asparagus spears, cooked
¾ cup non-chunky picanté sauce
½ cup diced fresh tomatoes
1 teaspoon oregano
1½ teaspoons cumin

2 tablespoons Healthy Choice Fat Free Cream Cheese
1¼ teaspoons cilantro
⅛ teaspoon garlic powder
Dash garlic salt and chili powder, or to taste
1 package dry Butter Buds

Blend all ingredients in blender or food processor until smooth. Chill and serve. Serves 8.

Per Serving: Cal 54; Fat 0; % Fat 0; Prot 5.1g; Carb 8.1g; Sod 469mg; Chol 0.

The Lite Switch

White Bean and Garlic Dip

1 cup canned white beans (cannelli), rinsed and drained well
2 large garlic cloves, boiled for 5 minutes, drained and peeled
1½ tablespoons extra virgin olive oil

½ teaspoon fresh lemon juice
⅛ teaspoon Tabasco, or to taste
Salt to taste
Assorted vegetables, cut into sticks

In a blender or food processor, purée beans, garlic, oil, lemon juice, Tabasco, and salt. Serve with assorted vegetables or chips of your choice. Makes 1½ cups.

From Generation to Generation

 Texas has desert, mountains, plains, forests, lakes, hills, beaches...no wonder people are so entranced with its world-in-a-state landscape. Author Mary Lasswell describes it as such: "I am forced to conclude that God made Texas on his day off, for pure entertainment, just to prove what diversity could be crammed into one section of earth by a really top hand."

Chili Hot Bean-Taco Dip

1 pound ground elk, deer or
  moose
Oil
1 (8-ounce) can tomato sauce
1 package taco seasoning mix
Salt, pepper, paprika, and
  garlic powder to taste
½ each: red and green bell
  pepper, sliced and chopped
4-6 green onions with tops,
  chopped
2 fresh tomatoes, peeled and
  chopped

2 stalks celery with leaves,
  chopped
1 (16-ounce) can Bush's Best
  Chili Hot Beans
1 (10-ounce) can Rotel
  tomatoes with green chilies
⅓ cup catsup
Dash Tabasco
Creole seasonings to taste
2 tablespoons fresh parsley,
  minced
1 small jar Spanish olives,
  pimiento-stuffed, sliced

In a skillet, brown meat in a small amount of oil. Add tomato sauce, taco seasoning mix and other seasonings to taste. In another skillet, sauté vegetables in a small amount of oil. Add a little water and steam until tender. Add beans, tomatoes with green chilies, catsup, Tabasco, and Creole seasonings to taste. Simmer to blend flavors. Add chopped parsley, olives, and meat mixture. Stir to blend. Serve hot in a chafing dish with chips for dipping. Serves a crowd. Delicious!

Note: Can use ground beef as alternate meat choice.

Gathering of the Game

Gazpacho Dip

1 (28-ounce) can tomatoes,
  mashed by hand
1 (8-ounce) can tomato sauce
2 tablespoons vinegar
3 tablespoons salad oil
1 clove garlic, minced
1 (4-ounce) can diced green
  chilies

1 (4-ounce) can chopped ripe
  olives
¼ pound mushrooms, diced
¼ teaspoon salt
¼ teaspoon garlic salt
1 bunch green onions, thinly
  sliced

Mix together all ingredients in a glass container. Cover and refrigerate overnight. Serve with tortilla chips. Yield: 1 quart.

Note: Prepare 8-10 hours ahead.

Deep in the Heart

Black-Eyed Pea Dip

1 pound Old English sharp
  cheese (3 jars)
½ pound butter or margarine
  (2 sticks)
4 cups cooked black-eyed
  peas

3 jalapeños, chopped or sliced
1 tablespoon jalapeño juice
½ medium onion, chopped
1 (4-ounce) can chopped
  green chilies

Melt together the cheese and margarine. Combine remaining ingredients. Stir cheese mixture into black-eyed pea mixture. Heat in crock pot and serve with tortilla chips.

Duck Creek Collection

Texas Caviar

1 pound dry black-eyed peas
2 cups Italian salad dressing
2 cups diced green pepper
1½ cups finely chopped
  green onion
½ cup chopped jalapeño
  peppers

1 (3-ounce) jar diced
  pimiento, drained
1 tablespoon finely minced
  garlic
Salt to taste
Hot pepper sauce to taste

Soak black-eyed peas in enough water to cover for 6 hours or overnight. Drain well. Transfer peas to saucepan, add enough water to cover. Bring to boil over high heat. Reduce heat, allow to boil until tender, about 45 minutes. Do not overcook. Drain well, transfer to large bowl. Blend in Italian dressing, and let cool. Add remaining ingredients; mix well. Refrigerate. Serve with tortilla chips.

Note: This dish can also be served on a lettuce leaf as a salad. Serve with grilled chicken for a cool summer meal. Yields 7½ cups.

Coastal Cuisine

Billy Archibald's Black-Eyed Peawheels

Black-Eyed Pea Festival Grand Champion, 1985.

1 (15-ounce) can black-eyed peas
½ stick butter (or margarine)
1 dash garlic
¼ teaspoon Lawry's Seasoned Salt
2 dashes cayenne
2 (3-ounce) packages cream cheese
2 packages imported ham
8 green onions

Heat peas in melted butter. Add garlic, seasoning salt, and cayenne. Simmer for 15 minutes. Cool and mix black-eyed peas and softened cream cheese together in food processor until mixture is creamy and well blended. Spread mixture onto each slice of ham. Roll green onion lengthwise in ham. Chill and cut into ½-inch peawheels. Serve these delicious Black-eyed Peawheels as appetizers any time of the year.

Eats: A Folk History of Texas Foods

Grand Marnier Cream Sauce

2 tablespoons Grand Marnier
1½ cups nonfat vanilla yogurt
½ cup powdered sugar
¼ cup evaporated skim milk

Blend the Grand Marnier, yogurt, and powdered sugar. Add milk, a little at a time, until you reach the desired consistency. Serve with fresh fruit as a dip, or over fruit as a sauce.

Duck Creek Collection

Piña Colada Fruit Dip

1 (8-ounce) can crushed pineapple, undrained
¾ cup milk
1 (3½-ounce) package instant coconut pudding mix
½ cup dairy sour cream

Combine all in a food processor; process for 30 seconds. Pour into a plastic bowl with a lid. Refrigerate several hours or overnight to blend flavors. Serve dip in hollowed-out pineapple; either using the bottom half to form a cup or cut lengthwise to form a boat. Serve with an assortment of fresh fruits.

Not Just Bacon & Eggs

Dill Dip

1 cup low-fat sour cream
½ tablespoon dried minced
  onion
½ teaspoon Beau Monde
  spice
½ tablespoon
  Worcestershire sauce

1 cup low-fat mayonnaise
2 tablespoons parsley flakes
½ teaspoon dill
Pinch of salt
1 large whole loaf of dark rye
  or pumpernickel bread

Mix all of the above ingredients (except the bread) and let sit in the refrigerator for about 3 hours.

Cut a big hole in the bread, scooping out the middle of the loaf. Fill the hole with the cold dip. Cut up the bread you scooped out and use that to eat the dip. This isn't good, it's Great!

The College Cookbook

The "Sizzler" Dip

2 (8-ounce) packages cream
  cheese, softened
¼ cup fresh lime juice
1 tablespoon cumin
1 teaspoon salt
1 teaspoon pepper
1 teaspoon cayenne pepper

1 (8-ounce) can whole kernel
  corn, drained
1 cup chopped walnuts
1 (4-ounce) can chopped
  green chilies
3 green onions, chopped (tops,
  too)

Whip the cream cheese until fluffy and beat in lime juice, cumin, salt, pepper, and cayenne pepper until smooth. Stir in corn, walnuts, green chilies, and onions. Refrigerate. Make at least 8 hours before serving. Serve with tortilla chips.

Southwest Sizzler

Southwestern Corn Dip

2 (10-ounce) packages frozen corn, cooked and drained
2 cups sharp Cheddar cheese, grated
1 (4-ounce) can diced pimentos, drained
1½ tablespoons jalapeños, chopped
2 tablespoons cilantro, chopped
1 cup sour cream
½ cup mayonnaise
¼ teaspoon Tabasco
Salt to taste
Tortilla chips for dipping

In large bowl, combine all ingredients; cover; refrigerate. Serve with chips. It's that simple! Yields approximately 7 sensational cups!

Great Flavors of Texas

Tortillas Au Gratin

This may be fixed a little ahead of time, refrigerated, then baked before serving.

8 ounces Monterey Jack cheese, grated
8 ounces Cheddar cheese, grated
½ cup sliced green onions
1 (4-ounce) can chopped green chilies, drained
8 (8-inch) flour tortillas
2 tablespoons butter or margarine, melted
Sour cream
Picante sauce

Combine cheeses, set aside. Combine onion and green chilies and set aside. Layer 4 tortillas into each of two 8-inch round cake pans. Sprinkle 2/3 cup of cheese mixture and 2 heaping tablespoons onion-chili mixture between each tortilla. Brush top tortilla in each stack with melted butter. Bake at 400° for 20 minutes or until cheese melts and tops of tortillas are brown. Cool 5 minutes, then turn out on plates and cut into wedges. Serve immediately with sour cream and picante sauce. Yield: 12-15 servings.

Raleigh House Cookbook II

Nachos Grande

1 cup guacamole
½ pound chorizo sausage
1 clove garlic, or 1 teaspoon
garlic salt
¼ pound Monterey Jack
cheese, (1 cup grated)
¼ pound Cheddar cheese (1
cup grated)

3 jalapeño peppers, fresh or
pickled
¼ cup pitted black olives
1 tablespoon minced onion
1 cup refried beans
½ pound tortilla chips
½ cup sour cream

Make the guacamole. Crumble or chop the sausage. Mince the garlic and grate the cheeses. Slice the peppers and olives, and cook the sausage over medium heat for 10 minutes. Drain on paper towels. Pour off all but ½ tablespoon of the rendered fat, add the onion and cook till soft, about 2 minutes. Add the garlic and cook 1 minute longer. Stir in the beans and cook till heated through, about 5 minutes. Heat the broiler.

After placing the tortilla chips on a baking sheet, sprinkle the cheeses over them and top with the peppers. Broil till the cheese melts, 2-3 minutes. Put bowls of guacamole, beans, chorizo, sour cream in the center of a large platter or tray and arrange nachos around them. Scatter olives around them. Yields 40 pieces.

The Mexican Collection

Jalapeño Pie

1 (11-ounce) can jalapeño
peppers
2 cups grated Cheddar cheese

3 eggs, beaten
Salt and pepper to taste

Seed and chop peppers. Place peppers in greased 9-inch pie plate. Sprinkle cheese over peppers. Pour seasoned eggs over cheese. Bake 20 minutes at 400°. Cut into small slices and serve.

The Four Ingredient Cookbook

Chili Parlor Nachos

Eating these nachos—mounded high, mortared together with melted cheese, and napped with steaming chili con carne—is an exercise in manual dexterity and greed. Provide plenty of napkins. In Texas there are some pretty good brands of canned chili for sale, but in the rest of the country, you may prefer to use homemade.

8 ounces unspiced, lightly salted, commercially prepared tortilla chips, or homemade tostaditas*

2½ cups (about 10 ounces) grated medium-sharp Cheddar cheese

6 pickled jalapeño chilies, stemmed and minced

1½ cups chili with beans

1 medium onion, peeled and diced (about 1 cup)

4 ounces sour cream, whisked until smooth and shiny

Position a rack in the upper third of the oven and preheat the oven to 425°. Layer half of the tostaditas in a round 10-inch ovenproof serving dish (we use a white ceramic quiche dish). Scatter half the cheese and half the jalapeños over these tostaditas. Bake 10-12 minutes, or until the cheese is melted and the tostaditas are lightly browned.

Meanwhile, in a small saucepan over medium heat, bring the chili to a simmer, stirring occasionally. Pour the chili evenly over the hot nachos. Sprinkle the onions evenly over the chili, top the entire business with the sour cream, and serve immediately. Serves 4-6.

*Tostaditas are corn tortilla chips, but they are *not* Doritos and they are *not* Fritoes. To make: Fry 6-inch yellow or blue corn tortillas cut into 6 wedges in deep hot corn oil till crisp; drain on absorbent paper and salt lightly.

Texas Border Cookbook

 The name El Paso is a shortened version of El Paso del Rio del Norte—the pass through the river of the north—the name given to the pristine river valley by conquistador Don Juan de Oñate more than four centuries ago. Through this pass, today marked as an historic monument, Spanish explorers found their way into what is now America, claiming it for the Crown.

Salsa Picante

In 1992 the folks who keep track of such things officially declared picante sauce as the number one condiment in the United States, surpassing catsup, mayonnaise, mustard, and the lot. The most amazing thing about this statistic, outside of the fact that it took 'em so long, is that most people have never even had the good stuff! Almost all commercially bottled hot sauces have to be cooked, for shelf-life reasons; and consequently they lack all the vitality, fresh taste, and crunch that a homemade salsa delivers. So make your own!

This recipe is at its very, very best the day it is made, but would keep in the refrigerator for about a week, if you let it, which you won't. Good fresh tomatoes, when you can get them, instead of the canned, make the very best of all salsas.

1 (14-ounce) can of tomatoes
with juice (or 4 fresh)
¼ onion, coarsely chopped
2 green onions, coarsely
chopped
1 large clove of garlic,
chopped
2 tablespoons tomato purée
(optional)

3 tablespoons fresh cilantro,
chopped
2 serrano peppers, chopped
Juice from ½ lime
Pinch of sugar
Pinch of salt

Pulse all ingredients in a food processor to the desired consistency. Yield: Approximately 3 cups.

Calories: 3. Fat per tablespoon: trace.

Lean Star Cuisine

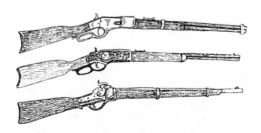

Brie with Sun-Dried Tomato Pesto

1 (2-pound) round of Brie
5 tablespoons minced parsley
5 tablespoons grated
  Parmesan cheese
10 oil-packed sun-dried
  tomatoes, minced

2½ tablespoons reserved
  oil, from tomatoes
12 garlic cloves, mashed
2 tablespoons minced basil
  leaves

Chill Brie thoroughly. Remove rind from top of Brie and transfer cheese to a serving platter. Let cheese stand for 30 minutes. In a large bowl, combine parsley, Parmesan cheese, tomatoes, oil, garlic, and basil. Spread mixture on top of Brie. Serve with crackers. Serves 16.

Buffet on the Bayou

Cream Cheese and Mushroom Logs

2 tubes crescent dinner rolls
1 small jar sliced mushrooms,
  diced, drained
8 ounces uncooked pork
  sausage, room temperature
1 (8-ounce) package cream
  cheese, softened

Savory salt and season salt, to
  taste
Egg, beaten
Poppy seed

Mix together mushrooms, sausage, cream cheese, and salt. With fingers, mash together perforations on rectangles of crescent rolls. Spread with sausage mixture. Roll lengthwise. Place on dish, seam-side-down and refrigerate several hours. When ready to bake, brush with beaten egg, and sprinkle with poppy seed. Cut each log into 6-8 smaller logs. Place on greased cookie sheet, seam-side-down. Bake in preheated 375° oven until golden brown, approximately 15-20 minutes.

Note: Can be made a day ahead and baked later.

More Calf Fries to Caviar

Chutney Cheese Ball

The combination of flavors makes this recipe one of our top ten. Very Good!

24 ounces cream cheese, softened
1 cup sour cream
1 cup raisins, chopped
1 cup salted peanuts, chopped
8 slices bacon, cooked very crisp, drained well, and crumbled
½ cup green onion, chopped, tops also
4 teaspoons curry powder, adjust to your own taste
Chutney
Coconut
Parsley

Mix cream cheese, sour cream, raisins, nuts, bacon, green onion, and curry powder. Shape into large balls. Wrap and refrigerate. Before serving, top with chutney. Sprinkle with coconut and parsley. Serve with unsalted crackers.

More Calf Fries to Caviar

Raspberry Cheese Ball

1 (8-ounce) package cream cheese, softened
2 tablespoons sherry
¼ cup chopped walnuts
¼ cup seedless raspberry preserves

Combine cream cheese, sherry and walnuts, mixing until well blended. Chill mixture for 30 minutes. At serving time, shape into a ball. Make a hollow on the top of the ball. Spoon preserves into hollow and around sides of ball. Serve with club crackers. Serves 24.

Per serving: Cal 60; Prot 1.82g; Carb 3.19g; Fat 5g; Chol 6.23mg; Sod 34.6mg.

Changing Thymes

Seafood Spread

1 (8-ounce) package cream cheese, softened
1/3 cup mayonnaise
1/3 cup sour cream
3 hard-boiled eggs, mashed
1 (8-ounce) can crabmeat, flaked
1 (8-ounce) can tiny shrimp, drained and chopped
1/4 onion, very finely chopped
1 stalk celery, very finely chopped
1 teaspoon Creole seasoning
Several dashes Tabasco

Combine cream cheese, mayonnaise, sour cream, and boiled eggs in mixer bowl. Beat until fairly smooth. Add crabmeat, shrimp, onion, celery, Creole seasoning, and Tabasco; mix well. Serve with crackers; this can also be used as a dip or to make good sandwiches.

I Cook - You Clean

Smoked Salmon Spread

Super, especially if you have Alaskan salmon.

1 (15½-ounce) can salmon or approximately 15 ounces leftover smoked or baked salmon
2 teaspoons prepared horseradish
½ medium onion, grated
1 tablespoon lemon juice
1/4 teaspoon liquid smoke
3 dashes Tabasco
1 (8-ounce) package cream cheese, softened
1/3 cup chopped pecans
3 tablespoons minced parsley

Drain and flake salmon. Combine next 6 ingredients and blend with salmon. Combine pecans and parsley. Mound the salmon on serving plate and sprinkle with nut mixture, pressing them into the salmon. Chill and serve with crackers. May be made the night before it is to be served or frozen to use at a later time.

Calories: 1825; Chol: 400mg; Sod: 2900mg

Cook 'Em Horns: The Quickbook

Shrimp-Crab Mousse

1 (10¾-ounce) can
condensed cream of
mushroom soup
1 (8-ounce) package cream
cheese
1 envelope unflavored gelatin

1 cup finely chopped onion
1 cup finely chopped celery
1 cup real mayonnaise
1 (6-ounce) can lump crab
meat
1 cup cooked salad shrimp

In saucepan, heat soup, cream cheese, and gelatin until warm and blended. Working with ½ mixture at a time, add remaining ingredients; mix until smooth. Grease a favorite seafood mold very well; fill with mousse mixture. Chill overnight. Unmold and garnish as desired. Serve with crackers or vegetable sticks. Serves 10-12.

Coastal Cuisine

Blue Cheese Cake

2 tablespoons butter or
  margarine
1 cup crushed cheese
  crackers
16 ounces cream cheese,
  room temperature
8 ounces blue cheese
3 eggs

¼ cup flour
½ teaspoon salt
¼ cup medium picante sauce
1 cup sour cream
½ cup chopped green onions
½ cup chopped walnuts
Parsley, cherry tomatoes or
  additional walnuts for garnish

Preheat oven to 325°. Butter an 8-inch springform pan. Sprinkle cracker crumbs on the bottom and sides. Blend cheeses, eggs, flour, salt, picante sauce, and sour cream together in a mixing bowl. Fold in the onions. Pour the mixture into the prepared pan and sprinkle with walnuts. Bake 1 hour. Cool and chill overnight. Garnish with parsley and tomato roses, or with additional chopped green onions, if desired. Serve at room temperature on crackers. Serves 20.

From Generation to Generation

Spinach-Stuffed Mushrooms

1 pound extra-large
  mushrooms
Vegetable cooking spray
1 (10-ounce) box frozen
  chopped spinach, thawed
3 tablespoons blue cheese
  fat-free salad dressing

1 tablespoon egg substitute
½ cup shredded Mozzarella
  cheese
¼ teaspoon salt
¼ teaspoon pepper
2 tablespoons bread crumbs
2 teaspoons melted margarine

Wipe the mushrooms with a damp paper towel. Remove the stems; chop finely and set aside. Coat the mushroom caps with the cooking spray and place the caps, stem-side-up, in a glass baking dish. Squeeze the spinach to remove most of the water; combine with the chopped mushroom stems. Combine the remaining ingredients, except bread crumbs and margarine. Mix with the spinach mixture. Mound the filling into the mushroom caps. Mix the bread crumbs and the margarine and sprinkle lightly over top of the spinach filling. Bake uncovered at 325° for 25 minutes. Three grams of fat per serving. Serves 4.

New Tastes of Texas

Sizzling Expensive Mushrooms

The name may draw attention to these mushrooms, but it's the flavor that you'll remember.

¼ pound oyster mushrooms
¼ pound shiitake
  mushrooms, stems removed
  and sliced
¼ pound Portobello
  mushrooms, stems removed
  and roughly chopped
¼ pound chanterelle
  mushrooms
½ red onion, sliced
1½ teaspoons minced garlic
2 tablespoons olive oil
1 teaspoon chopped fresh
  rosemary

1 teaspoon chopped fresh
  sage
1 teaspoon chopped fresh
  parsely
½ teaspoon chopped fresh
  thyme
1 tablespoon balsamic vinegar
A scant ½ cup dry white
  wine, or to taste
8 slices crusty bread, toasted
  on grill (optional)

Combine all ingredients except wine and bread in a non-metallic bowl. Place a fajita sizzle pan or a cast-iron skillet on the grill and heat until pan becomes very hot. Empty mushroom mixture onto hot pan and close grill cover. Cook until mushrooms are tender (about 5 minutes). Remove from grill and splash with wine to sizzle. Serve on fajita sizzle pan with toasted bread slices. Serves 3.

Recipe from Restaurant Biga, San Antonio.

San Antonio Cuisine

Tortilla Rollups

1 (8-ounce) package cream
  cheese, softened
1 teaspoon taco seasoning

⅓ cup picante sauce
12 flour tortillas

Beat cream cheese until smooth. Add taco seasoning, picante sauce and mix well. Spread mixture on each tortilla. Roll tortillas tightly. Place seam-side-down in airtight container. Chill at least 2 hours. Slice each roll into 1-inch slices forming a pinwheel. Arrange on plate to serve.

More of the Four Ingredient Cookbook

Tortilla Crisps

These little crisps may be used with soups and salads or made into a wonderful appetizer when spread with a cheese topping and reheated.

6 (10-ounce) flour tortillas
½ cup melted butter or
  margarine

½ cup corn oil

Cut each tortilla into 8 pie-shaped pieces. Place in a medium mixing bowl. Combine butter or margarine and oil, pour over tortilla pieces and soak for 20-30 minutes. Place pieces on a cookie sheet and bake at 400° for 10-12 minutes.

CHEESE TOPPING:

3 ounces shredded Cheddar
  cheese
3 tablespoons chopped ripe
  olives

¼ cup finely chopped green
  onion
½ cup mayonnaise

Combine ingredients, spread on Tortilla Crisps and bake at 400° for 3-4 minutes. Yield: 48 pieces.

More Tastes & Tales

In 1691 San Antonio was a remote Indian camp on a gentle river the Payaya Indians called Yanaguana—"The Clear Water." A Spanish explorer and a Franciscan padre discovered it on the feastday of St. Anthony and named it "San Antonio."

Mother's Cheese Straws

1 cup grated sharp Cheddar
  cheese
½ cup butter (do not
  substitute)
1 cup flour

1 egg yolk
½ - 1 teaspoon salt
Cayenne   .
Paprika

Mix together all ingredients except paprika. Chill. Roll out dough to approximately ⅛-inch thick. Slice into strips. Bake on cookie sheet at 400° for about 10 minutes. When done, sprinkle with paprika. Let cool on wire racks. Store in a tightly covered tin box and they will keep for weeks. Makes approximately 75 (½ x 2-inch) cheese straws.

Houston Junior League Cookbook

Mexican Party Mix

4 tablespoons margarine
2 teaspoons chili powder
¼ teaspoon garlic salt
¼ teaspoon onion salt
7 cups Kellogg's Crispix

2 cups Chili Cheese Fritos
¼ cup Parmesan cheese,
  grated
¾ cup peanuts

Melt margarine in microwave or saucepan; add the spices. Toss cereal, Fritos, and peanuts in a 9x13-inch pan or roaster pan. Pour margarine mixture over and toss to coat thoroughly. Bake in preheated oven at 250° for 15 minutes. Remove from oven; toss with Parmesan cheese to coat and return to oven for 30 minutes longer. Stir after 15 minutes. Spread on paper towels to cool. Yields about 10 cups.

The Mexican Collection

 You can still mosey through Judge Roy Bean's Jersey Lilly bar, courtroom, billiard parlor and jail in Del Rio. In 1885, he was The Law West of the Pecos in a county three times the size of Rhode Island and ten times as tough.

Zucchini Appetizers

3 cups zucchini, (about 4 small) unpeeled and sliced thin
1 cup prepared biscuit mix
½ cup finely chopped onion
¾ cup grated Parmesan cheese
2 tablespoons snipped parsley
4 eggs, beaten
½ teaspoon salt
½ teaspoon seasoned salt
Couple of dashes pepper, both black and cayenne
½ cup vegetable oil

Mix all ingredients together and spread in a greased 9x13-inch pan. Bake at 350° for about 25 minutes, or until golden brown. Makes about 4 dozen 2x1-inch appetizers. Serve hot out of the oven. Can be made ahead and reheated.

Collectibles III

Cricket's Marinated Shrimp

1 pound cleaned undercooked shrimp
1 medium onion, thinly sliced
1 lemon, thinly sliced
½ cup white vinegar
¼ cup water
2 teaspoons salt or to taste
1 teaspoon sugar
½ teaspoon dry mustard
¼ teaspoon ginger
½ teaspoon whole black pepper
1 bay leaf
Dash of Tabasco
¼ cup lemon juice
½ cup salad oil

Combine all ingredients and marinate for at least 24 hours. Turn at least twice. This will keep for 2 days in the refrigerator if tightly covered. (For 3 pounds of shrimp, use 1½ times the amount of marinade; for 9 pounds, use 4 times the amount.) Each pound serves 3-4.

The Star of Texas Cookbook

Bacon Appetizers

25 slices thin Roman Meal
  Bread
6 ounces cream cheese with
  chives, softened

1 tablespoon mayonnaise
25 slices bacon
Chopped parsley for garnish

Trim crusts from bread. Blend cream cheese with mayonnaise in bowl. Spread lightly on bread. Roll bread up to enclose filling. Wrap 1 slice of bacon around each bread roll; secure with toothpick if necessary. Place on rack in baking pan. Bake at 350° until bacon is crisp. Garnish with chopped fresh parsley. Serve warm. Yield: 25 servings.

Approx per serving: Cal 129; Prot 4g; Carbo 12g; Fiber 2g; T Fat 7g; Chol 13mg; Sod 230mg.

Texas Cookin' Lone Star Style

Chicken Bits a L' Orange

5 tablespoons flour
1 teaspoon chili powder
1 teaspoon salt
4 chicken breast filets, cubed
½ cup melted butter
½ teaspoon rosemary

1 teaspoon ginger
1½ tablespoons grated
  orange rind
2 tablespoons brown sugar
¼ cup Contreau
2 cups orange juice

Combine flour, chili powder, and salt in shallow bowl; mix well. Dredge chicken in flour mixture until well coated. Reserve remaining mixture. Brown chicken in butter in large skillet, turning to brown on all sides. Remove chicken; drain on paper towel. Stir reserved flour mixture, rosemary, ginger, orange rind, and brown sugar into drippings in skillet until smooth. Cook over medium heat for 1 minute, stirring constantly. Stir in Cointreau and orange juice gradually until thickened. Add chicken; reduce heat. Simmer for 30 minutes, stirring frequently. Spoon into chafing dish. Garnish with orange slices and parsley. Yield: 8 servings.

Approx per serving: Cal 238; Prot 11g; Carb 18g; Fiber 9g; T Fat 12g; 49% Fat; Chol 56mg; Sod 393mg.

Note: May double recipe and serve over rice as a main dish. May substitute orange liqueur for Cointreau.

Texas Accents

Armadillo Eggs

½ pound Monterey Jack
  cheese, grated
½ pound hot bulk Texas
  sausage
1½ cups buttermilk biscuit
  mix
15 medium jalapeño peppers,
  canned

½ pound Monterey Jack
  cheese, cubed (or with
  jalapeños)
1 box Shake 'n Bake for Pork
2 eggs, beaten

Mix cheese and sausage, add biscuit mix ½ cup at a time until thoroughly mixed. The mixture will become a very stiff dough and should be kneaded several minutes. Set aside. Slit and seed jalapeños. Stuff each pepper with a cube of cheese and pinch the pepper closed around the cheese. Pinch off a bit of the cheese-sausage mixture and pat into a flat pancake about ¼-inch thick. Place the cheese-stuffed pepper in the middle of the pancake and wrap pepper completely with dough, being sure that all edges and ends are sealed completely. Roll the dough covered pepper back and forth in your hands to mold egg shape. Roll each "egg" in Shake 'n Bake until coated. Dip armadillo eggs in beaten eggs and Shake 'n Bake again. At this point, the armadillo eggs may be baked or frozen. To serve, bake in slow oven about 300° for 20-25 minutes. If the cheese begins to bubble out, remove from the oven. The "eggs" will seem soft to the touch but upon cooling will crust nicely. Best served slightly warm. Yield: 15 eggs.

Potluck on the Pedernales

Party Puffs

1 cup water
½ cup butter or margarine
1 teaspoon sugar

½ teaspoon salt
1 cup flour
4 eggs

Bring water to boil in saucepan with butter, sugar, and salt. Remove from heat and quickly stir in flour. Stir vigorously with wooden spoon over low heat until mixture forms a ball. Remove from heat, beat in eggs, one at a time, until batter is smooth and shiny. Drop by rounded ½ teaspoon on ungreased baking sheet. Bake at 400° for 20-25 minutes. Puffs should be light and airy, slightly brown and dry. May freeze. If frozen, place in 425° oven 3-4 minutes to thaw and crisp. Yield: 70-80 puffs. Fill with one of the following:

TUNA OR CHICKEN FILLING:

1 (6½-ounce) can tuna or
  chicken
1 (3-ounce) package cream
  cheese

Salt and pepper to taste
3 tablespoons mayonnaise
Celery or onion, chopped,
  optional

Mix filling together, split puffs, fill and serve hot or cold. If served hot, place in 350° oven for 8 minutes.

HAM FILLING:

3 (4½-ounce) cans deviled
  ham
1 teaspoon onion salt

1 tablespoon prepared
  horseradish
½ cup sour cream

Blend all ingredients together, split puffs and fill. Serve cold.

Potluck on the Pedernales Second Helping

Shrimp Bubbles

1 (4½-ounce) cans tiny
  shrimp, drained and flaked
¼ cup real mayonnaise
1 teaspoon instant onion
½ teaspoon Accent

¼ teaspoon creamed
  horseradish
2 cans Pillsbury Crescent
  Rolls

Mix shrimp, mayonnaise, onion, Accent, and horseradish well. Cut each triangle of rolls in half to make 32. Place a scant amount of shrimp mixture on each triangle. Roll up and pinch dough to seal. Bake at 375° until brown. This also makes a good spread for crackers.

Feast of Goodness

Peter Rabbit's Pizza

Turn your food processor loose on this one.

2 (8-ounce) cans refrigerated
  crescent dinner rolls
2 (8-ounce) packages cream
  cheese, softened
1 (1-ounce) package
  ranch-style dressing mix
¾ cup salad dressing
¾ cup finely chopped
  broccoli
¾ cup finely chopped
  cauliflower

¾ cup finely chopped celery
¾ cup finely chopped onion
¾ cup finely chopped
  radishes
¾ cup finely chopped carrots
¾ cup finely chopped green
  pepper
¾ cup grated Cheddar
  cheese

Grease 11x15-inch cookie sheet with sides or a jelly roll pan. Unroll crescent rolls into 8 rectangles. Line bottom of cookie sheet with rectangles of dough, pinching perforations together to make a seal. Bake according to directions; cool. Combine cream cheese, dressing mix, and salad dressing. Spread over the crust. Mix chopped vegetables, and layer over cream cheese mixture. Top with cheese. Cover with plastic wrap and refrigerate overnight. Cut into 1x3-inch slices. Yield: 5 dozen pieces.

Note: Make the day before and refrigerate. For best results, chop green pepper by hand.

Homecoming

Caviar Pie

2 boiled eggs
1 pound cream cheese,
  softened
2-3 tablespoons Hellman's
  mayonnaise
Juice of ½ lemon
Dash Worcestershire

Dash Tabasco
2 bunches green onions
  sliced, green tops too (keep
  separate)
1 (4-ounce) jar of caviar, the
  red is pretty for Christmas

Grate the boiled egg whites and yolks separately and set aside. Mix cream cheese, mayonnaise, lemon, Worcestershire, and Tabasco. Add the white part of the onion. In a shallow glass bowl, make layers in the following order: cream cheese, caviar, egg white, egg yolk. Sprinkle green onion on top of second layer. Serve with Melba toast. Yield: 3 cups.

The Kimbell Cookbook

Queso Especial

Excellent!

1 small can evaporated milk
1 can Campbell's Cream of
  Chicken Soup
1 package (or 2 tablespoons)
  ranch dressing mix

1 (4-ounce) can chopped mild
  green chilies
1 large jar pimentos
1 pound Velvetta

Stir the milk, soup, dressing mix, chilies, and pimentos together over low heat first, then add the cheese, cut into small chunks, and heat until melted and blended. Stir often. If you have one, use a burner pad to protect from scorching. They are valuable for cheese dip, as well as cooking beans. Your microwave can do the job as well.

The Mexican Collection

Bread and Breakfast

Located at Fort Worth's Stockyards, Billy Bob's Texas is the largest honky tonk
in the world.

Texas Beer Bread

3 cups self-rising flour
¼ cup sugar
1 can Lite beer

1 egg, beaten
1 tablespoon water
Melted butter

Mix flour and sugar in bowl. Add beer; watch it foam, and mix just until blended. Pour into buttered loaf pan, preferably glass. Combine egg with water and brush top of loaf. Let rise 10 minutes. Bake at 350° for 40-45 minutes. Brush top with butter while hot. Great for last minute.

Lone Star Legacy

Mary Kay's Brittle Bread

2¾ cups flour
¾ teaspoon salt
2 tablespoons sugar
½ teaspoon baking soda

½ cup unsalted butter, softened
1 (8-ounce) carton plain yogurt (low fat)

Sift flour, salt, sugar, and soda together. Cut in butter until mix is the texture of cornmeal. Mix in yogurt until dough forms a soft ball. Chill 2-3 hours or freeze 30 minutes before continuing (I usually make 2 packages for easier handling). Roll dough out on well-floured board to thickness of pie crust. Bake 450° for 5 minutes on ungreased baking sheet. Cool on rack; salt slightly. When additional dough is baked, pile on a large jelly-roll-like sheet. When oven has cooled to 150°, return crackers to oven and leave overnight. Very important.

The Taste of Herbs

Cream Cheese Bread

1 cup sour cream	2 packages dry yeast
½ cup sugar	½ cup warm water
1 teaspoon salt	2 eggs, beaten
½ cup melted butter	4 cups flour

Heat sour cream on low heat; stir in sugar, salt, and butter—cool. Sprinkle yeast over warm water in a large mixing bowl, stirring until yeast dissolves. Add sour cream mixture, eggs, and flour; mix well. Cover tightly and refrigerate overnight.

Next day, divide dough into 4 equal parts; roll each part out on a floured surface into a 12x8-inch rectangle. Spread ¼ of the filling on each rectangle. Roll up jelly-roll fashion, beginning at long sides. Pinch edges together and fold ends under slightly. Place the rolls, seam-side-down, on greased baking sheets. Cover and let rise in a warm place until doubled, about an hour.

Best of Friends

Orange Bread

CANDIED ORANGE PEEL:

3 orange skins cut into thin strips	Water
	½ cup sugar

Peel oranges with a potato peeler to keep free of the bitter white pith. Cut peels into match stick-like pieces. Cover the peel with water in a saucepan, and boil for 10-15 minutes. Drain water from peel, add sugar, and simmer for 15-20 minutes, stirring occasionally.

2 cups flour, sifted	1 cup milk
1 cup sugar	1 cup Candied Orange Peel
2 teaspoons baking powder	1 egg
¼ teaspoon salt	

Sift all dry ingredients together. Add 1 cup candied orange peel. Add milk and egg and stir well. Place in a greased 4 ½x8 ½-inch loaf pan. Sprinkle lightly with sugar. Let stand 10-20 minutes. Bake at 350° for about 1 hour. Makes 1 loaf.

Pass it On...

Banana-Pecan Coffee Cake

2 eggs
½ cup shortening
1½ cups sugar
3 bananas, mashed
1 teaspoon vanilla extract
1 teaspoon soda
¼ cup buttermilk

1½ cups flour
¾ teaspoon salt
1 cup chopped pecans
1 cup packed brown sugar
½ cup margarine
1 (3-ounce) can coconut

Beat eggs, shortening, sugar, bananas, and vanilla in mixer bowl until well blended. Add soda dissolved in buttermilk; mix well. Add flour and salt; beat until well mixed. Stir in pecans. Pour into greased and floured 9x13-inch baking pan. Combine brown sugar, margarine, and coconut in saucepan. Cook over low heat until butter melts, stirring constantly. Spoon over batter. Bake at 350° for 45 minutes. This coffee cake gets better the older it gets. Yield: 15 servings.

Approx per serving: Cal 403; Prot 3g; Carb 53g; Fiber 2 g; T Fat 21g; 46% Fat; Chol 29mg; Sod 255mg.

Texas Accents

Memorable Banana Nut Bread

1½ cups flour
¾ cup Egg Beaters
½ cup light corn syrup
½-1 cup sugar
1 heaping cup bananas,
   mashed

1 teaspoon each: vanilla,
   soda, and baking powder
¼ cup 1% fat buttermilk
1 cup Grape Nuts
Pam no-stick cooking spray

Mix all ingredients; bake in large sprayed loaf pan at 350° for 50-60 minutes. Do not over-bake. Test for doneness with toothpick. Serves 16.

Per Serving: Cal 144; Fat 0.1g; 0% Fat; Prot 2g; Carb 34g; Sod 84mg; Chol 0.18mg.

The Lite Switch

Rich Pineapple Coffee Cake

Your guests will want this moist, very rich coffee cake recipe!

1½ cups sugar
2 cups flour
1 teaspoon baking soda
½ teaspoon salt
2 eggs, beaten

2 cups crushed pineapple,
 slightly drained
½ cup brown sugar
½ cup chopped pecans

TOPPING:
½ cup margarine
¾ cup sugar

1 cup evaporated milk
½ teaspoon vanilla

Preheat oven to 325°. In a large mixing bowl, combine sugar, flour, soda, salt, eggs, and pineapple. In a greased and floured 7x11-inch pan, pour mixture. In a separate bowl, mix brown sugar and pecans. Sprinkle over batter. Bake 30 minutes. Begin making topping about 10 minutes before cake is done. In a saucepan, mix together margarine, sugar, and evaporated milk. Boil over medium low heat for 2 minutes. Stir in vanilla. Spoon over hot cake. Yield: 8 servings.

Variation: Use ½ Topping.

Celebrate San Antonio

Date Rich Bran Bread

2 cups flour
¾ cup brown sugar, firmly
 packed
2 teaspoons soda
½ teaspoon salt

1½ cups bran cereal
1 cup dates, chopped
½ cup chopped pecans
1½ cups buttermilk

Combine all ingredients in a large bowl except milk. Stir well to combine. Add milk and mix well. Spoon into 3 well greased No. 2 cans. Cover tops of cans with foil. Bake at 350° for 60-70 minutes or until tops spring back when lightly touched in center. Remove from cans immediately.

Note: This bread can also be baked in a loaf pan. It has a spreadable texture and is very good spread with cream cheese.

Not Just Bacon & Eggs

Strawberry Bread with Spread

2 (10-ounce) packages frozen
   sliced strawberries, thawed
3 cups all-purpose flour
1 teaspoon baking soda
1 teaspoon cinnamon
2 cups sugar

1 teaspoon salt
1¼ cups vegetable oil
4 eggs, beaten
1 teaspoon red food coloring
Spread (recipe below)

Measure out ½ cup strawberry juice and reserve for spread. Mix all dry ingredients together. Make a hole in center of mixture. Pour strawberries, oil and eggs into the hole. Mix by hand until all ingredients are combined. Add food coloring. Mix well. Pour into 2 greased and floured 9x5x3-inch loaf pans. Bake at 350 for 1 hour. Cool thoroughly.

SPREAD:

½ cup reserved strawberry
   juice

1 (8-ounce) package cream
   cheese, softened

Mix until spreading consistency is obtained. Spread on cooled slices of strawberry bread.

Amazing Graces

Blueberry Bundt Delight

1¼ cups fresh blueberries	1 teaspoon baking powder
⅓ cup sugar	1 teaspoon soda
2 tablespoons cornstarch	½ teaspoon salt
1 teaspoon almond extract	1 (8-ounce) carton sour cream
½ cup softened butter	1 teaspoon almond extract
1 cup sugar	½ cup finely chopped, sliced
2 eggs	almonds
2 cups flour	Glaze (recipe follows)

Combine blueberries, ⅓ cup sugar, 1 teaspoon almond and corn-starch in a small saucepan. Cook on low 2-3 minutes until thickened, stirring constantly. Set aside. Cream butter; gradually add 1 cup sugar, beating until well blended. Add eggs, one at a time, beating after each addition. Combine flour, baking powder, soda, and salt. Add to creamed mixture alternately with sour cream, beginning and ending with flour. Stir in 1 teaspoon almond. Spoon half the batter into a greased Bundt pan, spoon on half the blueberry mixture and swirl with a knife. Repeat with the remaining batter and blueberry sauce, adding almonds to top. Bake at 350° for 50 minutes or until done. Let stand 5 minutes and remove from pan. Drizzle Glaze over the top.

GLAZE:

¾ cup sifted, powdered sugar	1 tablespoon warm milk
	½ teaspoon almond extract

Combine all ingredients, whisking well.

Best of Friends Two

The Yellow Rose of Texas was a pretty mulatta slave girl named Emily Morgan who belonged to a wealthy Texas landowner. In 1836 Mexican General Santa Anna claimed her as one of the spoils of war. Legend has it that he pitched his camp in a less than ideal location to indulge himself in her charms, and while he slept, the Texans advanced and crushed his soldiers at San Jacinto. She was indeed "the sweetest little rosebud that Texas ever knew."

Carrots-Oat Bran Muffins

1¼ cups oat bran
¾ cup flour
2 tablespoons brown sugar
½ teaspoon brown sugar
   substitute
2 teaspoons baking powder
1 teaspoon cinnamon

¼ teaspoon salt
¼ cup raisins
2 egg whites, slightly beaten
¾ cup skim milk
2 tablespoons honey
2 tablespoons vegetable oil
1 cup shredded carrots

In a large mixing bowl, combine oat bran, flour, brown sugar, sweetener, baking powder, cinnamon, salt, and raisins. Set aside.

In a small bowl, combine egg whites, milk, honey, oil, and carrots, blending well with a fork. Add egg-milk mixture to dry ingredients, and stir just until dry ingredients are moistened. Spray a 12-cup muffin tin, preferably nonstick, with vegetable cooking spray. Spoon batter into cups, each ¾-full. Bake in preheated 400° oven for 20-22 minutes, or until golden brown. Makes 12 muffins.

Per muffin: Cal 119; Fat 3g; Chol 0; Sat Fat 0. Food Exchanges: 1 bread; ½ fat.

Low-Cal Country

Banana Oatmeal Muffins

1 cup flour
½ cup sugar
2 teaspoons baking powder
½ teaspoon soda
½ teaspoon salt
²/₃ cup old-fashioned oats

¼ cup pecans, chopped fine
1 egg
½ cup milk
2 tablespoons oil
½ cup bananas, mashed

Combine flour, sugar, baking powder, soda, and salt in a medium mixing bowl. Stir in oats and nuts. In a small bowl slightly beat egg; add milk and beat. Stir in oil and bananas. Add to dry ingredients. Fill greased muffin tins ²/₃ full. Bake at 425° for about 15 minutes.

Not Just Bacon & Eggs

Troy's Apple-Cheese Muffins

1 (21-ounce) can pie-sliced
  apples
½ cup sugar
1 tablespoon ground
  cinnamon
¼ cup chopped walnuts
½ cup butter or margarine
½ cup sugar
2 eggs
1¾ cups flour
1 teaspoon baking soda

1 teaspoon baking powder
½ teaspoon salt
½ teaspoon ground
  cinnamon
¼ teaspoon ground
  cardamon
¼ teaspoon almond extract
1 cup sharp Cheddar cheese,
  shredded
¼ cup coffee

Heat oven to 375°. Drain apples; save 18 slices. Chop rest of apples; save. Combine ½ cup sugar and 1 tablespoon cinnamon in small bowl. Coat whole apple slices with mixture; set aside. Add nuts to remaining sugar-cinnamon mixture; set aside.

Cream butter and ½ cup sugar in large bowl; beat in eggs, one at a time, beating well after each addition. Stir in rest of spices and almond extract. Stir in chopped apples, cheese, and coffee. Line 18 muffin tins with paper liners. Fill tins ¼ full with batter. Press 1 sugared apple slice on each. Fill tins until 2/3 full with batter. Sprinkle tops with sugar-nut mixture. Bake about 20 minutes, or until wooden pick in center comes clean. Remove from tins; cool on wire rack.

Note: Can be wrapped in plastic wrap and kept in refrigerator for 1 week, or in freezer for 1 month.

Dallas Cowboys Wives' Family Cookbook

Raleigh House Orange Rolls

These rolls made Raleigh House famous. Patrons who had not had the opportunity to visit for several years asked if we still served the orange rolls before they ever sat down.

7/8 cup hot (105-115°) water	**1 teaspoon salt**
(1 cup less 2 tablespoons)	**1/3 cup vegetable oil**
½ cup sugar	**2 eggs**
2 packages dry yeast	**4 cups flour**

Put hot water in mixing bowl, add 2 teaspoons of the sugar, then sprinkle yeast over. Let stand until foamy, then add salt, sugar, and oil. Beat well. Add eggs and 2 cups flour and beat on high for 5 minutes. Stop mixer and add rest of flour; beat on high, until mixture starts to leave sides of bowl, about 10 minutes. In this way the dough does not have to be kneaded. Cover and let rise in a warm place until more than doubled. Turn out on lightly floured board and roll into a rectangle about ½-inch thick. Spread with soft margarine. Roll up in a tube-shape about 1½ - 2 inches thick; cut 1-inch slices with a floured pastry cutter or floured knife. Place on greased or parchment-lined cookie sheet about 2 inches apart. Let rise again until at least double. Bake at 375° about 20 minutes or until light brown. Serve hot with orange butter.

Note: If your mixer will not take the entire amount of flour, remove dough to a floured board and knead rest of flour in; continue kneading until dough is elastic.

ORANGE BUTTER:

1 pound box powdered sugar	**¼ cup frozen orange juice,**
1⅓ sticks margarine	**undiluted**

Mix margarine and sugar until creamy, add orange juice and beat until fluffy. This butter keeps well in the refrigerator and freezes well. Yield: about 4 dozen.

The orange butter is good spread on hot gingerbread and also on pancakes and waffles. It is my original recipe that I made in desperation. It was too time consuming to squeeze orange juice and grate the rind, as most orange butter recipes directed.

Raleigh House Cookbook

Quick Crescent Caramel Rolls

8 tablespoons margarine,
 divided
¾ cup firmly-packed brown
 sugar
¼ cup water
½ cup chopped pecans,
 optional

2 (8-ounce) cans refrigerated
 crescent dinner rolls
¼ cup sugar
2 teaspoons cinnamon

In ungreased 9x13-inch pan, melt 5 tablespoons margarine in oven. Stir in brown sugar, water, and pecans. Set aside. Separate each can of roll dough into 4 rectangles. Pinch perforations together to seal. Spread with 3 tablespoons softened margarine. Combine sugar and cinnamon; sprinkle over dough. Starting at shorter side, roll up each rectangle. Cut each roll into 4 slices, making 32 pieces. Place cup-side-down in prepared pan. Bake at 375° for 20-25 minutes until golden brown. Invert immediately to remove from pan. Serve warm. Yield: 32 rolls.

Hint: To reheat, wrap in foil and warm at 350° for 10-15 minutes.

Homecoming

Apricot Strudel

2¼ cups flour
1 cup sour cream
1 cup margarine
1 (16-ounce) jar apricot
 preserves

¾ cup coconut
1 cup pecans, chopped
Powdered sugar for garnish

Mix flour, sour cream, and margarine well and refrigerate at least one hour. Divide dough in four equal parts. Roll each part into a 13-inch long by 8-inch wide piece. Use a little flour when rolling out on plastic wrap or wax paper, so you can flip it over as you turn it. Spread apricot preserves along the narrow side. Sprinkle with coconut and pecans. Roll up jelly roll fashion and seal ends. Place on ungreased cookie sheet and bake at 400° for 30 minutes. Let cool and dust with powdered sugar, if desired. Slice diagonally. It is easy to double the recipe and prepare for freezer. Yield: 12-14 servings.

Potluck on the Pedernales Second Helping

Peach French Toast

This requires overnight refrigeration.

½ cup butter or margarine
1 cup dark brown sugar
2 tablespoons water
1 (29-ounce) can peaches or
   fresh peaches, sliced

1 loaf French bread (12-14
   slices)
5 eggs
1½ cups milk
1 tablespoon vanilla

In a saucepan, heat butter and sugar on medium-low heat; add water and continue until sauce comes to a full boil. Cook 10 minutes, then pour into a 9x13-inch baking dish and cool 10 minutes. Place drained peaches on top of cooled sauce and cover with slices of bread placed close together. Blend together eggs, milk, and vanilla, and pour over bread. Cover pan, and refrigerate overnight. To bake, place in a 350° oven for 40 minutes. Loosely cover with foil the last 10-15 minutes if mixture is browning too quickly. Serve with bread on the bottom and peaches on top. Serves 12-14.

Pass it On...

Laura's French Toast with Blueberry Sauce

½ cup egg substitute	8 slices firm bread
¼ cup ½% milk	Vegetable cooking spray
1 teaspoon brown sugar	Lemon wedges
Pinch of ground nutmeg	Powdered sugar

Combine the egg substitute, milk, brown sugar, and nutmeg in a wide, flat bowl. Beat until thoroughly mixed. Dip the bread slices into the milk mixture. Place on a hot griddle or in a large, nonstick hot skillet which has been thoroughly coated with cooking spray. Cook until golden brown on both sides.

Remove to the serving plates, cut the toast in half, arrange on the plates and sieve powdered sugar over the top. Add lemon wedges to squeeze over the top and serve with more powdered sugar. Or serve with the Blueberry Sauce below. Less than 1 gram of fat per serving. Serves 4.

BLUEBERRY SAUCE:

2 cups frozen blueberries	1 tablespoon fresh lemon
1 tablespoon cornstarch	juice
3 tablespoons sugar	⅓ cup orange juice

Combine the blueberries, cornstarch and sugar in a small saucepan. Stir in the lemon juice until the cornstarch is moistened. Add the orange juice and place over medium heat. Cook, stirring constantly, until the mixture is thickened and clear. Serve warm over waffles or pancakes. Refrigerate any leftovers. Makes 2½ cups.

New Tastes of Texas

Larry McMurtry's novel *Lonesome Dove* was reportedly based on the Charles Goodnight/Oliver Loving trail rides in and around Weatherford. Goodnight's 600-mile return by wagon to Parker County with Loving's body helped make the McMurtry novel a best seller and a favorite television drama. Loving is buried in the old Greenwood Cemetery in Weatherford.

Out of This World Pecan Waffles

2½ cups flour
4 teaspoons baking powder
1½ tablespoons sugar
¾ teaspoon salt

¾ cup oil
2¼ cups milk
2 eggs, beaten
½ cup ground pecans

Measure and sift dry ingredients together. Mix oil with milk and eggs. Stir into dry ingredients. Mix until smooth. Add pecans and mix well. Bake immediately or let set in the refrigerator overnight. They will keep well covered for 2 weeks. Easy and good.

The Authorized Texas Ranger Cookbook

Light Pancakes and Waffles

2 cups biscuit mix or pancake
  mix
1 egg

½ cup oil
1⅓ cups club soda

Mix all ingredients together by hand. For pancakes, heat griddle or heavy skillet and lightly brush with oil. Pour in about ¼ cup batter for each pancake. When bubbly on top and dry around the edges, turn over and brown on other side. For waffles cook according to waffle iron directions. Serve with butter and warmed syrup.

Note: This batter cannot be saved, so cook it all. The pancakes and waffles can be frozen. Wrap each pancake or waffle in foil and freeze. To have "just made" tasting pancakes or waffles, pop them in the toaster until warmed.

Not Just Bacon & Eggs

Magic Biscuits

5 cups all-purpose flour
1 teaspoon baking soda
1 to 3 teaspoons baking
  powder
1 teaspoon salt

5 tablespoons sugar
¾ to 1 cup shortening
2 cups buttermilk
1 to 1½ packages dry yeast
3 to 4 tablespoons hot water

Mix dry ingredients. Cut in shortening. Add buttermilk and yeast which has been dissolved in hot water. Put in oiled bowl, cover and refrigerate. You don't have to wait for rising. Bake in desired manner at 400° for 10 minutes.

Amazing Graces

Buttermilk Biscuits

2 cups flour
4 teaspoons baking powder or
  a small yeast cake

1 teaspoon salt
4 tablespoons fat
⅓ cup buttermilk

Mix the flour, baking powder, and salt. Cut in the fat with a knife. Continue to use the knife to slowly add in the buttermilk until a soft dough forms. Pat out the dough on a floured dough board until the dough is two-thirds of an inch thick. Take a biscuit cutter and cut out the shapes. Place the biscuits side-by-side in a heated skillet and bake in a moderate oven for about fifteen minutes. Serve hot with fresh butter.

Jane Long's Brazoria Inn

"Pass the Biscuits, Pappy!" Biscuits

Here is W. Lee O'Daniel's closely guarded biscuit recipe. Miriam thought that he was a knothead, but she sure liked these biscuits.

2 cups flour
2 teaspoons baking powder
1 teaspoon salt

2 tablespoons shortening
1 cup sweet milk

Sift flour, baking powder, and salt together. Rub the shortening into this, add the milk, mix lightly but well. Do not knead. Roll out 1-2 inches thick, cut into biscuits and bake in quick oven about 10 minutes.

Ma's in the Kitchen

Biscuits and Sausage Gravy

3 cups biscuit mix	⅓ cup flour
¾ cup milk	3½ cups milk
½ pound pork sausage	½ teaspoon salt
½ stick margarine	½ teaspoon pepper

Combine biscuit mix and milk; stir. Roll dough on floured wax paper to ¾-inch thickness; cut with biscuit cutter. Place on a greased baking sheet. Bake at 400° 12-15 minutes or until golden. For gravy, crumble and brown sausage in skillet. Drain, reserving 1 tablespoon dripping in skillet. Set sausage aside. Add margarine to drippings; melt margarine. Add flour and cook 1 minute, stirring constantly. Gradually add milk; cook over medium heat, stirring constantly until thickened. Stir in seasonings and sausage. Cook until heated, stirring constantly. Serve sausage gravy over cooked biscuits. Serves 6-8.

Great Tastes of Texas

Katy Kornettes

It has been a very long time since the last Missouri, Kansas, and Texas Railway ran passenger service in Texas. These little corn bread nuggets are now the thing of legend. They were served piping hot in the Katy dining car in a silver dish with a crisply starched linen napkin cover. You will love them no matter how they are served. Miriam sure did.

1 pound white cornmeal	½ cup butter
1 teaspoon sugar	1 quart boiling sweet milk
1 tablespoon salt	

Mix well first 4 ingredients. Add boiling sweet milk. Mix thoroughly, let stand five minutes. Drop through pastry bag about the size of a silver dollar (onto greased baking pan). Bake in a hot oven for about 20 minutes.

Ma's in the Kitchen

Batter Cakes

1 cup buttermilk
2 cups yellow or white
  cornmeal
1 egg

1 teaspoon salt
1 tablespoon shortening
1 teaspoon soda

Place milk in saucepan and heat; add to remaining ingredients and mix thoroughly. Fry spoonfuls in an iron skillet with a little bacon grease on medium heat until each cake is browned well on both sides.

Perfectly Splendid

Flash Pankaka

Delicious with a platter of fresh fruit for brunch.

3 eggs
1 cup flour
½ teaspoon salt
1 cup milk

1 tablespoon oil
¾ pound bacon, fried crisp
  and crumbled

Beat eggs. Add remaining ingredients except bacon and beat. Place bacon and some drippings into an 8x8-inch casserole. Pour batter carefully over the top. Bake at 400° for 25-30 minutes until golden. Batter will form a large bubble in casserole. Serve with a pitcher of maple syrup. Recipe can be doubled in a 9x13-inch glass casserole. Serves 3-4.

Delicioso!

Cowboy Cornbread

½ cup vegetable shortening
2 cups self-rising yellow corn
  meal mix
1 (8½-ounce) can
  cream-style corn
1 (8-ounce) carton sour cream

1 cup shredded sharp
  Cheddar cheese
2 eggs, beaten
1 (4-ounce) can chopped
  green chilies, undrained

Preheat oven to 400°. Melt shortening in a 9-inch square baking pan. Tilt pan to coat bottom evenly. Mix remaining ingredients. Add melted shortening. Mix until well blended. Pour into hot pan. Bake 30 minutes or until golden brown. Yield: 9 servings.

Wild About Texas

Maple Corn Cakes

These pancakes are delicious on their own, with just a sprinkling of powdered sugar, or try them with your favorite fruit preserves.

¼ cup coarse yellow
   cornmeal
1 cup water
3 tablespoons unsalted butter
¾ cup flour
½ teaspoon salt
½ teaspoon baking powder

¼ teaspoon baking soda
2 eggs, lightly beaten
½ cup milk
¼ cup sour cream
2 tablespoons maple syrup
½ cup fresh corn kernels

Combine the cornmeal and water in a small saucepan and cook, stirring over medium heat, until thick and porridge-like, about 3 minutes. Then add the butter and stir until smooth. Set the mixture aside to cool slightly.

Combine the flour, salt, baking powder, and baking soda in a bowl, and mix well. Stir the eggs, milk, sour cream, and maple syrup into the cooled cornmeal mixture. Then gently fold in the flour mixture and the corn. Stir thoroughly.

Lightly grease a griddle, and place it over medium heat. Drop the batter by tablespoons onto the hot griddle and cook until the edges of the pancakes are dry, the tops are bubbling, and the undersides are golden, 1 minute. Turn and cook 1 minute on the other side. Serve immediately. Serves 6-8.

From Generation to Generation

Megas

Surprise family and friends with this easy Tex-Mex breakfast.

5 tortillas, cut into ½-inch
   strips
Vegetable oil for frying
2 chicken breast halves
1 small onion, quartered
½ clove garlic

2 tomatoes, chopped
1 serrano chile, minced
½ white onion, chopped
3 tablespoons vegetable oil
4 eggs, beaten

Fry tortilla strips in hot oil until crisp. Boil chicken breasts, quartered onion, and garlic in water to cover for 20 minutes. Drain and dice the chicken breasts. Sauté tomatoes, serrano, and ½ onion in 3 tablespoons vegetable oil. Add tortilla strips and chicken. Add eggs and scramble. Serves 2.

Joe T. Garcia's, Fort Worth.

Variation: Bake tortillas with Pam, use only 1 teaspoon vegetable oil to sauté vegetables, and substitute Egg Beaters.

Fort Worth is Cooking!

Chorizo Con Papas

Popular potato and sausage dish.

½ pound chorizo Mexican
   sausage (or pork sausage)
6 tablespoons corn oil
1 large potato, diced
1 medium onion, diced
1 sweet pepper, diced

Fresh jalapeño, diced
2 tomatoes, chopped
6 eggs, well beaten
Flour tortillas
Picante sauce

Remove sausage from casing. Brown in skillet, crumbling with fork as it cooks. Remove from pan and drain. Heat oil in skillet. Add diced potato, onion, sweet pepper, jalapeño, and tomatoes and cook until tender. Add sausage and eggs. Cook until eggs are set. Serve on warm flour tortillas. Add picante sauce.

Variation: Add ½ cup chopped pimientos and ½ cup grated Cheddar or Monterey Jack cheese.

'Cross the Border

Tex-Mex Brunch or Supper

12 eggs, beaten
2 cups cream-style corn
4 cups (1 pound) sharp
  Cheddar cheese
2 (4-ounce) cans green
  chilies, drained and chopped

1 tablespoon Worcestershire
  sauce
1 tablespoon salt
½ teaspoon red pepper

Preheat oven to 325°. In large bowl, combine all ingredients; beat until well mixed. Pour into greased or Pam sprayed 9x13-inch baking dish. May prepare ahead of use up to this point; cover and can refrigerate up to 24 hours in advance. Bake 1 hour 15 minutes, or until firm to touch, at 325°. Serves 10-12.

Note: Good served with fresh fruit and buttered bread sticks.

Collectibles III

Torta a La Mexicana
(Mexican Omelet)

1 tablespoon onion, minced
1 tablespoon green chili
  pepper, diced
1 large tomato, chopped
2 tablespoons butter, divided

2 eggs
2 tablespoons milk
1 teaspoon salt
¼ teaspoon black pepper

In small skillet sauté onion, green chili peppers, and tomato in 1 tablespoon butter. Beat eggs, milk, salt, and black pepper. Heat an 8-inch skillet with flared sides. Add 1 tablespoon butter; tilt skillet to grease sides. Pour in egg mixture. Cook mixture slowly. Run spatula around edge, lifting to allow uncooked portion to flow underneath. Spoon sautéed mixture across center; fold sides of omelet over envelope-style, to hold filling. Tilt skillet and roll omelet onto hot plate. Serves 2.

South Texas Mexican Cook Book

24-Hour Wine and Cheese Omelet

Great for brunch or midnight breakfast. Serve with salad or fruit and rolls.

1 large loaf day-old French or Italian bread, broken into small pieces
6 tablespoons butter, melted
¾ pound Swiss cheese, shredded
½ pound Monterey Jack cheese, shredded
9 thin slices Genoa salami (¼-½ pound), coarsely chopped

16 eggs
3¼ cups milk
½ cup dry white wine
4 large whole green onions, minced
1 tablespoon spicy mustard
¼ teaspoon ground pepper
⅛ teaspoon red pepper
1½ cups sour cream
⅓ - 1 cup freshly grated Parmesan cheese

Butter two 13x9-inch baking dishes. Spread bread pieces over bottom and drizzle with butter. Sprinkle with Swiss and Monterey Jack cheeses and salami. Beat together eggs, milk, wine, green onions, mustard, and peppers until mixture is foamy. Pour egg mixture over cheese. Cover dishes with foil. Refrigerate overnight. Remove from refrigerator 30 minutes before baking. Bake, covered at 325° for 1 hour. Uncover, spread with sour cream and sprinkle with Parmesan. Bake uncovered until lightly browned, 10 minutes. Yield: 20 servings.

Wild About Texas

The Mansion on Turtle Creek Breakfast Taco

2 tablespoons corn oil
8 extra large eggs, beaten
  well
1 avocado, peeled, pitted, and
  cut into small dice
1 cup finely grated jalapeño
  Jack cheese

Salt to taste
Ground black pepper to taste
4 flour tortillas
Green Tomatillo Salsa
Red Tomato Salsa
Sprigs of fresh cilantro for
  garnish, if desired

Heat oil in a large skillet (preferably nonstick) over medium heat. When oil is hot, pour in eggs. Slowly stir eggs, scraping bottom and sides of skillet with a rubber spatula.

When eggs begin to take shape, fold in avocado and cheese and season with salt and pepper to taste. When cheese begins to melt, remove from heat.

Lay 1 warm flour tortilla on each of 4 warm dinner plates. Spoon scrambled eggs into the middle of each tortilla. Roll tortillas around eggs in the shape of a cigar and tuck the ends under. Place in centers of plates. Spoon Green Tomatillo Salsa on one side and Red Tomato Salsa on the other side of each tortilla. Garnish with sprigs of fresh cilantro, if desired. Serves 4.

GREEN TOMATILLO SALSA:

8 tomatillos, husked
1 clove garlic
1 shallot
1 serrano chili, seeded

1 tablespoon chopped fresh
  cilantro
Juice of 1 lime or to taste
Salt to taste

Place tomatillos in a large skillet over medium heat. Cook, shaking frequently, for 10 minutes or until skin starts to split. In a food processor, using the steel blade, chop cooked tomatillos, garlic, shallot, serrano chili, and cilantro very fine or grind in a food grinder to a very fine consistency. Do not purée.

Mix well and season to taste with lime juice and salt. If sauce is too thick, thin with a bit of chicken stock.

CONTINUED

RED TOMATO SALSA:

1½ very ripe tomatoes,
  peeled and seeded
1 clove garlic
1 shallot
1 serrano chili, seeded

1 tablespoon chopped fresh
  cilantro
Salt to taste
Juice of ½ lime or to taste

In a food processor, using the steel blade, chop tomatoes, garlic, shallot, serrano chili, and cilantro very fine, or grind in a food grinder to a fine consistency. Do not purée.

Mix well and season to taste with salt and lime juice.

The Mansion on Turtle Creek Cookbook

Brunch Eggs

16 slices white bread
1 (16-ounce) package grated
  sharp Cheddar cheese
1 pound bacon or sausage,
  cooked
½ cup green onions,
  chopped
½ cup chopped onions

1 can Rotel tomatoes
½ teaspoon salt
¼ teaspoon garlic powder
¼ teaspoon black pepper
Dash cayenne
6 eggs, beaten
3 cups milk
1 teaspoon dry mustard

Remove crusts from bread and butter one side. Arrange 8 slices, butter-side-down in baking dish. Cover with ½ of the cheese, then all of the meat, onions, and Rotel tomatoes (drain and cut up). Sprinkle with seasonings. Repeat bread and top with remaining cheese. Mix eggs, milk, and mustard well. Pour over and refrigerate overnight. Bake at 350° for 40 minutes. Serves 8.

Best of Friends

Egg, Bacon & Ham Brunch Bread

6 slices bacon, chopped
6 eggs, well beaten
¾ cup milk
1½ cups flour
2½ teaspoons baking
  powder

½ teaspoon salt
1 cup chopped ham
1 cup cubed Swiss cheese
1 cup cubed Cheddar cheese

Preheat oven to 350°. Brown bacon in skillet; drain. Combine eggs, milk, flour, baking powder, and salt in bowl, mixing by hand until smooth. Stir in bacon, ham, and cheeses. Pour into greased and floured loaf pan. Bake at 350° for 50-60 minutes or until bread tests done. Cool in pan on wire rack. Serves 12.

Note: Bread is delicious toasted.

Texas Sampler

Brunch in a Puffed Shell

10-12 puff pastry patty shells
½ pound bulk sausage,
  cooked
1 cup sour cream
8 ounces Monterey Jack
  cheese, grated
1 egg, beaten

2 tablespoons flour
2 tablespoons dry white wine
3 green onions, chopped
½ teaspoon garlic powder
¼ teaspoon dried basil
2 tablepoons diced pimentos

Prepare pastry shells as directed on package. Place on a baking sheet. Combine sausage, sour cream, cheese, egg, flour, wine, onions, spices, and pimentos; stir together well. Spoon filling into shells, fill to top. Bake at 325° for 30-40 minutes.

Note: Diced ham, cooked diced chicken or cooked shrimp can be substituted for the sausage.

Not Just Bacon & Eggs

White Cheese Casserole

The combination of cheeses in this recipe is unbeatable and different from most casseroles of its kind. It would be delicious served for a luncheon with a generous green or fruit salad.

6 (½-inch) slices of firm textured bread, crusts removed	1½ cups whole milk
	4 large eggs
	½ cup creamed small curd cottage cheese
8 ounces Monterey Jack cheese	½ of ¾ of a stick of butter or margarine
4 ounces cream cheese	

Cut bread into ½-inch cubes and cut the Monterey Jack and cream cheese in the same manner. Cut the butter in ¼-inch cubes. Set aside.

Beat eggs in a large bowl, add milk and mix again. Then add bread, cheeses, cottage cheese, butter and mix well. Pour into a buttered 11x7x2-inch casserole. Place in the refrigerator, covered, overnight.

Next day, bake in a preheated 350° oven for 45-50 minutes or until a knife inserted in center comes out clean. Let set 10 minutes before serving. Cut into portions or spoon onto plates. Yield: 6 servings.

Note: Recipe can be doubled for a 13x9x2-inch casserole that serves 12.

Raleigh House Cookbook

Duke of Windsor Sandwich

Helen Corbett created this light, attractive sandwich in 1958 for the Duke of Windsor's visit to Texas.

2 tablespoons sharp Cheddar
  cheese spread
2 slices egg or whole wheat
  bread, toasted
1 (½-inch thick) slice
  pineapple, grilled

2-3 ounces sliced turkey
2 tablespoons Major Grey
  chutney

Spread cheese on one slice of the toasted bread. Place pineapple, then turkey on this slice. Spread chutney on remaining slice of bread and place on top of turkey. Cut sandwich into 4 pieces and serve. Makes one sandwich.

Fort Worth is Cooking!

Super Subs "House Special"

1 (10-12-ounce) jar of green
  stuffed salad olives, drained
½ cup cooking or olive oil
½ teaspoon oregano
4 large onions
3-4 large bell peppers, red
  and green
3-4 medium tomatoes
1¼ pounds shaved, smoked
  turkey

1¼ pounds shaved, baked
  ham
¾ pound baby Swiss or
  Mozzarella cheese, thinly
  sliced
¾ pound Colby Longhorn,
  thinly sliced (shaved cheese
  is difficult to handle)
1 pint mayonnaise, if desired
Hoagie buns

Slice olives and reserve the oil. Marinate olives in cooking oil and oregano for 30-40 minutes. Thinly slice onions and bell peppers and sauté in the oil from the olives. Thinly slice the amount of tomatoes you will need. Butter both sides of your rolls. Layer meats on one side, top with vegetables and sliced olives and tomatoes. Top with the cheese slices of your choice. Wrap sandwiches in foil and bake in a preheated oven at 350° for 30 minutes.

Note: The amounts of ingredients listed here will serve 16-18 sandwiches. Adjust the amounts to your liking.

A Casually Catered Affair

Soups

Early autumn at Wichita Falls.

Gazpacho

The flavor of this soup is greatly heightened by fresh, ripe tomatoes. In lieu of those, I prefer to use a good brand of canned ones. If you like bell pepper, feel free to add some.

4 cups fresh tomatoes, peeled, seeded and chopped, or 4 cups canned, diced tomatoes
1 cup cucumber, peeled, seeded and chopped
½ cup chopped onion
1 garlic clove
1½ cups tomato juice
1 tablespoon each red wine vinegar and lemon juice

2 tablespoons olive oil
10 pimiento stuffed olives
2 tablespoons Pace's Medium Picante Sauce
½ teaspoon each basil and tarragon
Salt and Tabasco to taste
Buttered croutons, avocado slices for garnish

You may either chop the vegetables and mix all ingredients, or process them, or both, depending upon the consistency you desire. Yield: 7-8 cups; serves 4-6.

The Kimbell Cookbook

Golden Gazpacho with Serrano Chiles and Bay Scallops

Each spring, my friends Anne Lindsay Greer, Dean Fearing, Robert Del Grande, and I prepare a dinner together at the Texas Hill Country Food and Wine Festival in Austin. We each prepare a course, and in 1985, the first year we took this event on, this soup was my contribution to the meal. Soon afterwards, Craig Claiborne printed the recipe in the New York Times as part of a profile he wrote about me. The recipe can be made with red tomatoes if yellow ones are unavailable, and red bell pepper instead of yellow. The soup will not have its distinctive golden color, but it will still taste good. You can also substitute shrimp for the scallops. Chill the soup for at least 1 hour before serving.

CONTINUED

4 oranges
5 or 6 golden or yellow
  tomatoes, blanched, peeled,
  seeded, and diced
¼ cup diced yellow bell
  pepper
¼ cup diced cantaloupe
¼ cup diced papaya
¼ cup diced mango
⅓ cup diced chayote
1 cucumber, peeled, seeded,
  and diced (about ½ cups)

6 scallions (white part only),
  finely chopped
3 serrano chiles, seeded
2¾ cups chicken stock
¼ teaspoon powdered
  saffron
2 tablespoons fresh lime juice
½ teaspoon salt
1 tablespoon chopped cilantro
8 ounces fresh bay scallops

Zest one of the oranges, finely chop the zest, and reserve. Juice all of the oranges. Place the juice in a saucepan and reduce over high heat to about ¼ cup. Reserve the reduced juice. In a large mixing bowl, combine the tomatoes, bell pepper, cantaloupe, papaya, mango, chayote, cucumber, and scallions. Set aside.

In a blender, purée the serrano chiles in ¾ cup chicken stock. Transfer to a bowl, add the saffron, and allow to infuse for about 10 minutes.

In a blender or food processor, purée one half of the reserved tomato mixture. Return to the remaining tomato mixture in the bowl. Strain the chicken stock mixture into the bowl and stir in the lime juice, reserved orange juice, and salt. Let the soup chill for at least 1 hour. Meanwhile, place the cilantro and reserved orange zest in a bowl and mix together. Lightly poach the scallops in the remaining 2 cups of chicken stock for 1 minute. Remove the scallops, let cool, and coat in the cilantro and orange zest.

To serve, divide the soup into 4 chilled bowls and garnish each serving with 2 ounces of the scallops. Makes 4 servings.

The New Texas Cuisine

The name "Texas" is not of Spanish derivation, but traces to the Hasinai Indians who greeted Spanish explorers with "tejas," meaning friend. Called *Texians* in English and *Texiennes* in French, after statehood, Texas citizens were usually referred to as *Texans*; this designation became official in 1860.

Wild Game Gumbo

2 geese or 4 ducks or 12-16
  doves
3 quarts chicken stock
1 bay leaf
4 yellow onions
6 stalks celery
1 cup flour
½ cup bacon drippings
2 green bell peppers, chopped
¼ cup chopped parsley
4 cloves garlic, crushed
1 (8-ounce) can tomato sauce
3 cups fresh sliced okra or 2
  (10-ounce) packages frozen
  okra
2 tablespoons Worcestershire
  sauce
½ teaspoon Tabasco
1 tablespoon salt
1 tablespoon pepper

Boil game in chicken stock with bay leaf, 1 coarsely chopped onion, and 2 coarsely chopped stalks of celery until tender. Remove meat from bones, cut into small pieces, strain stock and discard vegetables. Return meat to stock to keep moist. In a heavy pan or iron skillet, cook flour in bacon drippings until glossy and chocolate-colored, stirring often. This takes about 30-45 minutes. Put this roux in a soup pot. Chop remaining onions and celery. Add to the roux along with peppers, parsley, and garlic. Cook for 10 minutes. Stir stock into roux by pints. Add remaining ingredients, including meat. Simmer for 1 hour. This freezes well. Yield: 4-5 quarts.

The Star of Texas Cookbook

Shrimp Bisque

1 pound shrimp, boiled and peeled
2 cups half-and-half
4 tablespoons butter
¼ cup chopped onion
3 green onions, finely chopped
2 stalks celery, finely chopped
1½ tablespoons flour
1 teaspoon Konriko Creole Seasoning
¼ teaspoon cayenne
½ teaspoon paprika
¼ teaspoon garlic powder
1 cup milk
1 cup heavy cream
4 tablespoons sherry or to taste

Purée shrimp in blender or processor with 1 cup half-and-half. Set aside. Melt butter—sauté onions and celery over medium heat until cooked (5-7 minutes). Blend in flour and seasonings, stirring well. Add shrimp, 1 cup half-and-half, milk and cream. Simmer until thick, stirring constantly. Add sherry just before serving. Garnish with whole shrimp and parsley sprigs. Serves 6 as a soup course.

Best of Friends Two

Black Bean Soup

2 cups dried black beans, washed, soaked overnight and drained
1 cup diced ham
1 onion, chopped
1 carrot, chopped
2 stalks celery, chopped
3 jalapeño peppers, seeded and chopped
10 cups water
2 (14½-ounce) cans chicken broth
1 teaspoon salt
2 tablespoons snipped fresh cilantro
1 teaspoon oregano
1 teaspoon chili powder
1 teaspoon cayenne pepper
2 teaspoons cumin
1 (8-ounce) carton sour cream

In a large, heavy soup pot, place all ingredients except sour cream. Bring to a boil; turn heat down and simmer for about 2 hours or until beans are tender. Add more water as needed and stir occasionally; make sure there is enough water in pot to make soup consistency and not too thick. Place a few cups at a time in a food processor (using the steel blade) or the blender and purée it until it is smooth. Add sour cream and reheat soup. Serve in individual bowls.

Southwest Sizzler

Drunken Bean Soup

1 (16-ounce) package dried
   pinto beans (2½ cups)
3 cups water
1 slice bacon, cut into 8
   pieces
2 teaspoons sugar
2 teaspoons salt
2 (12-ounce) cans beer

1 cup shredded cooked roast
   beef
1 teaspoon chili powder
¼ teaspoon garlic powder
1 teaspoon ground cumin
1 (10-ounce) can tomatoes
   and green chilies, undrained
Salsa
Shredded Cheddar cheese

Sort and wash beans; soak in Dutch oven covered with water by 2 inches for 8 hours. Drain beans and return to Dutch oven. Add 3 cups water; bring to a boil. Add bacon, sugar, and salt; cover, reduce to simmer for 30 minutes. Stir in beer, meat, chili powder, garlic powder, and cumin. Cover and simmer 1 hour, stirring occasionally. Stir in tomatoes and green chilies; cover and simmer an additional 30 minutes. Serve with salsa and cheese. Yield: 2 quarts.

Canyon Echoes

Green Chilies and Rice Soup

This recipe was originally a casserole. We added some chicken broth and milk and it became soup. Green chilies have a wonderful flavor. They are a little hot, so go lightly with the cayenne.

2 tablespoons butter
½ cup chopped onion
1 garlic clove, minced
2 cups chicken stock
1 cup milk
½ cup raw rice
2 (4-ounce) cans diced green
   chilies
2 cups whipping cream

½ cup (2 ounces) shredded
   Monterey Jack cheese
½ cup (2 ounces) shredded
   process American cheese
Salt, cayenne, cumin to taste
Garnishes: Diced tomatoes,
   avocado slices, tortilla chips,
   chopped cilantro

Sauté onions and garlic in butter over low heat for 10 minutes. Add stock, milk, and rice and simmer for about 20 minutes. Add remaining ingredients and heat through over medium heat. Taste for seasoning. Yield: 6 cups. Serves 3-4.

The Kimbell Cookbook

Taco Soup

1 pound lean ground beef
1 envelope taco seasoning
  mix
1 onion, chopped
1 (16-ounce) can pinto beans,
  undrained
1 (16-ounce) can kidney
  beans, undrained
1 (16-ounce) can golden
  hominy, undrained
1 (17-ounce) can cream-style
  corn

1 (14-ounce) can diced stewed
  tomatoes, undrained
1 (10-ounce) can diced
  tomatoes with chiles
  (optional)
1 envelope ranch-style
  dressing mix
Tortilla chips
1 cup (4-ounces) grated
  Cheddar or Monterey Jack
  cheese

Brown ground beef and chopped onion; drain. Add taco seasoning, mix thoroughly. Add without draining the cans of beans, hominy, corn, and tomatoes. Stir in the dry ranch dressing mix. Simmer over low heat until bubbly. Serve over tortilla chips and top with grated cheese. Serves 4-6.

Coastal Cuisine

Tortilla Soup

2 tablespoons oil
1 large onion, chopped
1 large bell pepper, chopped
1 green chili pepper, chopped
  (or ½ of a 4-ounce can of
  chopped green chilies)
3 garlic cloves, minced
2 quarts chicken broth
1 tablespoon parsley flakes

1 (12-ounce) plus 1 (6-ounce)
  can tomato paste
1 (2-inch) square Cheddar
  cheese, shredded
1 cup sour cream
1 large package of corn
  tortillas
Oil to deep fry

Sauté, onion, pepper, chilies, and garlic in oil. Add broth, parsley, and tomato paste. Simmer over low heat for 1 hour. Take out 1 cup of soup the last 15 minutes. Blend with cheese and sour cream until melted. Slowly return mixture to pot. Cut tortillas in 1-inch squares and deep fry until crisp. Drain well and set aside. Add a handful of chips to each bowl before serving soup.

Central Texas Style

Enchilada Soup

A low-cal wonderful creamy soup. Freezes well.

16 cups water
3 pounds chicken breasts
1 cup margarine
1 onion, chopped
2 cloves garlic, minced
3 stalks celery, diced
1½ cups flour
2 teaspoons paprika
2 teaspoons seasoned salt
¼ teaspoon cumin

1 (15-ounce) can tomatoes, chopped
1 (8-ounce) can diced carrots
1 (8-ounce) can chopped green chilies
2 pints sour cream
Tortilla chips
Grated Cheese
Fresh green onions, chopped

Cook chicken breasts in water. Save all of the broth for later. Chop chicken and set aside. Melt margarine in separate pan, add onion, garlic, and celery and cook until tender. Gradually add flour, paprika, and seasoned salt. Slowly add reserved broth. Cook until thickened, stirring constantly. Add cumin, tomatoes, carrots, chilies, and sour cream. Add chicken. Serve over crunched tortilla chips in individual bowls. Sprinkle with grated cheese and chopped green onions. This is a large recipe.

'Cross the Border

Mexican Potato Soup

Great on a cold day!

3 slices bacon, diced
3 large potatoes, peeled and
  cubed
5 cups water
1 cup tomato sauce
¼ cup onion, chopped

1½ teaspoons salt
1 (10-ounce) can green
  chilies, chopped
½ pound sharp cheese,
  grated

Brown bacon. Add potatoes and stir to coat. Add water, tomato sauce, onion, and salt. Reduce heat to simmer and cook 1 hour. Place chilies and cheese in bowls. Spoon hot soup over chilies and cheese to serve. Makes 6 servings.

The Wild Wild West

Baked Potato Soup

6 tablespoons (¾ stick)
  butter
8 level tablespoons flour
3 cups hot milk
2 cups chicken broth or 2
  cups hot water with 1
  tablespoon chicken base, not
  chicken bouillon
1 tablespoon butter

2 tablespoons grated onion
2 cups leftover baked
  potatoes cut into small cubes
⅛ teaspoon pepper
1 teaspoon salt
Bacon
Chopped green onion
Grated cheese

Make a buerre manié by creaming the butter and flour together. Heat milk in saucepan, add buerre manié in small pieces, stirring constantly, then add chicken broth and cook over medium heat, stirring, until thickened. Sauté onion in small skillet with an additional tablespoon butter and add to creamed mixture. Add baked potatoes, mix, and taste for seasoning. Serve in bowls topped with bacon, chopped green onion, and grated cheese. I serve additional toppings in bowls on the tables so guests can add, if they like. Yield: 6-8 servings.

Note: Do not use boiled potatoes. They do not have the flavor of baked ones. Next time you are serving baked potatoes, put some extra in the oven for a pot of soup.

Raleigh House Cookbook

Texas 1015 Onion Soup

¼ cup butter
3-4 large Texas Sweet Onions
  (8 cups), sliced
3 tablespoons sugar
1 cup white wine
8 cups chicken broth
1 teaspoon salt

2 teaspoons pepper
2 cups milk
⅛ teaspoon soda (to prevent
  curdling)
Garnish: Chopped chives and
  chive blossoms, if available

Melt butter in stockpot. Add onions and cook slowly until wilted and soft. Sprinkle sugar over onions. Cover surface of onions with piece of waxed paper while cooking over low heat for 45 minutes until onions are caramelized (golden).

Add wine, chicken broth, salt, pepper, and cook covered over medium heat for 15 minutes. Add milk and soda. Heat thoroughly and serve. Serves 10-12.

The Peach Tree Family Cookbook

Calabacitas Soup

This squash soup was inspired by the vegetable dish Hector's mother used to make.

4 slices bacon, diced
1 large onion, chopped
3 garlic cloves, minced
8 large yellow squash, sliced
2 large zucchini squash, sliced
10 cups chicken broth
½ cup green chilies, chopped
½ cup pimentos, chopped
5 teaspoons ground comino
2 teaspoons oregano

16 ounces frozen corn (or 2
  cups)
¼ teaspoon baking soda
2-4 cups evaporated milk
Salt to taste
2 teaspoons pepper
Garnish: Shredded Monterey
  Jack cheese and chopped
  green onions

In a large stock pot, sauté bacon, onion, and garlic. Add yellow squash, zucchini, chicken broth, chilies, pimentos, comino, and oregano. Bring to a boil. Then cook until squash is almost tender. Add corn. Simmer about 10 minutes. Add baking soda and evaporated milk and heat thoroughly. Taste for salt and pepper. Garnish with Monterey Jack cheese and green onions. Makes 16-18 cups.

The Peach Tree Family Cookbook

Mexican Corn Soup

4 cups fresh corn kernels
¼ cup chopped onion
2 tablespoons butter
2 tablespoons flour
Salt and pepper to taste
2 cups chicken broth

2 cups milk or cream
1 cup grated Cheddar cheese
1 (4-ounce) can green chilies,
   chopped, optional
Tortilla chips
½ cup crisp bacon, crumbled

Sauté corn and onion in butter until tender. Add flour, salt and pepper; cook 1 minute. Gradually add broth, alternating with milk or cream, until thickened. Add Cheddar cheese and green chilies; do not overheat. Serve soup in individual bowls, stirring in 4 or 5 tortilla chips; garnish with crumbled bacon.

Lone Star Legacy

Driskill Hotel Cheese Soup

From the historic landmark hotel in Austin.

4 cups milk
4 cups chicken stock
¼ cup butter
½ cup finely diced onions
½ cup finely diced carrots
½ cup finely diced celery
¼ cup flour
1½ tablespoons cornstarch

⅛ teaspoon baking soda
1 pound Old English or Kraft
   American cheese, cubed
½-1 teaspoon salt
White pepper
Dash of cayenne pepper
1 tablespoon dried parsley
Paprika

Milk and stock should be at room temperature. Melt butter. Sauté onions, carrots, and celery until tender. Stir in flour and cornstarch. Cook until bubbly. Add stock and milk gradually, blending into a smooth sauce. Add soda and cheese cubes. Stir until thickened. Season with salt, white pepper, and cayenne pepper. Add parsley. Before serving, heat thoroughly over boiling water. Do not boil. Garnish with paprika. Serves 6-8.

The Texas Experience

Zucchini Soup

Delicious served hot or cold.

7 chicken bouillon cubes
4 cups water
6 medium zucchini, thinly
  sliced
2 carrots, grated
1 onion, diced

1 (8-ounce) package cream
  cheese, cubed
Salt and pepper to taste
1 tablespoon fresh chives,
  optional

Dissolve bouillon cubes in boiling water. Add squash, carrots, and onion. Cook 15 minutes or until ingredients are tender. Put mixture in blender and purée. Add cream cheese a little at a time. Add salt and pepper. Garnish with chives. Yields 8 cups.

Necessities and Temptations

Roasted Red Pepper Soup

5 large red peppers
3 tablespoons olive oil,
  divided
2 cups chopped onion
2 cloves garlic, crushed
1 (10-ounce) can condensed
  chicken broth

1 can water
½ teaspoon salt
½ teaspoon cumin (optional)
5 whole peppercorns
Garnish: sour cream,
  chopped parsley, green
  onions or chives

Preheat oven to broil. Prepare peppers: cut in half, remove seeds and place cut-side-down on large ungreased cookie sheet. Brush lightly with 1 tablespoon olive oil. Broil 10 minutes (skins should be charred and blistered). Place peppers in paper bag immediately; crease bag securely. Let stand 10 minutes. Scrape away the blackened skins and rinse well. Slice peppers into strips.

Heat 2 tablespoons olive oil in stockpot; add onions and garlic. Cook over medium to high heat for 5 minutes. Add roasted peppers, cumin, salt, peppercorns, broth, and water. Simmer for 20 minutes. Remove from heat; purée soup with hand blender. Top bowls of soup with sour cream, chopped parsley, green onions or chives. Serves 4-6.

Texas Sampler

Tomato and Red Bell Pepper Soup

To serve, place thin slices of avocado or pieces of cooked asparagus spears (or both) in the bottom of each bowl. Then, pour in the hot soup, and garnish with a teaspoon of crème fraîche and fresh sprig of basil or mint.

2 tablespoons oil
1 cup coarsely chopped onion
2 cups peeled, deseeded, and coarsely chopped fresh tomatoes, or 1 (1-pound) can Progresso Peeled Italian-Style Tomatoes with Basil
1½ cups low-sodium chicken broth
2 large peeled and chopped red bell peppers

1 tablespoon chopped fresh garlic
½ cup light cream
¼ cup 2% milk
⅓ cup low-sodium chicken broth (additional)
½ teaspoon light salt
½ teaspoon dried basil
8-10 drops Tabasco sauce
Crème fraîche (optional)
Mint sprigs (optional)

In a large saucepan, heat oil over medium heat. Add onions and cook until tender. Add the tomatoes and cook for 10-15 minutes, stirring occasionally. Add the 1½ cups chicken broth, peppers, and garlic, and simmer for about 30 minutes. Transfer mixture into a food processor or electric blender and purée. Return the purée to the saucepan. Add all remaining ingredients, and cook, stirring occasionally until hot. Garnish with a dab of crème fraîche and a sprig of fresh mint. Makes 4 (1-cup) servings.

Per serving: Cal 166; Prot 4.75g; Carb 12g; Fat 11g; Chol 12mg; Fiber 1.23g; 60% Cal from Fat.

The 30-Minute Light Gourmet

Red Bean and Sausage Soup

We stole the idea for this recipe from some friends who own a fine local restaurant, The Inn at Brushy Creek. I don't know who they stole it from. You steal it from us. (It's too good a thing not to keep going).

2 cups cooked red beans
1 teaspoon olive oil
1 cup onion, diced
3 cloves garlic, minced
6 cups chicken or beef stock
  (or a mixture)
2 cups cabbage, diced
½ cup catsup
4 new potatoes, peeled and
  quartered
1 tablespoon brown sugar
1 tablespoon vinegar
Freshly ground black pepper
½ pound sliced Carabeef*
  sausage

Sauté onion and garlic in oil. Add stock, cabbage, catsup, and new potatoes. Cook until potatoes are almost done. Add remaining ingredients and heat thoroughly. Yield: 20 servings.

Cal: 97; Fat per 6-ounce serving: 1.8g.

Note: *Carabeef is the trade name for naturally raised water buffalo which is ounce-for-ounce leaner than boneless, skinless chicken breast. It is available at whole foods markets. Any lean sausage may be substituted.

Lean Star Cuisine

Golden Split Pea and Sweet Potato Soup

1 tablespoon vegetable oil	¼ teaspoon ground cinnamon
1 onion, chopped	7 cups water (or more)
1 tablespoon fresh ginger, minced	1 large sweet potato, peeled and diced
2 teaspoons ground cumin	1½ cups dry yellow split peas
2 teaspoons ground coriander	6 tablespoons non-fat yogurt
½ teaspoon tumeric	6 lime slices

Heat oil in a heavy large saucepan over medium-high heat. Add onion and sauté until tender, about 5 minutes. Stir in ginger and next 4 ingredients and cook 1 minute. Mix in 7 cups of water, sweet potato, and peas. Bring mixture to boil. Reduce heat to medium-low, cover and simmer until potato and split peas are tender, about 1½ hours.

Whisk soup vigorously for smoother texture. Thin with additional water if necessary. Season with salt and pepper. Can be prepared 1 day ahead. Refrigerate and return soup to simmer before serving. Ladle soup into bowls. Top each with 1 tablespoon yogurt and a lime slice. Serve immediately. Serves 6.

From Generation to Generation

Broccoli-Cheese Soup

½ cup butter or margarine	7 cups chicken broth
3 cups chopped onions	1 pound extra-sharp Cheddar cheese, coarsely shredded
2 cups chopped celery	
4 (10-ounce) packages frozen chopped broccoli, thawed and drained	1 cup half-and-half
	¼ teaspoon salt, or to taste
	Pepper, to taste

Melt butter in 5-6-quart pot or Dutch oven. Add onions and celery. Cook over medium heat, stirring occasionally, until tender. Add broccoli and chicken broth. Bring to a boil, reduce heat, cover, and simmer 8 minutes or until broccoli is very tender. Cool slightly. Purée about 2½ cups of broccoli mixture at a time in blender or food processor. Pour back into pot. Add cheese, half-and-half, salt, and pepper. Cook over low heat, stirring constantly with a wooden spoon, until cheese melts and soup is hot. (An extra-sharp cheese, like a New York Cheddar, adds the best flavor to the soup.) Serves 8. Can be frozen.

Central Texas Style

Peach Tree Chilled Avocado Soup

If I had to name our single most popular soup in the Tea Room, this would be the one. Our customers love it! It is one of our regular daily soups during the summer months.

4 medium ripe avocados,
   peeled and pitted
1 garlic clove, minced
4 green onions, chopped
5 tablespoons chopped fresh
   cilantro
1 tablespoon sliced pickled
   jalapeño with juice
½ teaspoon Tabasco

3 cups sour cream
1 cup buttermilk
8 cups chilled Swanson's
   chicken broth
Salt to taste
Garnish: Sour cream and
   finely minced green onions
   (green part only)

In a blender or food processor, combine avocados, garlic, green onions, cilantro, jalapeños with juice, and Tabasco. Process until smooth. Add sour cream and process again. Stir in buttermilk and chilled chicken broth. Taste for salt. Cover and refrigerate until very cold. Garnish with a dollop of sour cream and chopped green onions, green part only. Serves 12-14.

The Peach Tree Tea Room Cookbook

Cold Strawberry Soup

2 cups fresh strawberries
⅓ cup sugar
1 tablespoon lemon juice
1 cup water

1 cup dry Vermouth
1 teaspoon grated lemon peel
Whole strawberries
Fresh mint leaves

Purée first 6 ingredients in food processor. Refrigerate for 24 hours and serve cold. Garnish with whole fresh strawberries and mint leaves. Serves 4-6.

Buffet on the Bayou

Salads

Sand castles, like seagulls, make fleeting appearances on the beach at Galveston.

Caesar Salad

2 cups bread cubes
½ cup butter
2 cloves garlic, crushed
Juice of 2 lemons
½ cup olive oil
¼ cup vinegar
1 tablespoon Worcestershire sauce
2 whole garlic cloves, peeled
3 heads romaine lettuce
2 eggs
¼ cup grated Parmesan cheese
1 can anchovy fillets
Salt and pepper

Make croutons by sautéeing bread cubes and crushed garlic in butter until bread is crisp. Remove and set aside. To make dressing, shake lemon juice, olive oil, vinegar, Worcestershire sauce and garlic cloves together in a jar; chill. Tear romaine and lettuce into bite-sized pieces. Toss together the greens and croutons. Break eggs over greens and add cheese, anchovies, salt and pepper. Remove garlic from dressing. Pour dressing over salad; toss thoroughly. Serves 12.

Houston Junior League Cookbook

Creamy Gazpacho Salad

A great discovery!

1 can tomato soup
1 envelope plain gelatin
¼ cup cold water
1 (8-ounce) package cream cheese, softened
½ cup chopped celery
½ cup chopped bell pepper
1 tablespoon finely chopped onion
1 teaspoon lemon juice
½ cup chopped pecans
1 cup mayonnaise
⅓ cup sliced green olives

Heat soup, gelatin, and water; blend. Add cream cheese and stir constantly while leaving on medium heat. Blend well. Cool and add remaining ingredients. Pour mixture into a mold or a 9x9-inch Pyrex and let set overnight. Cut into squares to serve. Serves 8. To make a main dish, add 1 cup cooked shrimp.

A Little Taste of Texas

Gazpacho Salad with Avocado Mayonnaise

This tasty and unusual salad is also pretty and would make a nice start to a summertime brunch!

2 tablespoons unflavored
  gelatin
1 (18-ounce) cocktail
  vegetable juice
2 tablespoons wine vinegar
2 tablespoons lemon juice
1 teaspoon salt
Dash hot pepper sauce
2 tomatoes, peeled and diced

1 large cucumber, peeled and
  diced
1 green bell pepper, diced
¼ cup finely chopped green
  onion
Nonstick vegetable spray
1 avocado
½ cup mayonnaise

Sprinkle gelatin over 9 ounces of the cocktail vegetable juice. Add vinegar, lemon juice, salt, and remaining vegetable juice. Dissolve gelatin mixture over low heat, and then chill to consistency of egg whites. Fold in the tomatoes, cucumber, bell pepper, and green onion.

Pour mixture into a 1½-quart mold that has been sprayed with nonstick vegetable spray and refrigerate until firm.

In blender, purée 1 avocado with ½ cup mayonnaise until smooth.

From Generation to Generation

Pickled Beet Salad

1 (16-ounce) jar whole pickled
  beets, drain, reserve liquid
1 (3-ounce) package lemon
  gelatin
1 cup boiling water
1 teaspoon vinegar

1 cup chopped celery
1 teaspoon prepared
  horseradish
1½ teaspoons minced onion
3 hard-cooked eggs, sieved
3 tablespoons mayonnaise

Chop beets to measure 1 cup, set aside. Reserve remaining beets. Dissolve gelatin in boiling water. Stir in ½ cup of reserved beet liquid and vinegar. Chill until consistency of unbeaten egg white. Stir in chopped beets, celery, horseradish, and ½ teaspoon onion, pour into 10x6x2-inch baking dish. Chill until firm. Combine eggs, mayonnaise, and remaining 1 teaspoon onion; spread over salad. Makes 8 servings.

Jubilee Cookbook

Marinated Cucumber Salad

2 medium cucumbers, thinly
 sliced
1 medium onion, in rings
½ cup carrots, thinly sliced
½ cup celery, chopped
1 cup vinegar
2 tablespoons vegetable oil

2 teaspoons Sweet 'n Low
1 teaspoon celery seed
1 teaspoon salt
½ teaspoon pepper
Leaf lettuce, about 6 leaves to
 line salad bowl

Combine cucumber, onion, carrots, and celery in large bowl. Set aside. Combine vinegar, oil, sweetener, celery seed, salt and pepper. Pour over vegetables and toss gently. Cover the bowl tightly and chill for 10 hours.

When ready to serve, drain liquid off and serve in a lettuce-lined salad bowl. Makes 8 servings.

Per serving: Cal 53; Fat 4g; Chol 0; Sat Fat 0; Food Exchanges: 1 veget; ½ fat.

Low-Cal Country

Broccoli Salad Supreme

4 cups raw broccoli, chopped
1 cup celery, chopped
¼ cup green onions,
 chopped
1 cup seedless green grapes
1 cup seedless red grapes
⅓ cup sugar

1 cup good quality mayonnaise
1 tablespoon red wind vinegar
½ pound bacon, fried crisp
 and crumbled
⅔ cup almonds, slivered or
 sliced, toasted

Toss together the vegetables and grapes in a large salad bowl. Mix the sugar, mayonnaise and vinegar in a separate small bowl to make dressing. Pour dressing over vegetables and grapes and stir gently to allow dressing to coat evenly. Refrigerate overnight before serving, if time allows, for flavor to mix. Just before serving, add crumbled bacon and toasted almonds. Serves 10-12.

Amazing Graces

Cynthia's Jalapeño Potato Salad

In Fredericksburg, we have a Wild Game Dinner annually. We developed this recipe especially for this occasion and it turned out to be a real hit! Since then, we have fixed it often and it always gets raves from the men! It is great with barbeque and baked beans!

10 cups cubed, boiled and
  peeled potatoes (about 5
  pounds)
8 boiled eggs, coarsely
  chopped
10 ribs celery, diced
10 green onions, chopped
1 large yellow onion, diced
3-4 cups good quality
  mayonnaise

½ cup chopped pickled
  jalapeños
2 tablespoons juice from
  jalapeños
¼ cup chopped parsley
2 teaspoons comino
1 tablespoon black pepper
1 tablespoon salt

In large bowl, combine potatoes, celery, and both onions. Combine remaining ingredients and add to potato mixture. Mix well and chill several hours or overnight. Serves 24.

The Peach Tree Tea Room Cookbook

German-Style Potato Salad

With the strong German heritage of Central Texas, it's not uncommon to find German-style rather than mayonnaise-based potato salad in many barbecue restaurants. German potato salad is vinegar-based, a hot, tart blend of flavors that make a good complement to barbecue.

5 pounds potatoes, washed
  and peeled
1 large white onion, diced
3 large kosher dill pickles,
  diced

1 small jar pimientos, drained
½ cup white vinegar or
  pickle juice, or a combination
Salt and black pepper to taste

Quarter potatoes and boil until soft. Rinse potatoes and mash until chunky. Add onion, pickles, pimentos, and vinegar. Mix ingredients well. Season with salt and pepper (use pepper generously). Serve hot or cold. Serves 6-8.

Texas Barbecue

Texas Tabbouleh

Steve Southern, chef of Huntington's in the Westin Hotel Galleria in Dallas, developed this variation on the traditional bulgur salad.

¾ cup bulgur
1 cup freshly squeezed orange
  juice
²/₃ cup chopped tomatoes
²/₃ cup chopped cucumber
1 tablespoon tequila (optional)

1 jalapeño pepper, seeded
  and diced
1 heaping teaspoon chopped
  cilantro
Salt to taste

Place bulgur in bowl and mix with orange juice; let sit for 30 minutes. Add tomatoes, cucumbers, tequila, jalapeño, and chopped cilantro. Mix well. Refrigerate at least 1 hour. Serves 4.

Gourmet Grains, Beans, and Rice

Sunny Spinach Salad

1 pound spinach, torn into
  bite-size pieces
1 medium red onion, thinly
  sliced

1 (6-ounce) dried apricots,
  chopped
¹/₃ cup toasted salted
  sunflower seeds

Combine ingredients. Good served with vinaigrette dressing.

More of the Four Ingredient Cookbook

Coleslaw with Grapes

I sometimes add a chopped red-skinned apple to this slaw for additional color, but it is great as is.

COLESLAW:
6 cups shredded white cabbage

Crisp cabbage for about an hour with ice cubes.

DRESSING:

¾ cup cooked salad dressing (see below)
¾ cup dairy sour cream
1 tablespoon sugar
1 tablespoon vinegar

Salt and pepper
1 tablespoon chopped parsley
1½ cups seedless green grapes

COOKED SALAD DRESSING:

1 tablespoon flour
1 tablespoon sugar
½ teaspoon salt
½ teaspoon prepared mustard

½ cup water
3 tablespoons cider vinegar
1 egg, beaten
1½ tablespoons butter

In heavy saucepan, combine flour, sugar, salt, and mustard. Gradually blend in water and vinegar. Cook over low heat, stirring constantly, until mixture thickens and boils. Boil 1 minute, stirring, then remove from heat. Add a little of cream sauce gradually to beaten egg, then combine with rest of sauce. Add butter and return to heat, stirring, for 3 minutes or enough to cook egg. Cool before combining with sour cream.

Mix together the salad dressing and sour cream. Add the sugar, vinegar, and parsley. Chill to blend flavors. To serve, drain cabbage well and pat dry between paper towels. Pour dressing over cabbage. Add grapes, mix well and season with salt and pepper. Chill again before serving. Yield: 8 servings.

Raleigh House Cookbook II

Mandarin Orange Salad with Greens

½ cup sliced almonds
3 teaspoons sugar
½ head iceberg lettuce
½ head romaine lettuce
1 cup chopped celery

2 whole green onions,
  chopped
1 (11-ounce) can mandarin
  oranges, drained

In a small pan over medium heat, cook the almonds and sugar, stirring constantly until almonds are coated and sugar is dissolved.

Mix the lettuces, celery, and onions. Just before serving, add the almonds and oranges. Toss with Dressing.

DRESSING:
½ teaspoon salt
Dash of pepper
2 tablespoons sugar
Dash of Tabasco sauce

¼ cup vegetable oil
1 tablespoon chopped parsley
1 tablespoon vinegar

Eats: A Folk History of Texas Foods

Always Requested Cornbread Salad

1 (9x13-inch) pan cooked
  cornbread, crumbled
1½ cups mayonnaise
2 cups celery, sliced
1 green pepper, seeded and
  chopped
¾ cup green onions, chopped
1 (5-ounce) jar green olives
  and pimentos, drained,
  rinsed, and chopped

¾ cup pecans, toasted and
  chopped
2 large tomatoes, chopped
1 teaspoon sage
Pepper to taste
10 slices bacon, fried crisp
  and crumbled
1 jalapeño pepper, seeded
  and chopped

In bowl, combine all ingredients. Refrigerate 3-4 hours before serving. Wonderful! Serves 12.

Great Flavors of Texas

Crab and Wild Rice Salad

3 cups water
¾ pound unpeeled medium
  fresh shrimp
1 (8-ounce) package wild rice
12 ounces fresh lump
  crabmeat, drained
1 cup frozen tiny English
  peas, thawed

⅓ cup chopped green onions
1 (2-ounce) jar diced
  pimiento, drained
½ cup mayonnaise
1 tablespoon lemon juice
Leaf lettuce
Cherry tomatoes, cut into
  wedges

Bring water to a boil in a medium saucepan; add shrimp and cook 3 minutes or until shrimp turn pink. Drain well; rinse with cold water. Peel and devein shrimp; set aside. Cook rice according to package directions; let cool. Combine rice, shrimp, crabmeat, peas, onions, and pimento; stir gently. Combine mayonnaise and lemon juice. Gently stir into salad. Serve on lettuce leaves; garnish with cherry tomatoes. Serves 6.

Duck Creek Collection

Linda Martin's "Eyes of Texas" Salad

Black-Eyed Pea Festival Grand Champion, 1982.

1½ cups black-eyed peas,
  drained
1 cup chicken, boned and
  chopped
¼ cup celery, chopped
½ teaspoon salt

1 cup cooked rice
¼ cup onions, chopped
¼ cup mayonnaise
1 teaspoon pepper
1 dash hot sauce

Blend above ingredients and pack in mold. Let set for ½ hour. Ice with topping.

TOPPING:
1 avocado, mashed
½ cup sour cream
1 teaspoon garlic salt
½ cup mayonnaise

½ teaspoon Worcestershire
  sauce
¼ teaspoon salt
½ teaspoon lemon juice

Eats: A Folk History of Texas Foods

Corn-Black Bean Salad

This salad is great served with grilled meat, fish or quesadillas. Chill for several hours to capture the full flavor.

4 cups cooked black beans	Chopped fresh jalapeño
2 cups canned or frozen corn	pepper to taste (optional)
1 large red bell pepper, diced	Salt and black pepper to taste
1 large purple onion, chopped	Chopped avocados and
½ cup minced cilantro or	tomatoes (optional)
parsley	

Combine beans, corn, bell pepper, onion, cilantro, and jalapeño pepper. If canned beans are used, rinse and drain.

DRESSING:

2 cloves garlic, minced	Juice of 1 small lime
½ - ¾ cup vinaigrette	
dressing	

Prepare dressing by mixing garlic, vinaigrette and lime juice. Add dressing to vegetables. Chill for several hours before serving. Just before serving, add avocado and tomato. Makes approximately 8 cups.

Per ½ cup serving: Cal 115; Prot 4.65g; Carb 16.3g; Fat 4g; Chol 0; Sod 159mg.

Changing Thymes

Chicken Apricot Salad

The unusual combination of chicken and apricots is a treat! Attractive when served in avocado halves.

¼ cup milk	1 teaspoon salt
2 tablespoons lemon juice	1 cup dried apricots, diced
½ cup mayonnaise	3 cups cooked, diced chicken
1 cup sour cream	1 cup chopped celery
3 teaspoons prepared mustard	⅓ cup chopped green onions

Mix ingredients in order. Refrigerate several hours before serving. The mixture may appear soupy at first, but the apricots absorb most of the liquid while chilling. Serves 6-8.

Necessities and Temptations

Chicken Cantonese

5 cups diced, cooked chicken
1 cup chopped water
  chestnuts
2 cups pineapple tidbits,
  drained

½ cup chopped celery
¼ cup sliced green onions

DRESSING:
4 tablespoons Major Grey's
  Chutney
½ teaspoon curry powder

¾ cup sour cream
¾ cup mayonnaise

In a large mixing bowl, toss chicken, chestnuts, pineapple, celery, and green onions. In a separate bowl, combine chutney, curry powder, sour cream, and mayonnaise. Pour dressing over chicken mixture. Refrigerate. For the best results, make this salad at least 8 hours ahead. Serve on a lettuce leaf, garnish with radishes and/or cherry tomatoes. Serve with bran muffins. Yield: 8-10 servings.

Celebrate San Antonio

Cold Curried Chicken Salad

4 cups cooked, diced chicken
1 cup cooked rice
3 hard-cooked eggs, chopped
½ cup peanuts, crushed
1 bunch green onions, chopped
6 slices bacon, crisply cooked and crumbled

1 cup mayonnaise or to taste
2 teaspoons curry powder
½ teaspoon salt
1 teaspoon ground ginger
1 teaspoon white pepper
1 tablespoon lemon juice

Combine first 6 ingredients. Mix remaining ingredients and fold into chicken mixture. Chill and serve on lettuce leaves. Garnish with avocado slices or mandarin orange sections. Serves 10-12.

Necessities and Temptations

Horseradish Salad Mold

1 envelope unflavored gelatin
1 package lime Jello
2 cartons sour cream
¾ cup mayonnaise

¼ cup cold water
½ cup boiling water
1 (5-ounce) jar prepared horseradish

Sprinkle gelatin over ¼ cup water. Let stand 1 minute. Dissolve Jello in ½ cup boiling water. Add gelatin. Stir until dissolved. Add sour cream, horseradish, and mayonnaise. Stir to blend. Pour into lightly oiled mold until firm. Unmold and put onto purple cabbage leaves. Great served with brisket, as a spread for sandwiches, etc.

Feast of Goodness

Apricot Salad

Don't let anyone see you make this, for no one likes buttermilk and everyone loves this.

1 (3-ounce) package apricot gelatin

1 cup boiling orange juice
1 cup cold buttermilk

Dissolve gelatin in hot orange juice. Cool slightly. Add buttermilk. Pour into small mold and chill to set. Makes 4 servings.

Jubilee Cookbook

Elegant Blueberry Salad

1 (6-ounce) package
   raspberry gelatin
1 cup blueberry pie filling
1 (8-ounce) package cream
   cheese, softened

1 cup sour cream
½ cup sugar
½ cup chopped pecans

Dissolve gelatin in 1 cup of boiling water. Stir in pie filling and 2 cups of cold water. Pour into serving dish or mold. Chill until firm. Combine cream cheese and sour cream. Blend in sugar. Spread evenly over firm gelatin mixture. Sprinkle with pecans and chill. Serves 8.

Buffet on the Bayou

Booberry Salad

1 (15-ounce) can blueberries,
   reserve liquid
1 (8½-ounce) can crushed
   pineapple, reserve liquid
2 (3-ounce) packages black
   raspberry gelatin
1 cup boiling water

1 (8-ounce) package cream
   cheese softened
1 (8-ounce) carton sour cream
½ cup sugar
1 teaspoon vanilla extract
1 cup chopped pecans

Drain fruit and reserve liquid. In a saucepan, boil water and dissolve gelatin. Add enough water to reserved liquid to make 1¾ cups and add to dissolved gelatin. Pour into a 9x13-inch baking dish. When gelatin is slightly thickened, fold in fruit. Chill until firm. In a bowl, combine cream cheese, sour cream, sugar, and vanilla and beat well. Spread over gelatin and sprinkle with pecans. Spread over gelatin and sprinkle with pecans. Chill until set. Cut into squares and serve. Yield: 12 servings.

Celebrate San Antonio

 Native born Texan Howard Hughes did not get his fortune from his movies or aviator skills, but rather from the inheritance from his father's invention of the Hughes Drill Bit, which revolutionized the oil industry. Hughes, a brilliant businessman, invested wisely and acquired great wealth at an early age.

Angel Hash Salad

1 (#2) can crushed pineapple
1 (#2) can fruit cocktail
2 tablespoons cornstarch
¼ cup sugar
2 egg yolks, beaten

1 cup whipped topping
¼ cup chopped nuts
2 cups miniature marshmallows
3 bananas

Drain fruit and reserve juice. Combine cornstarch and sugar in pan; mix well. Add 1 cup juice and egg yolks. Blend well and cook over heat until thick, stirring constantly. Cool. Fold in whipped topping, nuts, marshmallows, bananas, pineapple, and fruit cocktail. Cover and chill overnight.

Chuckwagon Recipes

Frozen Cranberry Salad

1 (8-ounce) package cream cheese
2 tablespoons mayonnaise
2 tablespoons sugar
1 (16-ounce) can whole cranberry sauce

½ cup chopped pecans
1 (20-ounce) can crushed pineapple, drained
1 (13-ounce) carton Cool Whip

Soften the cream cheese and blend in the mayonnaise and sugar. Add cranberry sauce, pecans, and pineapple. Fold in Cool Whip. Pour into muffin papers and freeze. Store in Ziploc bag. To serve, unwrap and place on lettuce leaves. Yield: 20 servings.

The Gathering

Apple Salad

This is a 1860 recipe.

Chop together 4 large ripe apples, 1 cup of celery, and 1 cup of nuts. Make a boiled dressing as follows: Yolk of 2 eggs and 1 teaspoon mustard, 1 teaspoon salt, 2 teaspoons sugar, ¼ teaspoon pepper, 2 tablespoons butter, 1 cup of sweet cream, and the whites of 2 eggs beaten stiff. Add to the apple mixture.

A Pinch of This and A Handful of That

Fantastic Fruit Salad

2 cans mandarin oranges
2 (15-ounce) cans pineapple
  chunks
1 (16-ounce) packages frozen
  strawberries, thawed and
  drained

1 can peach pie filling
1 can apricot pie filling
2 bananas, sliced

Drain oranges, pineapple, and strawberries. In a mixing bowl, combine oranges, pineapple, strawberries, peach pie filling, apricot pie filling, and bananas; gently mix together. Place in a beautiful crystal bowl for serving. This is a wonderful fruit salad for special holiday dinners. Serves 16.

I Cook - You Clean

Alligator Pear Salad

The term "alligator pear" is a regional name for avocados. Alligator pears were probably so called because the peel resembles the hide of an alligator and they are somewhat pear shaped. One family member recalls as a child the name "alligator pear" brought romantic and dramatic possibilities to the imagination that "avocado" just never could match.

2 ripe alligator pears
1 teaspoon olive oil
½ teaspoon salt
¼ teaspoon sugar
Juice of ½ lemon

½ teaspoon onion juice
  (optional)
Few dashes hot red pepper
  sauce (optional)
Paprika

Mash pears fine with olive oil, salt, sugar, and lemon juice (onion juice and pepper sauce, if desired). Place on top of tomato slice in center of lettuce cup and serve with mayonnaise topped with paprika.

Perfectly Splendid

Copper Pennies

2 pounds carrots, sliced
  crosswise
1 small onion, finely chopped
1 medium bell pepper, finely
  chopped
3 ribs celery, finely chopped
1 cup tomato soup, undiluted

1 tablespoon dry mustard
1 tablespoon Worcestershire
  sauce
1 cup sugar
¼ cup oil
¾ cup apple cider vinegar
Lettuce

Cook sliced carrots in salted water until fork tender. Add chopped onion, bell pepper, and celery to the drained carrots. Set aside. Mix and bring to a boil soup, sugar, oil, vinegar, mustard, and Worcestershire sauce. Pour this hot mixture over above vegetables. Refrigerate overnight. Serve on lettuce. Serves 10-12.

Central Texas Style

Mary's Salad

1 medium head Boston or
  bibb lettuce, torn into pieces
½ avocado, peeled and thinly
  sliced
1 (11-ounce) can mandarin
  oranges, chilled and drained

½ cup chopped pecans,
  toasted
2 green onions, thinly sliced
Pepper to taste
⅓ cup Italian dressing

Combine all ingredients except dressing in a salad bowl. Just before serving add dressing and toss gently. Yield: 6 servings.

Deep in the Heart

Salad Sensation

Great way to dress a green salad. Dressing can double or triple.

1 clove garlic or garlic powder
½ teaspoon salt
¼ teaspoon pepper
2 tablespoons Parmesan
  cheese

1 tablespoon lemon juice
¼ cup salad oil
Pinch dry mustard

Mix ingredients with a whisk and put in the bottom of a wooden salad bowl. Break lettuce or romaine on top and add other salad ingredients. Cover and refrigerate as long as 2 hours. Toss just before serving.

This is a real time saver when you are rushed and having guests for dinner. All salad ingredients stay very crisp. Serves 6.

Collectibles III

Raleigh House Dressing

My customers say that this dressing is good with shrimp, fish, hamburgers, and hot dogs. Some of my college employees even eat this dressing on their baked potatoes. It keeps for months in the refrigerator.

1 quart Kraft or Hellman's
  Mayonnaise
½ cup plus 2 tablespoons
  Heinz Ketchup

⅛ teaspoon garlic powder or
  1 clove garlic, crushed
⅓ teaspoon dry mustard
¾ cup evaporated milk

Mix well by hand or in mixer. Replace in jar the mayonnaise came out of plus a smaller jar for the overage. Yield: 1 quart plus about 1 cup.

Raleigh House Cookbook

Four churches in Dallas have the distinction of having the largest congregation in its individual denomination in the world. They are: Highland Park Methodist Church, Highland Park Presbyterian Church, East Dallas Christian Church, and First Baptist Church.

Dijon Vinaigrette

If we had any sense we would keep this recipe as a trade secret; it's the most popular dressing at the resort by far, and deservedly so. Too good, really, not to share. You may substitute dried leaf basil for the fresh (halve the quantity and use more parsley) but it won't be quite the same. Use chives, thyme, and other fresh herbs also.

2 cloves garlic	1 cup Dijon mustard
¼ cup parsley sprigs, packed	1 cup balsamic vinegar
¼ cup basil leaves, packed	2 cups tomato juice
½ teaspoon cracked black pepper	2 tablespoons honey

Drop garlic into food processor or blender while motor is running. Add fresh herbs and process until finely chopped. Add the remaining ingredients and mix only until blended. Chill. It keeps well in the refrigerator for a week. Yield: 4 cups.

Cal: 7; Fat per tablespoon: .2g.

Lean Star Cuisine

Dressing for Cold Slaw

This is an 1899 recipe.

Beat up two eggs with two tablespoons of sugar, add a piece of butter the size of half an egg, a teaspoon of mustard, a little pepper, and lastly a teacup of vinegar. Put all of these ingredients into a dish over the fire and cook like a soft custard. Some think it improved by adding half a cupful of thick sweet cream to this dressing; in that case use less vinegar. Either way is very fine.

Seconds of A Pinch of This and A Handful of That

Vegetables

*Editor Barbara Moseley (right) gets into the swing of things with Texas friends
at The Market Square (El Mercado) in San Antonio.*

Greens

About a peck of greens are enough for a mess for a gathering of six folks. Almost any sort can be used. We've had the best of luck with dandelions, chicory, mustard or turnip greens. All greens should be carefully examined, and the tough ones thrown out. Thoroughly wash through several waters until they are entirely free from sand. Adding a handful of salt to each pan of water while washing the greens will free them of insects and worms.

When ready to boil the greens, put them into a large pot half full of boiling water, with a handful of salt, and boil them until the stalks are tender—anywhere from 5-20 minutes. Remember that over-long boiling wastes the tender nature of the leaves and lessens both the flavor and nourishment of the dish.

As soon as they are tender, drain them in a colander, chop them a little and return them to the fire. Season them with salt, pepper, and butter. The greens should be served as soon as they are hot.

As mentioned early on in this receipt, this serves 6 people, but could well serve 60. Just add a little more of everything in its measure.

Jane Long's Brazoria Inn

Raspberry Carrots

The hint of raspberry gives this vegetable dish a new twist.

6 carrots, thinly sliced	**2-4 teaspoons raspberry**
¼ cup water	**vinegar**
1½ teaspoons margarine	**2 teaspoons brown sugar**
Dash of salt	**Chopped parsley (optional)**

Place carrots and water in a covered dish and microwave for 5-7 minutes, just until tender. Drain water from carrots. Add margarine, salt, raspberry vinegar, and sugar; stir to combine. Microwave for 1-2 more minutes. Garnish with parsley, if desired. Yield: 3 servings.

Per serving; Cal 77; Fat 2g; Prot 1g; Carb 11g; Chol 0mg; Sod 107mg; Dietary fiber 3g.

More of What's Cooking

Apple-Carrot Casserole

This is a not-too-sweet and colorful casserole. Pretty any time, but especially on a buffet table.

2 tablespoons flour
¼ cup sugar
1 pound carrots, cut
   diagonally
½ teaspoon salt
½ cup water
4 medium cooking apples,
   peeled, cored and cut into
   ¼-inch slices

¼ cup butter or margarine,
   thinly sliced, divided
¼ cup frozen orange juice
   mixed with ½ cup water

Mix flour and sugar together in a small bowl. Set aside. Combine carrots, salt, and water in small saucepan. Cover and bring to a boil; reduce heat and simmer just until crisp-tender. Drain and set aside. Layer half of carrots, then half of apples in a lightly greased shallow 2-quart baking dish. (I use a 10x6x2-inch Pyrex dish). Sprinkle with half the flour mixture and dot with half the butter. Repeat layers. Drizzle with orange juice. Bake at 350° for about 35 minutes or until apples are tender, gently pressing apples down into syrup midway of cooking. Yield: 8 servings.

Raleigh House Cookbook II

Easy Carrot Casserole

1 cup water
8 medium carrots, pared and
   cut into 1-inch pieces
2 tablespoons butter

1 (16-ounce) can pie-sliced
   apples
½ cup sugar
½ cup raisins (optional)

Boil water and cook carrots for 15 minutes (can be steamed). Mix carrots, apples, and raisins. Turn into a 9-inch pie plate and sprinkle with sugar. Dot with butter. Bake at 375° for 1 hour. Can do ahead. Serves 8.

Collectibles III

Sesame Broccoli

1 tablespoon sesame seeds	2 teaspoons olive oil or
3 cups fresh broccoli,	safflower oil
trimmed and cut into spears	1 tablespoon vinegar
	1 tablespoon light soy sauce

Toast sesame seeds on a cookie sheet in oven on low heat; remove. Steam broccoli until tender-crisp. In a saucepan, combine oil, vinegar, soy sauce and toasted sesame seeds. Heat until boiling. Pour sauce over broccoli, turning to coat evenly. Yield: 4 servings.

Per serving: Cal 67; Fat 4g: Prot 5g; Carb 7g; Chol 0mg; Sod 163mg; Dietary fiber 3g.

What's Cooking at the Cooper Clinic

Chinese Braised Broccoli

1 bunch fresh broccoli	1 tablespoon gin
3 tablespoons oil	1 teaspoon sugar
2 chopped green onions	¼ cup water
2 tablespoons soy sauce	Salt and pepper to taste

Peel broccoli and cut into 1-inch thick slices. Heat oil and sauté broccoli and onions for 5 minutes. Mix soy sauce, gin, sugar, and water. Pour over broccoli, cover, and cook for 2 minutes. Serves 4.

The Denton Woman's Club Cookbook

Walnut Broccoli

So good, you hardly know it's broccoli.

3 (10-ounce) packages
  chopped broccoli
½ cup butter
4 tablespoons flour
1½ teaspoons instant
  chicken bouillon or 2 cubes

2 cups milk
1 (8-ounce) package
  commercial cornbread stuffing
  mix
1 cup chopped walnuts

Cook broccoli according to package directions. Drain and place in a greased 9x13-inch baking dish. In saucepan, melt butter, add flour, and stir to blend. Add chicken bouillon and milk, stirring constantly. Cook until smooth and thick. Pour over the broccoli. Prepare the cornbread stuffing mix according to package directions, using lowest amount of water. Add walnuts and spread over the broccoli mixture. Bake at 350° for 30 minutes. Pecans or almonds may be used instead of walnuts. Yield: 12 servings.

Cook 'em Horns: The Quickbook

Harvard Beets

¼ cup sugar
1 tablespoon cornstarch
½ teaspoon salt
Dash of white pepper
¾ cup drained liquid from
  beets plus water
¼ cup vinegar

¼ cup concentrated,
  undiluted frozen orange juice
1 (16-ounce) can sliced beets,
  drained
1 teaspoon grated orange
  rind, optional

Combine sugar, cornstarch, salt, and pepper into a 1-quart pan. Stir the beet liquid, vinegar, and orange concentrate into sugar mixture. Cover. Cook 5-7 minutes, or until mixture is glossy and slightly thickened, stirring twice. Add sliced beets and heat until beets are hot. Sprinkle orange rind over top before serving. Serve warm or chilled. Keeps well in the refrigerator.

The Second Typically Texas Cookbook

Skillet Cabbage Plus

3 tablespoons butter
6 thin strips bacon
2/3 cup coarsely shredded
 carrots
1½ cups thinly sliced celery
4 cups finely grated cabbage,
 firmly packed
½ cup sliced green bell pepper

½ teaspoon sugar
1 teaspoon instant chicken
 broth granules
¼ cup water
1 teaspoon salt
⅛ teaspoon pepper

In a 12-inch skillet, melt butter and slowly cook the bacon, carrots, and celery until slightly softened, about 5 minutes. Add cabbage, bell pepper, and a mixture of the sugar, chicken granules, water, salt and pepper. Mix well. Cover tightly and simmer just until tender crisp, 8-10 minutes. Serve at once. Serves 6-8.

Lone Star Legacy II

Spicy Hot Eggplant Casserole

1 medium eggplant (about
 1½ pounds) peeled and cut
 into ¼-inch thick slices
1 (10-ounce) can tomatoes
 with green chiles, drained,
 chopped, and divided
¼ cup soft bread crumbs,
 divided
¼ teaspoon dried oregano,
 divided

½ cup no-salt-added tomato
 sauce, divided
2 tablespoons grated
 Parmesan cheese, divided
½ cup (2 ounces) shredded
 reduced-fat Cheddar cheese,
 divided
Vegetable cooking spray

Cook eggplant in a small amount of boiling water 5 minutes; drain well. Layer half each of eggplant, tomatoes, and next 5 ingredients in a 1½-quart casserole coated with cooking spray. Repeat layers, omitting top layer of Cheddar cheese. Bake at 350° for 15 minutes; sprinkle with remaining Cheddar cheese and bake 5 minutes. Yield: 3 servings.

Duck Creek Collection

Greenback Tomatoes

This is a good vegetable dish for a buffet supper because it is colorful, tasty and arranged in individual servings.

2 (10-ounce) packages frozen chopped spinach	¼ cup Parmesan cheese
	¼ teaspoon Worcestershire
2 cups Progresso bread crumbs	1 teaspoon salt
	½ teaspoon pepper
6 green onions and tops, chopped	1 teaspoon thyme
	¼ teaspoon Tabasco
6 eggs, slightly beaten	12 large thick slices of tomato
½ cup melted butter	

Cook spinach and drain well. In large mixing bowl combine crumbs, onions, eggs, butter, Parmesan, Worcestershire, salt, pepper, thyme, and Tabasco. Arrange tomato slices in buttered shallow baking dish. Mound spinach mixture on top of each tomato slice. Bake at 350° about 15 minutes. Serves 12.

Variation: Great for hors d'oeuvres. You may use it to stuff little cherry tomatoes. Reduce cooking time accordingly.

The Texas Experience

Summer Tomatoes

6-8 tomatoes

DRESSING:

½ teaspoon dried oregano	½ teaspoon salt
2 teaspoons dried basil or 2 tablespoons shredded fresh basil	1 teaspoon sugar
	2 green onions, finely diced
½ teaspoon garlic, minced	2 tablespoons finely diced red onions

Blanch tomatoes and peel skins. Blend dressing ingredients. Pour dressing over whole tomatoes and marinate overnight. Serve in a large bowl garnished with fresh parsley and basil. No further dressing is necessary. Makes 6-8 servings.

Pass it on... Slice and drizzle with balsamic vinegar and olive oil and sprinkle with bits of Mozzarella cheese.

Pass it On...

Gourmet Filled Tomatoes

Quick to fix.

3 tomatoes
½ cup herbed stuffing mix
1 clove garlic, minced
3 tablespoons parsley, minced

¼ teaspoon thyme leaves
¼ teaspoon salt
Pepper, freshly ground
⅓ cup olive oil

Preheat oven to 400°. Cut tomatoes in half and gently squeeze out the juice and seeds. Blend stuffing mix, garlic, parsley, thyme, salt and pepper to taste. Fill each tomato half, and sprinkle with olive oil. Arrange in baking dish; bake for 12 minutes or until tops are golden.

Note: The filled tomatoes can be made ahead, and baked when needed. They are great for brunch with chicken, fish or pork.

Coastal Cuisine

Spinach-Tomato Bake

10-12 ounces fresh spinach
2 tablespoons lemon juice
4 tablespoons sour cream
1 (3-ounce) can
  broiled-in-butter mushrooms

3 fresh tomatoes, peeled and
  thinly sliced
Salt and pepper
Parmesan cheese

Chop spinach in blender or with scissors. Mix with lemon juice, sour cream and mushrooms. Season with salt and pepper. Place in buttered casserole and cover with tomato slices. Dust with salt and pepper and a thick layer of Parmesan cheese. Bake at 300° until brown and bubbly, about 15 minutes. Serves 4-6.

Houston Junior League Cookbook

Sensational Spinach

3 (10-ounce) packages frozen
  chopped spinach
1 pint sour cream

1 envelope onion soup mix
Bacon bits

Cook and drain the spinach well. Combine all ingredients and bake 25 minutes at 350°. May top with bacon bits. Also good with chopped broccoli. Serves 6.

Amazing Graces

Spinach Stuffing Casserole

This is yummy with baked chicken.

1 cup melted butter
1½ cups chicken broth
6 eggs, beaten
1 teaspoon thyme (optional)
2 tablespoons garlic salt
Grated black pepper
2 cups grated Cheddar cheese
1 large onion, chopped

2 tablespoons butter
1 cup chopped pecans
2 packages frozen chopped
   spinach, cooked and drained
4 cups bread crumbs
2 cups Pepperidge Farm Herb
   Stuffing Mix

Mix together butter, broth, eggs, thyme, garlic salt, pepper, and cheese. Sauté onion in butter. Add onion and pecans to broth mixture, spinach, bread crumbs, and stuffing mix. Pour into 11x14-inch casserole and bake at 325° for 40 minutes or until set. Serve hot or cold. Can be cut into squares and freezes well. This will serve 10-12 as a side dish with turkey or will serve 8 for lunch with fruit salad.

Delicioso!

Artichoke-Spinach Casserole

Terrific...a tasty, rich recipe.

2 sticks butter
½ medium onion, chopped
1 (8-ounce) package cream
   cheese
4 (10-ounce) packages frozen
   chopped spinach, cooked and
   drained

½ teaspoon salt (or to taste)
¼ teaspoon pepper (or to
   taste)
1 (14-ounce) can artichoke
   hearts, drained and chopped

Sauté onions in butter, add cream cheese, then spinach and seasonings. Line bottom of buttered casserole dish with artichokes and pour spinach sauce over all. Heat at 350° until hot through, about 20 minutes. Yield: 10 servings.

Cook 'em Horns: The Quickbook

111

Artichoke Casserole

This dish is a tradition with all holiday meals. The only disagreement is who gets to bring it! We rarely have leftovers, and when we do, they don't last long.

1 (14-ounce) can artichoke
   hearts, drained and quartered
3 hard-cooked eggs, sliced
½ cup pimiento-stuffed
   green olives, sliced
¼ cup water chestnuts,
   sliced

1 (10¾-ounce) can cream of
   mushroom soup, undiluted
¼ cup milk
½ cup buttered breadcrumbs
½ cup (2 ounces) grated
   Cheddar cheese

Layer artichoke hearts, eggs, olives, and water chestnuts in greased 9x9x2-inch baking dish. Blend soup and milk together. Pour over ingredients in casserole dish. Top with breadcrumbs and cheese. Bake, uncovered, at 350° for 25-30 minutes or until bubbly and browned. Serves 8.

Per ½ cup serving: cal 144; Prot 6.55g; Carb 10.8g; Fat 9g; Chol 88.4mg; Sod 646mg.

Changing Thymes

Okra and Tomatoes

5 strips bacon, chopped
2 medium onions, chopped
9 medium okra pods

1½ cups cooked tomatoes
1 teaspoon salt
¼ teaspoon pepper

Cook bacon and onion in a skillet until onion is yellow. Add thinly sliced okra and cook for 2 minutes. Add tomatoes, salt and pepper and bring to boiling point. Cook on medium for about 25 minutes, simmer until serving.

Perfectly Splendid

Ochra and Tomatoes

Use equal quantities of each, slice the ochra and skin the tomatoes. Stew without water three-quarters of an hour, then add butter, salt and pepper.

The First Texas Cook Book

Green Peas with Celery and Ripe Olives

1 tablespoon butter
1 tablespoon oil
2 cups celery, cut at an angle in ¼-inch slices
2 (10-ounce) packages frozen green peas, broken apart and slightly thawed
20 large pitted ripe olives, halved
½ teaspoon salt
¼ teaspoon pepper

Melt butter; add oil and celery. Cover and cook slowly over low heat for 10 minutes, shaking the pan occasionally. Add peas and continue cooking until peas are just done. Add olives, salt, and pepper; check seasonings, adding more salt, pepper, and butter if needed. Serves 6-8.

The Denton Woman's Club Cookbook

Emmitt Smith's Sour Cream Green Beans

2 pounds green beans
1 medium onion, thinly sliced
1 tablespoon parsley, chopped
2 tablespoons melted butter or margarine
2 tablespoons flour
2 tablespoons lemon rind, grated
1 teaspoon salt
¼ teaspoon pepper
1 cup lite sour cream
1 cup buttered bread crumbs

Prepare beans as usual; cook in slightly-salted water until tender. Drain; set aside. Sauté onions and parsley in butter. Reduce heat; add flour, lemon rind, salt, and pepper. Stir until bubbly. Combine sour cream and beans; stir well. Pour into a greased baking dish; sprinkle with bread crumbs. Bake at 350° for 20 minutes.

Dallas Cowboys Wives' Family Cookbook

Garlicky Green Beans

Serve this with broiled steak and herbed potatoes for a delicious meal.

2 tablespoons peanut oil or
  canola oil
1 (16-ounce) package thawed
  French-style green beans
6 cloves garlic, chopped

Scant ½ teaspoon salt
1 tablespoon soy sauce
2 tablespoons slivered
  almonds

Heat oil in wok or skillet and stir-fry beans with garlic for about 5 minutes. Keep high to singe beans. Add salt, soy sauce, and almonds. Cover wok, lower heat and simmer for 5 minutes. Yield: 4 servings.

From Generation to Generation

Green Bean Revenge

Hot!

3 (16-ounce) cans green
  beans, drained
1 (8-ounce) can sliced water
  chestnuts, drained and
  chopped

2 (8-ounce) jars jalapeño
  Cheez Whiz
1 cup cracker crumbs
2 cans onion rings

Place green beans in a 9x13-inch baking dish and cover with water chestnuts. Heat both jars of cheez in the microwave just until they can be poured. Pour Cheez Whiz over green beans and water chestnuts. Sprinkle cracker crumbs over green beans, water chestnuts, and cheez. Arrange onion rings over casserole and bake at 350° for 25-30 minutes. (For the "faint of heart," you might want to use 1 jar of the jalapeño Cheez Whiz and 1 jar of the regular Cheez Whiz.) Serves 12.

A Little Taste of Texas

 Austin is home to the nation's largest urban bat colony—up to 1.5 million of these creatures find shelter under the Congress Avenue bridge. They come from their winter home in Mexico in March and stay in Austin till October.

Corn, Green Chilies, and Cheese

1 onion chopped
1 can diced green chilies
2 tablespoons butter
1 can whole kernel corn

½ pound grated Monterey
  Jack cheese
½ cup sour cream

Sauté onion and chilies in 2 tablespoons butter or enough to cover bottom of skillet. Add corn. Fold cheese into mixture until it melts. Add salt and pepper to taste. Just before serving, mix in ½ cup of sour cream. Serve immediately.

Down-Home Texas Cooking

Chimayo Corn Pudding

1½ cups creamed corn
1 cup yellow cornmeal
1 cup (2 sticks) butter, melted
¾ cup buttermilk
2 medium onions, chopped
2 eggs, beaten

½ teaspoon baking soda
2 cups grated sharp Cheddar
  cheese
1 (4-ounce) can green chilies,
  drained

Preheat oven to 350°. Grease a 9-inch square baking pan. Combine first 7 ingredients and mix well. Turn half the batter into the greased pan; cover evenly with half the cheese, all the chilies, then remaining cheese. Top with remaining batter. Bake 1 hour. Let cool 15 minutes before serving. This is a spicy side dish that's sure to become a family favorite...delish served with any and all Bar-B-Q. Makes 8-12 servings.

Collectibles III

Corn Pudding

This is an 1888 recipe.

Use 6-8 ears of corn, grated and scraped. Boil in half water and half milk until soft. Add 2 eggs, ½ cup of flour, butter, and some salt and pepper. Bake about 45 minutes or until firm.

A Pinch of This and A Handful of That

Mexican Zucchini Corn

5 large zucchini (4-5 cups)
½ onion, chopped
1 (16-ounce) can cream-style
    corn
1 (8-ounce) package cream
    cheese, softened

1 can chopped green chilies,
    drained
1 teaspoon salt
½ teaspoon seasoned pepper
1½ cups cracker crumbs

Cook squash and onion just until tender-crisp. Drain well. Add corn, cream cheese, and cornstarch and leave on low burner; stir until cream cheese is melted. Add green chilies, salt and pepper and pour into a large casserole and top with cracker crumbs. Bake 45 minutes at 350°. Serves 8-10.

Southwest Sizzler

Quick and Easy Zucchini Casserole

1 small onion, chopped
1 tablespoon oil
14-15 small zucchini squash
1 (14-ounce) jar Ragu
    Spaghetti Sauce

½ cup Mozzarella cheese,
    grated

Sauté onion in oil. Dice or slice zucchini and spread in 13x9x2-inch baking dish. Sprinkle onion over zucchini. Pour entire jar of spaghetti sauce over dish. Bake at 350° for 30-40 minutes or until tender. Sprinkle cheese over casserole and place back in oven until cheese is melted. Cool 5-10 minutes. Serve and enjoy. Yield: 8 servings.

Potluck on the Pedernales Second Helping

Zucchini Smart

2 zucchini
2 tablespoons Italian extra
  virgin olive oil

¼ cup chopped onions
4 mushrooms, diced
Parmesan cheese

Steam the zucchini for about 10 minutes. Cut in half lengthwise.
Scoop out the inside and put in a bowl. Heat oil in a skillet and
sauté onions until soft and golden brown, add the mushrooms
and cook over medium heat for about 2 minutes. Combine
mushrooms and onions with the zucchini. Spoon the mixture
back in the zucchini "boats," top with Parmesan cheese and
bake for 10 minutes at 350°. Serves 2.

The College Cookbook

Spinach-Stuffed Zucchini

1 (10-ounce) package frozen
  chopped spinach
4 zucchini squash
3 tablespoons chopped onion
3 tablespoons margarine
3 tablespoons all-purpose
  flour

1 cup milk
½ cup (2 ounces) shredded
  Swiss cheese
Salt and black pepper to taste
1 tablespoon grated Parmesan
  cheese

Prepare spinach according to package directions. Drain well
and press to remove excess moisture. Cook whole zucchini in
boiling water for 5 minutes. Drain. Trim ends and cut in halves
lengthwise. Remove and discard pulp, leaving ¼-inch thick
shells. Place in 13x9x2-inch baking dish. Sauté onion in margarine until tender. Add flour and cook for 1 minute. Add milk,
stirring until thickened. Add spinach, Swiss cheese, salt, and
black pepper to mixture. Spoon mixture into zucchini shells and
sprinkle with Parmesan cheese. Bake, uncovered, at 350° for 25
minutes. Serves 8.

Per serving: Cal 126; Prot 5.48g; Carb 10.6g; Fat 7.5g;Chol 10.9mg; Sod
150mg.

Changing Thymes

Summer Squash Torta

Proof that a quesadilla by any other name would taste as sweet. This has become one of the most popular and widely requested recipes at the resort, deservedly so. Serve it with black beans and a fruit salad. (If this dish is served as a leftover, it becomes known as a "re-torta.")

1 large zucchini, cut in half across, then sliced lengthwise
1 large yellow squash, cut in half across, then sliced lengthwise
½ red bell pepper, sliced into thin rings
2 ounces low-fat Cheddar cheese, grated
2 ounces low-fat cottage cheese

2 tablespoons Parmesan cheese
1 teaspoon cumin
2 cloves garlic, minced
1 serrano pepper, seeded and minced (optional)
2 whole wheat flour tortillas
Vegetable cooking spray

Steam first 3 vegetables together until just tender. Blend next 6 ingredients together. Spread cheese mixture on one tortilla. Top with vegetables and cover with other tortilla.

Spray a nonstick skillet with vegetable spray. Slide in the torta, cover and cook over medium heat for a few minutes. Remove torta from the skillet, re-spray, invert torta, slide it back into the skillet, cover and cook until cheese is melted and tortillas are browned. Cut into quarters and serve with salsa. Yield: 4 servings.

Cal: 190; Fat per serving: 6.5g.

Lean Star Cuisine

Squash Casserole

6 medium yellow squash, sliced
1 small onion, chopped
1 cup Velveeta cheese, cut in ½-inch cubes

1 (4-ounce) can chopped green chiles

Boil squash and onion until tender. Drain well and mix with cheese and chiles. Pour into buttered baking dish. Bake 15 minutes at 375°. Serves 6-8.

The Four Ingredient Cookbook

Baked Squash Olé

4-5 cups cooked squash, drained	1 cup grated Monterey Jack cheese
1 teaspoon salt	1 (10¾-ounce) can cream of chicken soup
½ teaspoon pepper	
1 onion, chopped	1 cup sour cream
1 (4-ounce) can chopped green chilies, drained	1 stick margarine, melted
	1 package herb dressing mix

Place cooked squash in a mixing bowl and season with salt and pepper; add onion, green chilies, cheese, soup, and sour cream. Blend well. Mix margarine and herb dressing mix. Place ½ of the dressing mix in a 9x13-inch greased baking dish; pour squash mixture on top. Sprinkle with remaining dressing mix. Bake at 375° for 30 minutes. Serves 10.

Great Tastes of Texas

French-Fried Onion Rings

Onion rings fried in peanut oil taste better than those fried in shortening and they have less cholesterol.

6 medium Spanish onions, thinly sliced	1 egg, beaten
	1 cup all-purpose flour
1 cup milk	2-3 cups peanut oil
1 cup buttermilk	Salt to taste

Separate onion slices into rings. Combine milk, buttermilk, and egg in a medium mixing bowl. Add onion rings and refrigerate for 30 minutes. Spread flour on a plate. Heat oil to 375° in a medium saucepan or deep-fat fryer. Remove onion rings from milk mixture and dip one at a time into flour. Fry in hot oil until golden brown. Cook no more than 8-10 rings at one time to prevent oil from cooling below 375°. Remove from oil, drain on paper towels and sprinkle with salt. Yield: 6-8 servings.

More Tastes & Tales

Carole's Roasted Vegetables

A tasty way to enjoy your "5 a day."*

8 yellow squash, sliced
6 zucchini, sliced
3 red onions, cut into wedges
1 red bell pepper, cut into strips
1 poblano pepper, cut into strips

Nonstick vegetable cooking spray
1½ tablespoons olive oil
1 tablespoon minced garlic
¾ teaspoon salt
¾ teaspoon pepper
8 ounces whole mushrooms

Place squash, zucchini, onion, and peppers in an oversized (larger than 9x13-inch) baking dish, or 2 smaller ones, that have been coated with cooking spray. In a small bowl, stir together oil, garlic, salt and pepper. Pour over vegetable mixture and stir to coat all vegetables. Bake, covered, at 400° for 15 minutes, stirring twice. Remove vegetables from oven and add mushrooms. Stir to coat vegetables. Bake an additional 10 minutes. Yield: 12 servings.

*The National Cancer Institute recommends that we consume a variety of fruits and vegetables. Strive for a minimum of 5 servings per day.

Per serving: Cal 58; Fat 2g; Pro 3g; Carb 7g; Chol 0mg; Sod 287mg; Dietary fiber 2g.

More of What's Cooking

Apple Mallow Yam Yums

2 apples, sliced
⅓ cup chopped pecans
½ cup brown sugar, packed
½ teaspoon cinnamon

2 (16-ounce) cans yams
¼ cup butter
2 cups miniature marshmallows

Toss apples, nuts, brown sugar, and cinnamon together. Alternate layers of apples and yams in a buttered casserole. Dot with butter. Bake at 350° for 35-40 minutes. Sprinkle marshmallows over all and broil until lightly brown. Serves 6-8.

Delicioso!

Creamy Baked 1015 Onions

Texas 1015 onions are wonderfully mild, sweet onions grown in the Rio Grande Valley. Their name comes from the date the onions are planted, October 15th. Because the days are short during the growing season, the onions have less acidity than those grown in the long, hot days of summer. In taste tests of the Texas 1015, the Vidalia onion of Georgia and the Walla-Walla of Washington, the Texas onion wins again and again. Onions are usually used to enhance other flavors, but this dish makes the onion the culinary star.

4 large Texas 1015 onions	2 teaspoons sodium-reduced
2 tablespoons margarine	soy sauce
2 garlic cloves, minced	½ teaspoon black pepper
1 cup chicken broth	½ cup seasoned bread
1 packet Lipton's Cream of	crumbs
Chicken Cup-a-Soup Mix	
¼ cup grated Parmesan	
cheese	

Peel and slice the onions. Separate some of the slices into rings. Reserve 1 tablespoon of margarine for the topping. Place 1 tablespoon of margarine, the garlic, the chicken broth and the contents of the packet of soup mix in a large saucepan; stir. Add the onion rings and simmer until tender.

Transfer the onion rings to a 2-quart casserole leaving some of the broth mixture in the pan. Mix the Parmesan cheese, soy sauce, and pepper with the broth mixture and pour over the onions. Melt the reserved margarine and mix with the bread crumbs. Sprinkle the bread crumb mixture over the top of the onion mixture and bake at 350° for 30 minutes. 4.2 grams of fat per serving. Serves 6.

New Tastes of Texas

Sherried Baked Fruit

Elegant for buffet dinner parties, large or small.

2 (20-ounce) cans chunk
  pineapple
1 (29-ounce) can sliced
  freestone peaches
1 (17-ounce) can apricots,
  sliced
1 (16-ounce) can pitted Bing
  cherries or blueberries

2 (15-ounce) jars spiced apple
  rings
½ cup butter
4 tablespoons all-purpose
  flour
1 cup brown sugar
¼ cup sherry

Preheat oven to 350°. Drain fruit. Arrange in layers in a 3-quart baking dish. Melt butter. Add flour and stir until well blended. Add brown sugar and sherry. Cook until thick. Pour over fruit. Bake 30 minutes. Serves 20.

Necessities and Temptations

Praline Sweet Potato Casserole

FILLING:

3 cups mashed, cooked sweet
  potatoes
1½ cups sugar
¾ stick oleo
1 cup evaporated milk

3 eggs, beaten
½ teaspoon nutmeg
½ teaspoon cinnamon
½ teaspoon salt
1 teaspoon vanilla

TOPPING:

1 cup crushed cornflakes
½ cup brown sugar

¾ stick melted oleo
½ cup chopped pecans

Mix all ingredients and put into 9x12-inch ungreased casserole dish. Bake 15 minutes at 375°. Remove from oven and layer topping over mixture. Return to oven and bake for 15 minutes more.

From Cajun Roots to Texas Boots

Sweet Potato Casserole

No Thanksgiving dinner was complete at the Commercial without this special dish, and it's been a tradition in our family ever since. (The bourbon was later added by my mother to give it a little zing-g-g.)

5 large sweet potatoes	1 teaspoon vanilla extract
6 tablespoons butter	1 teaspoon cinnamon
½ - ¾ cup canned milk	1 teaspoon nutmeg
2 eggs	1 cup chopped pecans
1 ½ cups brown sugar	½ cup bourbon
2 cups marshmallows, cut up*	Marshmallows (for topping)

Gently boil sweet potatoes until tender. Peel the hot potatoes and mash. Melt the butter and, along with the milk and the eggs, add to the potatoes. Beat until fluffy. Stir in the other ingredients, reserving the large marshmallows. Pour into a 2-quart casserole. Top with marshmallows and bake at 350° until marshmallows brown.

*They didn't have miniature marshmallows back then.

Boardin' in the Thicket

Stuffed Baked Sweet Potatoes

6 medium sweet potatoes	½ cup pecans, chopped
2 tablespoons margarine	1 (8-ounce) can crushed pineapple, drained

Bake potatoes for 1 hour at 375°. Cut a 1-inch lengthwise wedge from the top of each potato. Carefully scoop pulp from shells. Mix potato pulp, margarine, and pineapple. Beat until fluffy. Stuff back into potato shell and sprinkle with pecans. Bake for 12 minutes at 375°.

More of the Four Ingredient Cookbook

Texas is probably more Western than Southern. It is not part of "Dixie" even though it was a slave state and fought on the side of the Confederacy during the Civil War.

Garden Ratatouille

The roadside stands and farmers' markets overflow with an abundance of produce during the Texas summer and fall. The combination of vegetables in this recipe is a good way to enjoy the bounty. Remember to double the recipe and freeze half; it's wonderful served over pasta or a baked potato for a quick meal. It can be served hot, cold, or at room temperature and has very little fat.

1 tablespoon canola oil
2 medium onions, sliced
1 medium red pepper, chopped
1 tablespoon minced garlic
1 small eggplant, cubed
3 medium zucchini, cut into ½-inch slices
¾ cup canned whole tomatoes, undrained

2 tablespoons fresh minced parsley
1 teaspoon dried basil
½ teaspoon dried oregano
2 large tomatoes, skinned and chopped
½ teaspoon salt
Freshly ground black pepper

Heat the oil in a large skillet; add the onions, red peppers, and garlic; sauté for 3 minutes. Add the eggplant, zucchini, canned tomatoes, parsley, basil, and oregano. Simmer for 10 minutes, stirring occasionally. Add the remaining ingredients and simmer for another 10 minutes. 2.2 grams fat per serving. Serves 6.

New Tastes of Texas

Peppy Potatoes

4 cups boiled, sliced red
  potatoes
½ cup slivered bell pepper
1 small (2-ounce) can pimento
⅛ teaspoon pepper
1 teaspoon salt
1 tablespoon flour

½ cup butter
1 cup milk
4 ounces cubed processed
  cheese
4 ounces cubed jalapeño
  cheese
¼ teaspoon garlic powder

Layer potatoes in 2-quart buttered casserole with slivered bell peppers and pimento. Salt and pepper each layer. Melt butter in saucepan. Add flour and stir until smooth. Gradually add milk to make a smooth white sauce. Add cheeses and garlic, stirring constantly. Cook until melted (don't overcook or it will become stringy). Pour cheese over the vegetables. Bake at 350° for 45 minutes to 1 hour. Yield: 4-8 servings.

Canyon Echoes

Mexican Hash Browns

5 slices bacon
3-4 tablespoons oil
4 medium potatoes, peeled
  and cut into ¼-inch slices
2 tablespoons margarine
1 medium onion chopped
¼ cup green pepper,
  chopped

1 clove garlic, crushed
2 tablespoons chopped
  pimento
¼ teaspoon salt
Pepper to taste

Cook bacon in a large skillet until crisp; drain on paper towels. Add oil to bacon grease if not enough to cook potatoes, if not now, oil may be needed while potatoes are cooking. Heat skillet over medium heat, when hot, add potatoes and cook until golden brown. Drain potatoes on paper towels. Melt margarine in skillet; add onion, green pepper, and garlic. Sauté until tender. Stir in potatoes, crumbled bacon and pimentos. Sprinkle with salt and pepper. Toss to combine. Serve immediately.

Not Just Bacon & Eggs

Herbed New Potatoes

8 new potatoes
1 teaspoon salt
2½ tablespoons melted
  butter
2½ tablespoons chopped
  fresh herbs such as parsley,
  chives, thyme or sage or 2
  teaspoons dried herbs of your
  choice

4 tablespoons grated Cheddar
  cheese
1½ tablespoons Parmesan
  cheese

Scrub and rinse potatoes. Cut them into thin slices but not all the way through. Use a handle of a spoon to prevent knife from cutting all the way. Put potatoes in a baking dish, fan them slightly. Sprinkle with salt and drizzle with butter. Sprinkle with herbs. Bake potatoes at 425° for about 50 minutes. Remove from oven. Sprinkle with cheeses. Bake potatoes for another 10-15 minutes until lightly browned, cheeses are melted and potatoes are soft inside. Check with a fork.

The Taste of Herbs

Creamy Mashed Potatoes

These potatoes are great for a buffet as they hold the heat so long.

5 pounds potatoes, peeled
  and quartered
2 teaspoons salt, divided
2 (3-ounce) packages cream
  cheese with chives, cubed
4 tablespoons butter or
  margarine

½ teaspoon garlic salt
½ teaspoon pepper
2 cups heavy cream
2 tablespoons butter or
  margarine
Paprika

Cook potatoes with 1 teaspoon salt in boiling water. Drain. Mash until smooth. Add cream cheese, butter, garlic salt, 1 teaspoon salt and pepper. Mix until smooth and add heavy cream gradually. Spoon in a greased 13x9x2-inch dish. Dot top with butter and sprinkle with paprika. At this point you can refrigerate up to a day ahead of time. Bake, uncovered, at 325° for 30 minutes. Increase heat to 375° for 30 more minutes. Serves 10-12.

Potluck on the Pedernales

Microwave Parmesan Potatoes

Not the usual plain old potatoes.

2 tablespoons margarine
2 medium unpeeled potatoes,
  sliced ¼-inch thick
⅓ cup chopped onion
¼ teaspoon salt

¼ teaspoon pepper
¼ cup grated Parmesan
  cheese
Paprika
Chopped parsley

Melt butter in shallow 7x11-inch dish in microwave oven. Add potatoes, onion, salt and pepper. Cover loosely with plastic wrap. Place in microwave on HIGH for 5 minutes. Turn and microwave on HIGH 3 minutes. Uncover and gently mix in cheese, paprika, and chopped parsley. Microwave, uncovered 3 more minutes. Let rest 2 minutes before serving. Yield: 3 servings. Cal: 150; Chol: 3mg; Sod: 400mg

Cook 'em Horns: The Quickbook

Garlic Mashed Potatoes

I serve these potatoes often to company and my family. They can be prepared several hours ahead. Cover tightly with a lid or aluminum foil. Heat in a moderate oven for about 20-30 minutes. Remove cover just before serving.

4 pounds red potatoes, cut
   into 1-inch pieces, unpeeled
4-6 large garlic cloves, whole
1 cup milk
½ cup butter

Salt and pepper to taste
4 large garlic cloves, thinly
   sliced
1 tablespoon olive oil

Place potatoes and garlic cloves in a large pot. Cover with water and bring to a boil. Cook until potatoes are tender, about 12-15 minutes. Drain potatoes and garlic. Mash until the large lumps are gone. (This is where personal preference comes in—I really prefer some lumps in my mashed potatoes!) Add milk and butter and beat well to combine. Add salt and pepper to taste. Place in a baking dish.

   In a small skillet, sauté the sliced garlic with the olive oil until light golden brown. Sprinkle garlic and oil over the mashed potatoes. Serve and relish the raves you'll receive!!! Serves 8-10.

The Peach Tree Family Cookbook

A Change From Baked Potatoes

And such a tasty change!

6 potatoes, peeled and cubed
4 tablespoons margarine
4 tablespoons bacon drippings
1 small onion, sliced in rings

6 green onions, sliced
   including tops
Seasoned salt
Cracked pepper

Preheat oven to 350°. Melt margarine and bacon drippings in 9x13-inch Pyrex dish while oven is preheating. Mix potatoes and onions with margarine and bacon drippings to coat. Season to taste. Bake in oven for 45 minutes to 1 hour, stirring occasionally. Serves 6-8.

Delicioso!

Southwest Scalloped Potatoes

8 medium potatoes, peeled
  and thinly sliced
⅓ cup butter
⅓ cup flour
¾ teaspoon garlic salt
3 cups milk

2 cans condensed Cheddar
  cheese soup
1 (4-ounce) can green chilies
1 small onion, finely chopped
Buttered bread crumbs
1 cup grated Monterey Jack cheese
Dash of paprika

Cook potatoes until tender. Melt butter in a saucepan and stir in flour and garlic salt. Cook until bubbly. Stir in milk and cook until in thickens and bubbles, about 3 minutes. Stir soup in with a whisk. Add chilies and onion. Drain potatoes and layer with sauce in a 13x9x2-inch pan. Top with bread crumbs, cheese, reserved chilies and paprika. Cover with foil and bake at 350° for 1 hour, uncover and bake 30 minutes longer. Yield: 12 servings.

Per serving: Cal 372; Fat 8g; Carb 47g; Prot 9g.

Diamonds in the Desert

Frijoles Rancheros

This recipe is adapted from Concha's Mexican Kitchen Cookbook which was written by Catharine Stoker in 1946. In the book's "Foreword," Stoker wrote of her many years in Mexico which included the heyday of Pancho Villa and Zapata (circa 1910).

She recalled living only 40 kilometers from Villa's headquarters and asking the name of the commanding officer of every invasion force that passed through "so that I might 'Viva' the right side!...It was a great life, with all the excitement of hoping to find oneself alive and ready for breakfast in the morning," she wrote.

1 pound dried pinto beans (4 cans of beans may be substituted)	2 cloves garlic, chopped
	½ teaspoon cinnamon
	2 whole cloves
1 jalapeño, chopped	Juice of 1 lemon
1 onion	2 tablespoons olive oil
2 tomatoes	Salt to taste

Cook beans in water for 4 hours over low heat if using dried beans. Add jalapeño, onion, tomatoes, and garlic. Add cinnamon and cloves, lemon juice and olive oil. Cook 20 minutes. Add salt to taste. Serve with warm tortillas. Yield: 4-6 servings.

Canyon Echoes

Brown Beans By Bullock

It ought not to be necessary to have a recipe for cooking a pot of pinto beans. But it must be. Bob Bullock (former Lieutenant Governor of Texas) has come to that conclusion after the many times he's been served mushy pintos that don't even deserve to be recycled on a nacho.

Soaking beans overnight is the #1 killer of a good pot of beans. Don't do it! This old soaking overnight mistake is a hangover from the days when beans were sold in bulk straight from the fields without washing. Today's packaged beans are free of dirt and rocks and need only a little rinsing.

The second enemy of a good pot of pintos is cooking them too long in the name of making them just soft enough to eat. How *long* they cook isn't the answer—*how* they cook is.

CONTINUED

Put your beans in a pot and cover them at least three times higher with water. Bring to a rapid boil for 5 minutes covered. After 5 minutes of boiling, turn out the fire and *do not open the lid*. If you open the lid, forget it. You've ruined it.

Let the covered pot set for 1 hour. Then turn the fire back on just a little higher than a simmer. When the pot starts boiling again and the lid starts jumping around and sputtering over on the stove, put in a tablespoon of oil. This will cut down the sputtering.

After a couple of hours—a little longer if you're busy doing something else—you should need to add more water. Add only *hot* water. Never put cold water in a boiling food.

This is also a good time to add some onion, a slab of salt pork or whatever else you like. The salt pork sold in most markets today is so sorry that you get about the same good out of a couple of strips of bacon.

Now turn the fire down to a simmer, and thicken the juice. A tablespoon or two of brown sugar works fine. It doesn't taste in the beans. Some folks like to use 2 or 3 tablespoons of masa flour worked into a paste. You can taste this in the beans, but it is good. (Incidentally, if you don't keep masa flour around, you can get the same effect by pulverizing a handful of Fritos.) Now the beans can simmer until they are exactly like you want them. They will not get mushy.

At this point you can also decide if you want just plain beans or if you want to go another route. If you like something off in the sweet direction, put in some more brown sugar or a little molasses. If you want something with a little zing, put in whatever is your favorite of barbecue sauce, steak sauce, chili powder, jalapeños, or the like.

When all this is simmered in good, you're ready to eat. If you're planning ahead, you can now put the beans in the icebox and warm 'em up when ready. Just warm them; don't cook 'em to death. They won't get mushy, but the juice will get thick.

Good Eating!

Raider Recipes

Mayan Ranch Barbecue Beans

For over 50 years, the Mayan Ranch in Bandera, Texas, has given visitors the opportunity to be cowboys. This hill country dude ranch serves up the best of the West with old-fashioned barbecue dinners. They say this recipe isn't too sweet like baked beans, but just right for eating with brisket.

2 (23-ounce) cans ranch-style
  beans
1 onion, chopped and sautéed
  until tender
1 link Opa-brand sausage

2 tablespoons prepared
  mustard
½ cup maple syrup
½ cup picante sauce

Combine beans, onion, sausage, mustard, and maple syrup in a glass baking dish or pan. Top with picante sauce. Bake in a 350° oven for 1½ hours. Serves 10-12.

Note: Beans can also be cooked in an iron skillet outside until onions are tender.

Texas Barbecue

Salsa Verde
(Green Enchilada Sauce)

6 fresh green tomatillos,
  cooked and chopped
2 green chili peppers, minced
¼ cup onion, chopped

¼ cup fresh coriander
  (cilantro)
1 teaspoon salt
¼ cup chicken broth

(Tomatillos are green tomatoes which have a dry husk-like covering.) Remove husk covering, rinse, and boil tomatoes in 2 cups water until tender. Drain and chop tomatoes. Blend tomatoes, onion, chili peppers, coriander, broth, and salt in a blender. Cover; blend till puréed. Transfer to saucepan; heat thoroughly. Serves 3-4.

Note: Use this sauce for Green Enchiladas or Green Mole dishes.)

South Texas Mexican Cook Book

Hot Chili Beans with Cornbread

½ pound ground beef, pork,
  or chicken (optional)
1 tablespoon vegetable oil
1 cup chopped onion
2 (16-ounce) cans hot chili
  beans
2 (10-ounce) cans tomatoes
  with green chilies, crushed
Nonstick cooking spray
1 egg

⅔ cup milk
1 (6-ounce) package yellow
  corn bread mix or
  approximately 3 cups batter
Optional toppings: grated
  cheese, sour cream, sliced
  black olives, cilantro,
  shredded lettuce, chopped
  tomato, chopped green onion,

Preheat oven to 400°. Brown meat, if using, in nonstick skillet.
Drain off any fat and reserve browned meat.

Heat oil in skillet over medium-high heat. Add onion and
cook just until soft, 3-5 minutes. Add beans, tomatoes, and
meat. Cook over medium heat until bubbly, stirring occasionally. Reduce heat to low, cover, and simmer 5 minutes. Pour
bean mixture into 9x13x2-inch baking dish that has been sprayed
with nonstick cooking spray.

Beat egg in small mixing bowl. Add milk and cornbread mix;
stir until smooth. Spoon cornbread batter over bean mixture
and spread evenly. Bake 15 minutes or until lightly browned.
Cool 10 minutes before serving.

If desired, top with the grated cheese, sour cream, sliced black
olives, cilantro, shredded lettuce, chopped tomato, or chopped
green onion and picante sauce. Serves 6-8.

Gourmet Grains, Beans, and Rice

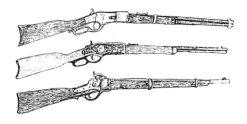

Tomatillo-Jalapeño Chutney

This was one of the first condiments we developed at Routh Street Cafe, and we served it for some time with grilled quail and warm goat cheese. This chutney goes well with any game dish.

12 medium tomatillos (about 1 pound), husked, rinsed, and chopped

2 small red bell peppers, seeded and diced

1 small green bell pepper, seeded, and diced

8 scallions, thinly sliced

4 jalapeño chiles, seeded and minced

⅔ cup red wine vinegar

½ cup fresh corn kernels (1 small ear)

¼ cup firmly packed light brown sugar

1 tablespoon chopped cilantro

1 teaspoon salt

1 clove garlic, minced

¼ teaspoon cayenne powder

¼ teaspoon ground cumin

In a large saucepan, bring all the ingredients to a boil, stirring frequently. Reduce the heat and boil gently until thick, stirring occasionally, 30-35 minutes. Let cool completely. Cover and refrigerate until ready to serve. Makes about 2 cups.

The New Texas Cuisine

Pepper Relish

This is delicious when served over beans and peas.

4 cups green pepper, chopped

4 cups sweet red pepper, chopped

4 cups onion, chopped

4 cups celery, chopped

¼ cup salt

3 cups sugar

3 cups vinegar

Cover peppers, onions, and celery with boiling water. Drain after 5 minutes and add the rest of the ingredients. Boil rapidly for 10 minutes. Pour into sterilized jars and seal.

The Honey Island Boarding House, Honey Island.

Boardin' in the Thicket

Cranberry Chutney

1 pound cranberries
2 cups sugar
½ cup orange juice
4 oranges, peeled, chopped
2 apples, peeled, chopped
2 pears, peeled, chopped

1 tablespoon grated orange rind
1 teaspoon Tabasco sauce
2 teaspoons curry powder
¼ teaspoon ginger

Combine cranberries, sugar, and orange juice in saucepan. Cook until cranberries pop, stirring occasionally. Add oranges, apples, pears, orange rind, Tabasco sauce, curry powder, and ginger; mix well. Cook for 2-3 minutes. Spoon into 6 hot sterilized 1-pint jars; seal with 2-piece lids. Yield: 50 servings.

Approx Per Serving: Cal 50; Prot <1g; Carbo 13g; Fiber 1g; T Fat <1g; 1% Calories from Fat; Chol 0mg; Sod 1mg.

Gatherings

Cranapple Pepper Jelly

Super!

1 cup chopped jalapeño peppers (mild variety if you can locate)
1 quart cranapple juice cocktail

7 cups sugar
1¼ cups vinegar
7 ounces Certo (liquid)
Red food coloring

In blender container, process peppers and cranapple juice till peppers are finely chopped. Strain into large kettle. Stir in sugar, vinegar, Certo, and food coloring to tint as desired. Bring to a rolling boil, then boil 3-5 minutes. Pour into sterilized jelly glasses and seal with paraffin. When cool, cover with lids. Makes 8 half-pints.

Note: Cover ball of cream cheese with this jelly. Serve with crackers.

The Mexican Collection

Prickly Pear Jelly

This is an 1852 recipe.

Gather about a half-bushel of dark red or purple prickly pear apples. My grandfather Hardt always built a small fire and singed the thorns off by putting the apples on a long-handled fork and holding them over the flames. Then the residue of the thorns was cut off before the apples were washed and quartered. Put apples in a kettle or large pot, cover with water, and boil for about 20 minutes. Press the pulp through four thicknesses of cheesecloth and let the juice drip from jelly bag. Grandmother Vetter saved her sugar sacks for jelly bags. For each 4 cups of juice, use 1¾ ounces boiled-down strained grape or pear juice, and let it dry some in a cool place. Bring to rough boil. Add 3½ pounds of sugar (7 cups) and bring back to a hard boil for 5 minutes. Skim and pour into clean jars. Let set for a spell and then cover with hot beeswax.

I remember that after the beeswax or paraffin had set, my grandmother would stretch a rag across the glass and tie it with a string. Then the rag would be pulled down all the way around until it was tight.

A Pinch of This and A Handful of That

Paul Bosland, a New Mexico State University chili breeder, ranks chilies according to their spiciness, with 1 being mild to 10 as the firehouse hottest! 1) bell peppers, pimento; 2) NuMex R Naky; 3) Anaheim; 4) Ancho; 5) Santa Fe Grande; 6) Serrano; 7) Jalapeno; 8) Tabasco, cayenne peppers; 9) Piquin; 10) Habanero. *The Mexican Collection* also tells us not to gulp down cold beverages after a hot bite, as it just tends to spread the heat. Instead have bread, rice, or other absorbent foods ready to cool the fire.

Pasta, Rice, Enchiladas, Etc.

Editor Gwen McKee takes a stroll back through history
at the San Jose Mission in San Antonio.

Angel Hair Pasta with Goat Cheese Cream Sauce and Sun-Dried Tomatoes

1 cup dry white wine
¼ cup white wine vinegar
3 shallots, trimmed and
   minced
2 tablespoons chopped garlic
¼ teaspoon salt
¼ teaspoon white pepper

1 bay leaf
3 cups heavy cream
8 ounces goat cheese
1½ pounds angel hair pasta,
   cooked
4-5 sun-dried tomatoes,
   softened and sliced thin

In a medium saucepan, combine wine, vinegar, shallots, garlic, salt, pepper, and bay leaf. Bring mixture to a boil, then reduce heat, and simmer for 15-20 minutes, or until liquid is reduced by half.

Add cream and bring again to a boil. Reduce heat and simmer for about 4 minutes longer, or until liquid thickens. Remove from heat and strain through a fine sieve.

Transfer sauce to a clean saucepan and warm over low heat. Whisk in goat cheese and simmer for about 10 minutes. (Be careful not to scorch.)

Arrange cooked pasta and sauce on plates and garnish with strips of sun-dried tomatoes. Serves 4-5.

Dallas Cuisine

Macho Fettucine

1 package fettucine
1 pound Italian sausage

1 can cream of chicken soup
2 cups sour cream

Cook fettucine and drain. Cut up Italian sausage into small pieces. Brown sausage over medium-high heat for about 8 minutes. Place on paper towel to drain grease. Mix all ingredients together. Put into a 6x18-inch Pyrex dish. Bake 30 minutes at 350°. Serves 4-6.

The College Cookbook

Creamed Pasta with Fresh Basil

Fresh basil may be difficult to obtain in the winter. If so, substitute another fresh herb or use pesto.

8 ounces thin, flat pasta (such as linguine), cooked al dente
1 large clove garlic
15 fresh basil leaves
1 cup half-and-half or light cream

2 tablespoons unsalted butter
Salt and freshly ground pepper to taste
1⅓ cups grated Gruyère cheese

Mince together garlic and basil with scissors or chop on a board. Using the still-hot saucepan the pasta cooked in, pour in half-and-half, butter, basil-garlic mixture, salt, pepper, and pasta. Reheat and serve immediately, accompanied by a bowl of grated Gruyère. Serves 2-4.

Recipe from La Madeleine French Bakery & Cafe, San Antonio.

San Antonio Cuisine

Chicken Broccoli Quiche

3 cups grated Cheddar cheese
1½ cups cooked chicken, diced
⅔ cup chopped onion
1 package frozen chopped broccoli, thawed and drained

1⅓ cups milk
3 eggs
¼ teaspoon pepper
¾ cup Bisquick

Mix 2 cups of the cheese, chicken, onion, and broccoli in 10-inch deep greased pie plate. Beat remaining ingredients except cheese with hand mixer until smooth. Pour over mixture in pie plate. Bake 350°, 20-30 minutes or until knife inserted in center comes out clean. Top with remaining cup of cheese. Bake until melted 1-2 minutes. Cool 5 minutes. Serves: 6-8.

M. D. Anderson Volunteers Cooking for Fun

Juarez Quiche
(Microwave)

Too tired for kitchen duty? Try this one.

1 pastry shell
1 cup Cheddar cheese
1½ cups Monterey Jack
  cheese
1 cup milk

1 (4-ounce) can chopped
  green chilies
Salt and cumin
3 eggs, lightly beaten

Bake pastry shell in a microwave pie plate according to directions. Grate cheeses and sprinkle in bottom of shell. Heat milk, chilies, salt and cumin, but do not boil. Whisk eggs into hot mixture. Pour mixture over cheese. Microwave at 70% power for 10-12 minutes, turning every 3-4 minutes. Pie will be soft in center but will set up during standing time. Let stand at least 30 minutes.

'Cross the Border

Denise's Deep Dish Pizza

1 package active dry yeast
1 cup warm water
2 tablespoons oil
1 teaspoon salt
1 teaspoon sugar
2½ cups flour

1 pound ground beef or
  sausage
1 small can tomato sauce
1 (4-ounce) Mozzarella
  cheese

Dissolve yeast in water. Stir in oil, salt, sugar, and flour. Beat twenty strokes. Let rise 5 minutes. Cook 1 pound ground beef or sausage. Drain. Press dough into lightly greased oblong pan. Add tomato sauce, meat mixture, and any extras you desire (olives, mushrooms, peppers, onions, etc). Bake 15 minutes at 400°. Add cheese and bake another 5 minutes.

Gingerbread...and all the trimmings

Three Cheese Casserole

1 pound ground beef
½ cup chopped onion
2 (8-ounce) cans tomato sauce
1 teaspoon sugar
¾ teaspoon salt
¼ teaspoon garlic salt
¼ teaspoon pepper
4 cups raw noodles

1 cup cream-style cottage
  cheese
1 (8-ounce) package soft
  cream cheese
¼ cup sour cream
⅓ cup chopped green pepper
¼ cup grated Parmesan
  cheese

In a large skillet, cook meat and onion till meat is lightly browned and onion is tender. Stir in tomato sauce, sugar, salt, garlic salt, and pepper. Remove from heat. Cook and drain noodles. Combine cottage cheese, cream cheese, sour cream, and green pepper. Spread ½ of noodles in a 11x7-inch dish. Top with a small amount of the meat sauce. Cover with the cheese mixture. Layer remaining noodles, then meat sauce. Top with Parmesan. Bake at 350° for 30 minutes. Serves 8-10.

Gingerbread...and all the trimmings

Beef, Noodle & Cheese Casserole

Something like lasagna, but easier to prepare.

1 (8-ounce) package egg noodles	¼ cup dairy sour cream
1 pound lean ground beef	1 (8-ounce) package cream cheese
1 teaspoon salt	½ cup chopped green onions
1 tablespoon butter	1 tablespoon chopped bell pepper
2 (8-ounce) cans tomato sauce	2 tablespoons melted butter
1 cup cream-style cottage cheese	

Cook noodles according to package directions. Brown meat in butter. Add tomato sauce. Remove from heat and set aside. Combine cottage cheese, sour cream, onion, bell pepper, and cream cheese in a separate bowl. Using a 2-quart buttered casserole, spread with half of the noodles. Cover with the cheese mixture. Spread with the remainder of the noodles. Drizzle with melted butter. Top with meat mixture. Bake 30 minutes in 350° oven. Yield: 6 servings.

Calories: 700; Cholesterol: 165mg; Sodium: 1300mg

Cook 'em Horns: The Quickbook

Rice with Mushrooms

1⅓ cups long grain rice, uncooked	1 (4-ounce) can mushrooms, drained
2 (10½-ounce) cans beef consommé	1 medium onion, chopped
	1 stick margarine

Mix uncooked rice, consommé, mushrooms, and onion in 2-quart casserole dish. Cut stick of margarine into slices (about 10) and place on top. Cover. Bake at 425° for 45 minutes or until consommé is absorbed. Yield: 6 servings.

Deep in the Heart

Chicken Spaghetti "Carole Curlee Special"

BROTH:

1 (3 - 4-pound) chicken	Salt to taste
1 onion	Water to cover
2 stalks celery	

Boil till chicken is tender. Cool to handle; bone chicken, reserving broth.

1 large onion, chopped	Salt and pepper to taste
3 ribs celery, sliced	½ teaspoon garlic salt
3 tablespoons oleo	1 small jar pimientos, chopped
1 grated carrot, optional	1 small can sliced
2 cans cream of chicken soup	mushrooms, optional
1 can or more saved broth or	3-4 chicken bouillon cubes,
evaporated milk	optional
1¾ cup grated Cheddar	1 (12-ounce) package
cheese	spaghetti, cooked
1 teaspoon chili powder	

Sauté onion, celery, and carrots in oleo. Add soup and broth (or milk). Add 1 cup grated cheese to the sauce mixture and heat. Also, add chili powder, salt, pepper, garlic salt, pimientos, and mushrooms. Add the boned chicken. Taste for seasoning; can add chicken bouillon cubes for more flavor. Toss the sauce with cooked spaghetti. Put a ladle of extra sauce on top for eye appeal, and toss ¾ cup grated cheese on top. Either refrigerate until later, or cook at 325° for 25 minutes or until bubbly and hot. You can add a little more liquid if you want thinner sauce. This is super! Serves 8.

A Casually Catered Affair

Mother's Chicken Filled Shells

2½ cups cooked chicken
  breasts
1 small jar pimento
½ cup minced onion
½ cup mayonnaise
14 cup sliced almonds
¼ cup chopped mushrooms
¼ cup chopped water
  chestnuts

1 (12-ounce) package jumbo
  pasta shells, cooked and
  cooled
Stuffed olives, sliced
1 can cream of chicken soup
½ cup water
Chopped parsley

Mix first 6 ingredients and stuff shells. Place sliced olive in each. Arrange in single layer in 9x13-inch casserole dish. Combine soup and water and carefully pour over shells. Cover with foil and bake at 325° for 30 minutes. Sprinkle with chopped parsley before serving. Yum, wonderful!

From Cajun Roots to Texas Boots

Santa Fe Chicken

4 boneless, skinless chicken
  breasts
1 teaspoon paprika
1 teaspoon salt
¼ teaspoon pepper
2 teaspoons olive oil or oleo
1 small onion, chopped
1 small bell pepper, chopped

1 garlic clove, minced
1 (10-ounce) can Rotel
  tomatoes and green chilies
Chicken broth
1½ cups Uncle Ben's
  instant rice
¾ cup (3 ounces) shredded
  Monterey Jack cheese

Cut cooked chicken into strips or chunks. Sprinkle with paprika, salt and pepper. Heat oil in 10-inch skillet over medium-high heat. Cook chicken in oil for 2 minutes. Add onion, bell pepper, and garlic; cook until tender (about 4 minutes), stirring frequently. Drain tomatoes, reserving liquid. Add chicken broth to tomato liquid to equal 1½ cups of liquid. Add liquid to skillet; bring to boil. Stir in rice and reserved tomatoes. Cover and remove from heat. Let stand until liquid is absorbed (about 5 minutes). Sprinkle with cheese. Yields 4 servings.

From Cajun Roots to Texas Boots

Michael's Rice Pilaf

1 cup fine noodles, broken in
   pieces
1 cup raw rice
½ cup onion, finely-chopped
2 cloves garlic, minced
½ teaspoon ground cumin
3 tablespoons butter or
   margarine, melted

2 (10½-ounce) cans
   condensed chicken broth
²/₃ cup water
Dash of crushed red pepper,
   optional
½ cup cilantro or parsley,
   chopped
6 green onions, thinly-sliced

Cook and stir noodles, rice, onion, garlic, and cumin in butter or margarine in saucepan until noodle mixture is lightly brown. Add broth, water, and red pepper. Bring to a boil; stir. Reduce heat. Cover; cook over low heat for 20-25 minutes, or until liquid is absorbed. Stir in cilantro and green onions. Makes 4-6 servings.

Dallas Cowboys Wives' Family Cookbook

Green Rice Casserole

2 cups uncooked rice
1½ cups milk
½ cup salad oil
1 cup chopped fresh parsley
   (or flakes)
1 cup chopped green pepper

2 cloves of garlic, minced
1 pound Cheddar cheese,
   shredded
1 cup chopped whole green
   onions
Salt and pepper, to taste

Cook rice, following package directions; rinse and drain. Add milk, oil, and other ingredients; mix well. Pour into greased 2-quart casserole. Cover with foil and bake 1 hour. Serves 10-12. Can be made the day before, but do not bake. Store, covered, in refrigerator. Heat thoroughly (at 350°) when time to serve.

Central Texas Style

 Gail Borden, a Texas surveyor and patriot, discovered that milk could be condensed by evaporation, and patented condensed milk in 1856. He was the founder of the Borden Milk Company.

Black Beans & Yellow Rice

½ cup diced bacon
1 cup chopped onions
2 cloves crushed garlic
2 cups uncooked rice
2½ teaspoons salt
¼ teaspoon ground turmeric
⅓ teaspoon crushed red
  pepper

4 cups water
1 cup chopped green peppers
2 medium fresh tomatoes,
  chopped
½ cup fully-cooked ham
1 pound dry black beans
  cooked and well-seasoned or
  4 (16-ounce) cans black beans

Cook bacon in heavy pan (preferably iron) until almost done; discard fat. Add onions and garlic; cook over low heat until tender-crisp. Stir in rice, seasonings and water. Bring to a boil, reduce heat, cover and simmer 10 minutes. Add green peppers, tomatoes, and ham; simmer 5 minutes longer or until rice is tender and liquid is absorbed. Serve yellow rice in deep bowls and spoon beans in center. Yield: 12 servings.

Canyon Echoes

Broccoli and Rice Casserole

1 cup uncooked rice
2 cups water
1 teaspoon salt
½ cup minced onion
½ cup celery, chopped
3 tablespoons butter or oleo
1 package frozen chopped
  broccoli

1 can cream of mushroom
  soup
1 can cream of chicken soup
1 (8-ounce) jar Cheez Whiz or
  ½ pound Velvetta

Cook rice in salted water; bring to boil, lower heat, cover and simmer 15 minutes; turn off heat, let stand for 10 minutes. Cook broccoli as directed on package. Sauté onion and celery in butter. Mix all together; add soups and cheese. Place in casserole. Heat in 300° oven until bubbling, about 30 minutes. May be frozen.

Variation: Paprika, pimentos, garlic powder may be used.

Decades of Mason County Cooking

Company Casserole

1 (6-ounce) package wild rice
1 (10-ounce) package frozen
  chopped broccoli
2 cups chopped cooked ham
1 (4-ounce) can mushrooms,
  drained
1 cup diced Cheddar cheese
1 can cream of celery soup
1 cup mayonnaise
2 teaspoons prepared mustard
1 teaspoon curry powder
¼ cup grated Parmesan
  cheese

Cook rice according to package directions. Spread on bottom of a buttered 9x13-inch pan. Top with broccoli, ham, mushrooms, and cheese. Blend soup with mayonnaise, mustard, and curry. Pour soup mixture over all. Sprinkle with Parmesan cheese; bake at 350° for 45 minutes. Serves 6-8.

Lone Star Legacy

Brown Rice Pilaf with Raisins and Nuts

¼ cup chopped onion
2 tablespoons butter
1 tablespoon oil
1 cup raw brown rice
2½ cups chicken stock or
  water
¼ teaspoon black pepper
½ cup yellow raisins
½ cup dry white wine
¾ cup almonds, sliced and
  toasted

Sauté onions in butter and oil until clear. Add rice and cook over low heat for 3 minutes, stirring constantly, until lightly browned. Add chicken stock. Season with pepper. Bring to a boil. Cover, reduce heat, and simmer for 45 minutes. While rice cooks, plump raisins in white wine for about 45 minutes. Drain. When rice is cooked, stir in raisins and toasted almonds. Yield: 4 servings.

Note: One (14½-ounce) can of clear chicken broth may be used for the stock. Add water to make 2½ cups.

Homecoming

Tuna and Rice Quickie

Filling, pretty and good!

1 (10¾-ounce) can cream of
  mushroom soup
1 (5-ounce) can evaporated
  milk
2½ cups cooked rice
2 (7-ounce) cans tuna, drained
  and flaked

¼ pound processed
  American cheese, grated
¼ cup finely chopped onion
¼ cup finely chopped
  pimiento
2 dashes Tabasco

In large mixing bowl, combine all ingredients, mixing well. Turn into greased 1½-quart baking dish. Bake 30 minutes at 350° or until hot throughout. Yield: 6 servings.

Calories: 350; Cholesterol: 60mg; Sodium: 1200mg

Cook 'em Horns: The Quickbook

Fiery Tex-Mex Rice

1 (16-ounce) can whole
  tomatoes, chopped with juices
1 (8-ounce) can tomato sauce
Water
2 tablespoons olive oil
1 cup chopped onion
½ cup chopped green pepper

1 small jalapeño, whole
1 cup rice
½ teaspoon salt
1 teaspoon ground cumin
1 teaspoon chili powder
Leaves from 2-3 sprigs fresh
  cilantro for garnish

Place tomatoes and their liquid along with tomato sauce in 3-cup measure. Add enough water to equal 2½ cups liquid; reserve.

Heat oil in large skillet over medium heat. Add onion, green pepper, and jalapeño, cooking until vegetables are wilted, about 5 minutes. Add rice, stirring to coat grains evenly. Cook about 5 minutes or until rice and vegetables begin to brown. Add salt, cumin, and chili powder and stir to coat all ingredients.

Gradually stir in reserved tomatoes and liquid. Be careful to avoid spatters. Reduce heat, cover and simmer until rice is tender and liquid is absorbed, about 14-16 minutes. Remove whole jalapeño. Garnish with snipped cilantro leaves.

Serves 4-6.

Gourmet Grains, Beans, and Rice

Spanish Rice

A Mexican dinner would not be complete without this dish.

1 cup rice
2 tablespoons oil
1 onion, chopped
2 cloves garlic, minced
1 (16-ounce) can stewed
   tomatoes, chopped

1 (14-ounce) beef broth
Salt and pepper
½ teaspoon cumin powder

Place rice, oil, onion and garlic in skillet and brown. Add tomatoes, beef broth, salt and pepper, and cumin. Cover and simmer 20 minutes or until tender and juice is absorbed.

'Cross the Border

Jambalaya

2 medium onions, chopped
½ medium green pepper,
   chopped
1 clove garlic, finely chopped
3 tablespoons olive or
   vegetable oil
1 pound fresh or frozen
   medium raw shrimp, peeled
   and deveined
1 cup uncooked rice

2 cup chicken broth
1 (16-ounce) can tomatoes
1 teaspoon salt
⅛ teaspoon pepper
⅛ teaspoon ground thyme
⅛ teaspoon red pepper
   sauce
1 bay leaf, crumbled
1½ cups cubed cooked ham

Cook onions, green pepper, garlic, and 2 tablespoons of oil in 4-quart Dutch oven over low heat for 3 minutes. Add shrimp. Cook, stirring frequently, until shrimp are pink. Turn shrimp mixture into bowl and reserve. Cook remaining 1 tablespoon oil and rice in Dutch oven over medium-high heat, stirring frequently, until rice is light brown. Stir in chicken broth, tomatoes (with liquid), salt, pepper, thyme, pepper sauce, and bay leaf. Heat to boiling. Reduce heat. Cover and simmer 15 minutes. Stir in reserved shrimp mixture and ham. Cover and cook until hot. Yield: 6 servings.

Wild About Texas

Southwestern Risotto

Can be served as a main meal with a green salad.

½ cup chopped onion
2 cloves garlic, crushed
2 tablespoons butter or
  margarine, melted
1 cup medium-grain rice,
  uncooked
½ cup dry white wine
6 cups chicken broth, divided
½ cup whipping cream
2 medium tomatoes, seeded
  and chopped

1 jalapeño pepper, seeded
  and minced
½ cup sliced green onions
½ cup grated Parmesan
  cheese
3 tablespoons minced cilantro
Garnish: fresh cilantro
  sprigs, cubed tomatoes

Cook onion and garlic in butter in a large skillet or saucepan over medium heat, stirring constantly, until tender. Add rice; cook 2-3 minutes, stirring frequently with a wooden spoon. Add wine and cook, uncovered, until liquid is absorbed. Add one cup broth; cook, stirring constantly, over medium-high heat 5 minutes or until broth is absorbed. Add remaining broth, 1 cup at a time, cooking and stirring constantly until each cup is absorbed, about 25-30 minutes. (Rice will be tender and have a creamy consistency).

Stir in whipping cream and next 5 ingredients. Cook 2 minutes. Serves 6.

Texas Sampler

Wild Rice Cakes

These savory cakes are baked, rather than sautéed or fried.

¾ cup cooked wild rice
½ cup finely diced red and
  yellow bell pepper
½ cup finely diced zucchini

Pinch of arrowroot
Salt and pepper
2 egg whites, beaten until stiff
1½ teaspoons olive oil

Place wild rice, bell pepper, zucchini, and arrowroot in a mixing bowl, and season with salt and pepper. Fold in egg whites. Spoon small cakes onto greased pan and bake at 375° until golden brown. Serves 6.

Fort Worth is Cooking!

Mexican Lasagna

2 pounds lean ground pork
  (beef may be substituted)
1 (16-ounce) can refried beans
2 teaspoons dried oregano
1 teaspoon cumin
1 teaspoon garlic powder
1 (8-ounce) package lasagna
  noodles, uncooked

2½ cups salsa
2½ cups water
1 (16-ounce) container sour
  cream
2 cups Monterey Jack cheese
½ cup chopped green onion
1 (2.2-ounce) can sliced black
  olives

Mix uncooked ground pork, beans, and seasonings. Line bottom of 13x9x2-inch pan with uncooked lasagna noodles, spread half of meat mixture over noodles, make another layer of noodles and spread with remaining meat mixture; if you have noodles left over, layer them on top.

Mix salsa and water, pour over casserole, cover tightly. Bake at 350° for 1½ hours. Cover with sour cream and shredded cheese. Top with green onions and olives. Bake for 5 more minutes to melt cheese. Yield: 12-14 servings.

Canyon Echoes

Quick Enchilada Casserole

1 (9-ounce) package corn
  chips
1 large onion, peeled and
  chopped

1 (1-pound) can chili without
  beans
Grated American cheese

Place corn chips in bottom of a greased casserole. Top with onions. Pour in chili. Cover with cheese, using as much as desired. Bake at 375° for 15-20 minutes, or until cheese is melted and casserole is well heated. Serves 2-4.

Down-Home Texas Cooking

Tortillas de la Hacienda

Luncheon for a gathering.

5 tablespoons oil
10 cups cubed cooked
   chicken or turkey
2½ cups chopped onion
2½ cups chopped celery
2½ cups chopped cilantro or
   parsley
5 (2-ounce) jars diced
   pimiento, drained

5 teaspoons lemon juice
5 cups mayonnaise
2½ teaspoons each ground
   cumin, paprika and black
   pepper
10 garlic cloves, minced
40 flour tortillas

Preheat oven to 350°. Heat oil in skillet; cook chicken, onion, and celery 3-5 minutes until onion is transparent and celery softens slightly. Remove from heat and add cilantro, pimiento, lemon juice, mayonnaise, cumin, paprika, pepper, and garlic. Stir well. Place ½ cup chicken mixture on each tortilla and roll up. Place seam-side-down in lightly buttered baking dishes.

SAUCE:

5 (10¾-ounce) cans cream
   of chicken soup
2½ soup cans water
5 cups grated Cheddar cheese
2½ teaspoons each ground
   cumin, paprika and garlic
   powder

10 large mushrooms, sliced,
   or 5 (2-ounce) cans sliced
   mushrooms, drained

Pour soup into a pan and stir vigorously until smooth. Add water and stir until blended. Heat until barely simmering. Add cheese and remaining spices, stirring until cheese melts and is blended. Pour over tortillas. Bake at 350° for 20 minutes. Arrange mushrooms on top and bake 3 minutes more. Yield: 25-30 servings.

The Gathering

Sour Cream Chicken Enchiladas

4 chicken breasts
1 onion, chopped
1 tablespoon margarine
1 (4-ounce) can chopped
  green chilies
2 (4-ounce) cans sliced
  mushrooms, drained
1¼ cups shredded Cheddar
  cheese
½ teaspoon garlic powder
½ teaspoon chili powder

1 cup sour cream
12 flour tortillas
¼ cup flour
¼ cup melted butter
1 cup shredded Monterey
  Jack cheese
1½ cups sour cream
Chili powder to taste
1½ cups shredded
  Monterey Jack cheese

Rinse chicken and pat dry. Cook in water to cover in saucepan until tender. Drain, reserving 1½ cups broth. Cool and chop chicken. Sauté onion in margarine in skillet. Add chicken, green chilies, mushrooms, Cheddar cheese, garlic powder, ½ teaspoon chili powder, and 1 cup sour cream; mix well. Microwave tortillas on HIGH for 1 minute or until softened. Spoon chicken mixture onto tortillas. Roll to enclose filling. Place seam-side-down in greased 9x13-inch baking dish. Blend flour into butter in saucepan. Stir in reserved broth. Cook until thickened and bubbly, stirring constantly. Stir in 1 cup Monterey Jack cheese, 1½ cups sour cream and additional chili powder to taste. Pour over enchiladas. Bake at 350° for 30 minutes. Sprinkle with remaining 1½ cups Monterey Jack cheese. Bake just until cheese melts. Yield: 6 servings.

Approx per serving: Cal 1001; Prot 44g; Carbo 76g; Fiber 5g; T Fat 61g; Chol 164mg; Sod 1168.

Texas Cookin' Lone Star Style

153

Chicken Enchiladas

3 chicken breasts, cooked
  and diced (save stock)
2 cans cream of chicken soup
½ pint sour cream
2 small cans green chilies

1 soup can of water
2 cups Cheddar cheese,
  grated
1 cup onion, chopped
12 tortillas

Boil chicken in seasoned water. Make sauce of soup, sour cream, chilies, and water. Add diced chicken. Combine cheese and onion. Dip tortillas in chicken stock. Stuff with sauce and 1 tablespoon of cheese and onion. Roll up in casserole and cover with remaining sauce. Bake 325° for 30 minutes.

Gingerbread...and all the trimmings

Green Enchiladas

(Rolled)

½ pound Velveeta cheese
1 can cream of chicken soup
1 small can evaporated milk
1 small can green chilies,
  chopped
1 small can pimentos,
  chopped

1 pound ground meat
2 onions, chopped
½ pound Cheddar cheese
1 package tortillas

Make sauce of Velveeta, soup, and milk over low heat. Add green chilies and pimentos. Brown meat lightly; add onion and grated cheese. Dip tortilla in hot water and place small amount of meat in each one and roll. Place in baking dish. Pour sauce over enchiladas, cover with foil and bake at 350° for 30 minutes. Serves 6-8.

Decades of Mason County Cooking

The Tyler Municipal Rose Garden is the largest rose garden in the United States. Tyler is the Rose Capitol of the World.

Open-Face Enchiladas

This is great served with a green salad.

SAUCE:

2-4 tablespoons New Mexico chili powder or to taste
3 tablespoons flour
¼ teaspoon oregano
¼ teaspoon garlic powder

2 tablespoons oil
1 teaspoon salt
¼ teaspoon cumin
⅓ teaspoon pepper
2 cups water

Combine sauce ingredients and cook about 15 minutes.

4 corn tortillas
Hot oil
½ pound Longhorn cheese, grated

½ pound Monterey Jack cheese, grated
1 small onion, grated

Soften tortillas in hot oil. Dip a tortilla in sauce and place in a pie dish. Divide cheeses and onions equally and spread on top of each tortilla. Pour remaining sauce on top and bake 10-15 minutes at 350°. Serves 4.

Potluck on the Pedernales

Mango Chutney

It's so easy to make chutney in the microwave you'll probably never use the stove-top method again. The flavor of the mangoes in this sweet-spicy chutney is a good accompaniment to poultry or pork dishes.

1½ cups chopped fresh mangoes
¼ cup light brown sugar
¼ cup finely chopped onion

½ cup golden raisins
2 tablespoons white vinegar
½ teaspoon ground ginger
½ teaspoon dry mustard

Peel and seed the mangoes and cut into ½-inch cubes. Combine with the other ingredients in a deep 2-quart microwave-safe dish. Mix well. Cook, uncovered, on HIGH for 6 minutes. Cool, cover and refrigerate. Makes about 2 cups.

New Tastes of Texas

Richardson Woman's Club Pickles

We started selling these at bake sales in 1958!

1 gallon whole dill or sour pickles	1 teaspoon allspice
5 pounds sugar	3 tablespoons celery seed
3 tablespoons mustard seed	3 tablespoons whole cloves
8 sticks cinnamon	8 cloves garlic
	4 jalapeño pods, optional

Drain and discard juice from pickles. Cut into ¾-inch thick slices and place in a 2-gallon crock. (Don't use aluminum!) Pour sugar and spices over pickle slices. After 24 hours stir with wooden or stainless steel spoon. Then stir 2 or 3 times daily. They are ready to eat after the third day. May be left in crock (covered) or put into four 1-quart jars and sealed.

Note: There will be lots of juice left when pickles are gone. Don't throw it away! It's wonderful for basting a baked ham. Also gives a delightful flavor to tuna or chicken salad. (Put some pickles in the salad, too!)

The Texas Experience

Poultry

The Tower at the University of Texas at Austin.

Chicken in Lime

This is such an easy dish but will impress anyone who tastes it.

6 chicken breast halves, skinned and boned	8 tablespoons butter
½ teaspoon salt	⅓ teaspoon garlic powder
½ teaspoon white pepper	¾ teaspoon minced green onions
⅓ cup oil	½ teaspoon dill weed
1 lime, juiced	

Sprinkle chicken, both sides, with salt and pepper. Place oil in a large skillet and heat to medium; add chicken and sauté until lightly browned. Turn chicken, cover and reduce heat to low. Cook 10 minutes or until done. Remove chicken and keep warm; drain off oil. In same pan, add lime juice and cook over low heat until juice begins to bubble. Add butter, stirring, until butter becomes opaque and forms a thickened sauce. Stir in garlic, green onions, and dill. Spoon over chicken. Serves 6.

Best of Friends Two

Yvette's Crunchy Chicken

2 cups sautéed Butterball boneless, skinless chicken breasts (approximately 1 package)	1 tablespoon lemon juice
	1 teaspoon onion, grated
	1 (3½-ounce) can sliced mushrooms
1 can cream of mushroom soup	½ cup sliced almonds, toasted
¾ cup mayonnaise	1 cup cornflakes, crumbled
1 cup diced celery	3 tablespoons butter
1 cup rice, cooked in chicken broth	

Combine first 9 ingredients. Place in casserole dish. Sprinkle cornflakes and butter on top. Bake at 350° for 30 minutes. Makes 6 servings.

Dallas Cowboys Wives' Family Cookbook

Chicken Fajitas #1 Favorite

This recipe is so good that you can even stir-fry it inside and people will love it! Anything is best grilled outside, but this succeeds either way.

1 cup soy sauce
1 cup water
2½ tablespoons honey
1 tablespoons Worcestershire
  sauce
½ tablespoon granulated
  garlic

¼ teaspoon ground ginger
1½ tablespoons liquid
  smoke
⅓ cup (2 tablespoons) lemon
  juice
6-8 chicken breast halves

Mix ingredients and marinate the chicken for 1 hour. This marinade can be refrigerated and used once or twice more within the week. Serves 6.

Note: To serve, provide guests with warm flour tortillas and bowls of salsa, refried beans, guacamole, grilled onions and bell pepper strips, grated cheese and chili conqueso to make their fijitas just as they want them. Don't forget the Pico de Gallo! Also good with skirt steak, good round steak or flank steak. Allow ⅓ pound of meat per person.

The Mexican Collection

Jalapeño Chicken

2 cups chopped onions
2 tablespoons butter
1 (10-ounce) package frozen
chopped spinach, cooked and
drained
6 jalapeño peppers
1 pint sour cream
2 cans cream of chicken soup

4 green onions, tops only
½ teaspoon salt
1 (12-ounce) package Doritos
4-6 cups chopped, cooked
chicken
2 cups grated Monterey Jack
cheese

Sauté onions in butter; blend in spinach, jalapeños, sour cream, soup, onion tops, and salt. In a large Pyrex pan alternate layers of Doritos, chicken, spinach mixture and cheese. Layer again ending with cheese. Bake at 350°, 30-40 minutes. Serves 10-12.

Lone Star Legacy

Pollo Pizziolla

8 boneless, skinless chicken
breasts
1 cup all-purpose flour
Salt and pepper to taste
½ cup olive oil
3 tablespoons chopped garlic

2 (24-ounce) cans plum
tomatoes, drained and cut into
½-inch pieces
1½ teaspoons dried oregano
3 tablespoons finely chopped
parsley

Trim fat from chicken breasts, rinse in cold water, and pat dry with paper towels. Season flour generously with salt and pepper, mixing well, and spread onto a plate or piece of waxed paper. Dip chicken breasts in flour to lightly coat all sides.

Heat olive oil in a large skillet over medium-high heat. Place chicken breasts in a single layer in skillet along with garlic. Fry until chicken becomes golden around the edges, then turn and cook other side. Stir in tomatoes and oregano, and cook uncovered for 10 minutes. Sprinkle with fresh parsley and serve immediately. Serves 8.

Massimo da Milano, Dallas.

Dallas Cuisine

Microwave Chicken Kiev

Pat Swinney's "micro-quick" recipe for the working girl. Very impressive dish for those unexpected guests.

4 whole chicken breasts
1 cup cheese crackers,
  crushed
1½ tablespoons taco
  seasoning mix, dry
3 tablespoons butter
3 tablespoons soft Cheddar
  cheese

2 teaspoons instant minced
  onion
1 teaspoon monosodium
  glutamate
2 tablespoons chopped green
  chilies
1 teaspoon salt

Skin, bone and half chicken breasts; pound flat. Set aside. Combine crackers and taco seasoning; set aside. Mix together butter, cheese, onion, MSG, green chilies, and salt. Divide butter mixture into 8 balls. Roll chicken breasts around each butter-cheese ball. Tuck in ends and fasten with a toothpick. Dip each chicken piece in melted butter and roll in cheese-cracker/taco seasoning mix. Lay in pan and cover with wax paper. Microwave on HIGH for 10-12 minutes.

More Calf Fries to Caviar

Chicken Florentine with Mushroom Sauce

½ cup minced onion
1 tablespoon margarine
2 (10-ounce) packages frozen
  chopped spinach, thawed and
  drained

1 cup (4 ounces) shredded
  Swiss cheese
½ teaspoon ground nutmeg
4 skinless, boneless chicken
  breast halves, pounded flat

Sauté onion in margarine. Remove from heat and add spinach, cheese, and nutmeg. Spoon spinach mixture into 4 mounds in lightly-greased 13x9x2-inch baking dish. Place chicken piece over each mound. Bake at 350° for 20-30 minutes or until chicken is done.

MUSHROOM SAUCE:

2 cups sliced fresh
  mushrooms
1 tablespoon margarine
2 teaspoons lemon juice

1 cup chicken broth
1 cup milk
½ cup dry white wine
White pepper to taste

Sauté mushrooms in margarine until liquid evaporates. Add lemon juice, broth, milk, wine, and white pepper to mushrooms. Bring to a boil and cook until liquid is reduced by 2/3 and sauce is slightly thickened. Spoon ¼ of sauce over each serving.
   Serves 4.

Per serving: Cal 540; Prot 47.6g; Carb 19.2g; Fat 29.5g; Chol 124mg; Sod 578mg.

Changing Thymes

Pecan Chicken

This recipe is a real winner!

1 cup flour
1 cup ground pecans
¼ cup sesame seeds
1 tablespoon paprika
1½ teaspoons salt
⅛ teaspoon pepper
1 egg beaten

1 cup buttermilk
8 (5-ounce) chicken breasts,
  boned and skinned
⅓ cup butter
¼ cup coarsely chopped
  pecans

Combine first 6 ingredients. Mix together egg and buttermilk. Dip breasts in egg mixture and then coat well in flour mixture. Melt butter in baking dish. Place breasts in dish, turning once to coat with butter. Sprinkle with coarsely chopped pecans. Bake in a preheated 350° oven for 30 minutes. Do not overcook. Serve with cream sauce, if desired. Serves 8.

The Peach Tree Tea Room Cookbook

Fiesta Chicken

1 stick margarine, divided
1¾ cups finely crushed
  Cheddar cheese crackers
2 tablespoons taco seasoning
  mix
8 chicken breasts, boned,
  skinned and flattened
5 green onions, tops too,
  chopped

1 (4-ounce) can chopped
  green chilies
2 cups heavy cream
1 teaspoon instant chicken
  bouillon
2 cups grated Monterey Jack
  cheese

Melt margarine in a 9x13-inch baking dish and set aside. Combine cracker crumbs and taco mix. Dredge chicken in this mixture—pat this on so you get plenty of crumbs to stick on chicken. Place chicken in baking dish with margarine. In a medium-size saucepan, take out a couple tablespoons of the melted margarine and place in saucepan. To the melted margarine in saucepan, add chopped onions and sauté. Then add the green chilies, heavy cream, instant chicken bouillon and the Monterey Jack cheese; mix well. Pour this mixture over chicken breasts. Bake uncovered at 350° for 50-55 minutes. Serves 6-8.

Great Tastes of Texas

Breast of Chicken Olé

CHICKEN:

1 cup cracker crumbs
2 tablespoons taco mix

8 (4-6-ounce) boneless
  skinless chicken breasts

In a shallow dish combine crumbs and taco mix. Mix well. Dip chicken in crumbs and place in a greased 13x9x2-inch baking dish.

SAUCE:

4 green onions, white only,
  chopped
2 tablespoons margarine
2 cups whipping cream or
  evaporated milk, undiluted
1 cup (4 ounces) Monterey
  Jack cheese, grated

1 cup (4 ounces) Velvetta
  cheese, cut into small dice
1 (4-ounce) can green chilies,
  drained

Place margarine in saucepan over low heat until melted, add onions, and sauté until tender. Add cream and remaining ingredients; pour over chicken, making sure that cheese is well distributed. Bake at 350° about 15-20 minutes or until chicken is just firm to the touch.

Note: If you are substituting evaporated milk for the heavy cream, one 12-ounce can of evaporated milk contains 1½ cups. A 5-ounce can contains 2 tablespoons more than a half cup. Also, there are 5 tablespoons of taco mix in a package.

Raleigh House Cookbook II

Monterey Chicken
(Lone Star Legacy's)

4 chicken breasts, skinned,
  boned and halved
Salt and pepper
½ cup flour
½ cup butter, divided
½ cup chopped onion
1 clove garlic, minced
8 ounces mushrooms, chopped
2 tablespoons flour

1 teaspoon salt
½ teaspoon white pepper
½ cup chicken stock
½ cup white wine
1 avocado, mashed
1½ cups grated Monterey
  Jack cheese, divided
¼ cup chopped green chilies,
  optional

CONTINUED

Place chicken between 2 sheets of waxed paper and pound until about ¼ to ½-inch thick. Sprinkle with salt, pepper, and flour. Quickly sauté in ¼ cup butter until golden. Remove to plate and add remaining ¼ cup butter to pan and sauté onion, garlic, and mushrooms slowly until cooked but not browned. Stir in flour, salt, pepper, chicken stock, and wine. Cook until thickened, about 5 minutes. Stir in mashed avocados and ½ cup cheese. Arrange chicken breasts in glass baking dish. Top with sauce, remaining cheese and green chilies if desired. Bake at 350° for 10 minutes. Serves 8.

Lone Star Legacy II

Monterey Chicken
(Coastal Cuisine's)

¼ cup flour
1 (1¼-ounce) package taco
  seasoning mix

4 skinned chicken breasts
¼ cup (½ stick) margarine
1 cup crushed tortilla chips

Combine flour and taco seasoning in a bag. Add chicken, shake to coat. Melt margarine in baking pan. Place chicken in pan, and turn to coat. Roll each piece in crushed chips and return to baking pan. Bake at 375° about 30 minutes.

CHEESE SAUCE:
2 tablespoons chopped onion
1 tablespoon vegetable oil
2 tablespoons flour
¼ teaspoon salt
1 (13-ounce) can evaporated
  milk
¼ teaspoon hot pepper
  sauce

1 cup (4 ounces) grated
  Monterey Jack cheese
¼ cup sliced olives
1 teaspoon lemon juice
Shredded lettuce

Cook onion in oil until tender but not brown. Stir in flour and salt. Add milk and hot pepper sauce. Heat, stirring constantly, until bubbly. Cook an additional 1-2 minutes. Stir in cheese, olives, and lemon juice; cook until cheese melts. Serve chicken on shredded lettuce, and pour cheese sauce over top. Serves 4.

Coastal Cuisine

Cilantro Chicken Cutlets

1 teaspoon seasoned pepper	¼ cup flour
2 teaspoons cilantro	½ teaspoon salt
1 teaspoon cumin	1 teaspoon seasoned pepper
6 boned chicken breasts,	¼ teaspoon cumin
halved, pounded into ¼-inch	1 teaspoon cilantro
thick pieces	2 cups milk
2 cups bread crumbs	⅓ cup dry white wine
Oil	1 cup grated Monterey Jack
3 tablespoons margarine	cheese

Mix together seasoned salt, seasoned pepper, cilantro, and cumin. Sprinkle seasonings over chicken cutlets and dip in bread crumbs. Pour oil into a large skillet and brown chicken. Remove to a 9x13-inch greased baking dish. In a saucepan, melt margarine, blend in flour and seasoning. Add milk and stirring constantly, cook until thickened. Remove from heat and stir in wine. Pour sauce over chicken and bake at 350° for 45 minutes. Remove from oven and sprinkle cheese on top of each piece of chicken; return to oven for 5 minutes. Serves 6.

Southwest Sizzler

East Texas Fried Chicken

In our travels through Texas, we've found fried chicken seasoned with oranges, jalapeños, garlic, mustard, cayenne, and cumin. We've found it butter-dipped and cornmeal-coated, pan-fried and deep-fried, and cooked in lard, bacon drippings, shortening, and a multitude of oils, mainly corn, canola, safflower, and sesame. Forget the gimmicks. Nothing tops this recipe.

3-4 cups buttermilk	3½ - 4 pounds chicken parts
2 teaspoons Tabasco or other	1½ cups all-purpose flour
hot pepper sauce	1½ pounds (3 cups)
2-3 teaspoons salt	shortening preferably Crisco
1 teaspoon fresh-ground	3 tablespoons bacon drippings
black pepper	

At least 2½ hours (and up to 12 hours) before you plan to eat, mix the buttermilk, Tabasco or other sauce, ½ teaspoon of the

CONTINUED

salt, and ¼ teaspoon of the pepper in a shallow dish. Add the chicken parts, turning to coat them well with the mixture. Cover the dish, and refrigerate it.

About 20 minutes before you plan to fry the chicken, bring it to room temperature. Sprinkle the remaining salt and pepper into a medium-size paper bag, and add the flour. Set the bag aside.

In a 10- to 12-inch cast-iron skillet, melt the shortening over high heat. Add the bacon drippings to the skillet. When small bubbles form on the surface, reduce the heat slightly. Place a large brown paper sack near the stove for draining the chicken. Starting with the dark pieces, take a piece of chicken out of the marinade, shake off the excess liquid, and drop it into the bag of seasoned flour. Shake the bag well so that the piece is coated thoroughly. Remove it from the bag, and lower it gently into the skillet, skin-side down. Repeat until all the chicken is in the skillet, arranging it so that all the pieces cook evenly. The pieces should fit snugly together, although they shouldn't stick to each other. Reduce the heat to medium, and cover the skillet. Fry the chicken exactly 17 minutes.

Lower the heat slightly, take off the cover, and use tongs to turn over the chicken gently. Fry it uncovered for another 17 minutes. Remove the chicken with the tongs—it will be a deep, rich brown—and lay it on the paper sack to drain.

Variation: Among all the possible variations of fried chicken, we're partial to the jalapeño-garlic version we enjoyed a few years ago at the Kerrville Folk Festival. Just add to the buttermilk a couple of minced pickled jalapeños with 1 or 2 tablespoons of their pickling liquid and a half-dozen garlic cloves. Serve the chicken with pickled jalapeño slices.

Texas Home Cooking

Rip's Barbecued Chicken (Texas Style)

1 (5-ounce) bottle
  Worcestershire sauce
5 ounces water (halfway
  between ½ and ¾ cup)
5 ounces vinegar
2 tablespoons margarine
2-3 slices uncooked bacon,
  chopped
½ teaspoon salt

½ teaspoon black pepper
½ teaspoon celery salt
½ tablespoon prepared
  mustard
Grated rind of ½ lemon
1-2 dashes Tabasco sauce
1-2 cloves garlic, crushed
3-4 chickens, about 1½
  pounds each

Combine first 12 ingredients and simmer for 30 minutes. In the meantime split chickens in half and season with salt and pepper. Place chickens on hot grill, skin down, and brown on both sides, turning occasionally (takes about 15 minutes). Baste first with oily part of sauce that has floated to top. Continue basting and turning over gentle coals until done. Chickens will be tender and a deep rich brown (takes about 45 minutes). Serves 6-8.

M. D. Anderson Volunteers Cooking for Fun

Apple Glazed Barbecued Chicken

6 ounces frozen apple juice
  concentrate, thawed
¼ cup firmly packed brown
  sugar
¼ cup ketchup
1 tablespoon cider vinegar

1 teaspoon dried thyme,
  crumbled
⅛ teaspoon hot pepper
  sauce
3 pounds of chicken pieces
Vegetable oil

In a heavy saucepan, combine apple juice, brown sugar, ketchup, vinegar, thyme, and pepper sauce; heat until sugar completely melts. Cool. In a shallow baking dish, place chicken in one layer. Pour ½ of the cooled sauce over the chicken, turning once to coat both sides. Cover and marinate for up to 24 hours.

Prepare the grill. Remove chicken from marinade, brush each piece with oil; season generously with salt and pepper. Grill until chicken is almost cooked through, turning occasionally, about 20 minutes. Brush with reserved glaze; continue grilling until chicken is tender and cooked through, turning and brushing with glaze frequently, about 10 more minutes. Serves 4.

From Generation to Generation

Beer-In-The-Rear-Chicken

Don't cook just one—there won't be enough to go around!

Buy a whole frying-size chicken. This will work equally well on the BBQ pit or in the kitchen oven. You can prepare the chicken to suit individual tastes. You are limited only by your imagination. Some suggestions are to rub the chicken with olive oil and sprinkle with rosemary and thyme, or sprinkle with onion flakes and garlic flakes (inside and out). Place slice of onion, apple, or celery in cavity of the chicken. After preparing chicken, open a can of light beer (removing tab and opening one or two additional holes) and insert can of beer upright into cavity of the chicken and place upright in shallow pan in oven at 325° for 2 hours or until done. If BBQing, place chicken upright on grill (after placing beer can in cavity). Baste with sauce about 30 minutes before done.

Variation: Slit the skins and put seeded quarters of jalapeño between the skin and meat. Then rub dry Hidden Valley Dressing. Mix all over the chicken for seasoning and set each chicken on a can of beer on the pit.

The Authorized Texas Ranger Cookbook

Chicken Bundles

An elegant and delicious recipe that is easy to make. There is nothing complicated about using puff pastry sheets, and they add such a special touch.

1 (17¼-ounce) package Pepperidge Farm Frozen Puff Pastry Sheets
2 cooked chicken breasts, skinned and boned
2 tablespoons peanut oil
¼ cup chopped onion
¼ cup chopped mushrooms
½ cup sour cream
1½ teaspoons prepared mustard
½ teaspoon garlic salt
¾ teaspoon salt
¼ teaspoon pepper
¼ pound Monterey Jack cheese

Thaw puff pastry sheets until flexible. Chop chicken into small, bite-size pieces. Pour oil into a small skillet, heat and add onion and mushrooms. Sauté for 3-4 minutes. Mix sour cream, mustard and seasonings and add to onion and mushrooms.

Cut each pastry sheet in half. Place a mound of ¼ of the chicken in center of each sheet. Spoon skillet mixture over chicken. Slice cheese and place on top. Bring ends of puff pastry together over chicken and fold twice. Crimp sides of pastry to seal chicken mixture inside. Place on a lightly greased cookie sheet and bake at 350° for 20-25 minutes or until richly browned. Yield: 4 servings.

More Tastes & Tales

Texas Strudel

Plan to do this for a summer party. It can be done a day before, and baked when ready for your guests.

6 green onions, finely
  chopped
2 tablespoons butter
4 cups chicken breasts,
  cooked, cubed
½ teaspoon salt
¼ teaspoon pepper
2 tablespoons fresh parsley,
  chopped
2 teaspoons ground comino
1 teaspoon garlic, minced
2 eggs

1½ cups Monterey Jack
  cheese, shredded
2 cups green chilies
½ cup black olives, halved
½ cup golden raisins
½ cup almonds, chopped
20 sheets filo pastry
½ cup butter, melted
Garnish: Sour cream and
  black olives; or fresh sprig of
  oregano or cilantro

Preheat oven to 400°. Sauté onions in butter until tender. In a bowl, combine the sautéed onion, chicken, salt, pepper, parsley, comino, and garlic. Stir in the eggs, cheese, chilies, olives, raisins, and almonds. In a 9x13-inch baking dish, brush butter on the sides and the bottom. Cut filo pastry sheets in half widthwise. Begin by laying one piece of filo pastry flat in the dish. Brush melted butter onto the dough. Repeat this process until 10 layers have been buttered. Spoon the filling over the layers and spread evenly. Lay a sheet of filo pastry over the filling and brush with melted butter. Repeat this process until 10 more layers have been buttered, including the top layer. Cut into desired serving sizes before baking.

Bake for 35 minutes, or until the crust is golden brown. Garnish with a dollop of sour cream and a black olive, or with a fresh sprig of oregano or cilantro. Serves 8-10.

The Peach Tree Family Cookbook

With over 823,000 acres, the King Ranch is the largest in the US and covers all or part of four Texas counties.

Gingered Chicken Ragout with Linguine and Bean Sprouts

6 tablespoons peanut oil
2 red onions, finely diced
1 stalk leeks, diced
1 stalk celery, diced
1 tablespoon minced fresh
  gingerroot
4 cloves garlic, minced
1½ quarts chicken stock
3 bay leaves
2 teaspoons salt
1 teaspoon crushed white
  peppercorns

2 whole chicken fryers (about
  6 pounds total), washed and
  cleaned
2 red peppers, cleaned and
  diced
2 yellow peppers, cleaned and
  diced
1 cup bean sprouts
1 pound linguine, cooked and
  rinsed

In large stockpot heat oil and cook onions, leeks, celery, ginger-root, and garlic over low heat. Add chicken stock. Slowly bring to a boil. Add bay leaves, salt, and peppercorns.

Cut fryers into 8 pieces each. Place into stock mixture and simmer gently for 45 minutes. Remove from heat. Remove chicken and cool. Remove skin and meat from bone. Place red and yellow peppers into stock and bring to a boil; add chicken pieces. Heat thoroughly. Adjust seasoning with salt and pepper. Keep warm.

Wash and clean bean sprouts. Place onto a large serving platter. Season cooked linguine with a little peanut oil, salt, and pepper. Place on platter. Place chicken pieces on top and pour hot stock over chicken. Serve at once. Serves 8.

Cuisine Actuelle

King Ranch or Mexican Chicken

1 dozen tortillas
Chicken broth
1 cup onions, diced
1 can green pepper, diced
1 can cream of mushroom
  soup
1 can cream of chicken soup
1 tablespoon chili powder
1 (2- to 3-pound) fryer, cooked
  and diced
¾ pound Cheddar cheese,
  grated
1 can Rotel tomatoes and
  green chilies or 1 can tomato
  soup mixed with 1 tablespoon
  chili powder

Line large baking dish with layer of tortillas. Sprinkle with chicken broth. Sauté onions and green pepper and add soups and chili powder. Pour layer of soup mixture over tortillas, then layer chicken, then layer cheese. Repeat layers. Pour over the Rotel tomatoes or the tomato soup with chili powder. If a milder taste is desired, you may use ½ can Rotel tomatoes and ½ can plain tomatoes. Bake 1 hour in 350° oven. Serve with vegetable salad and Mexican rice or beans.

Decades of Mason County Cooking

Chicken with Apple Pecan Stuffing

The wonderful aroma this dish creates will call your family to the table before the table is set.

2 Granny Smith apples,
  chopped
1 cup chopped onion
⅓ cup raisins
3 tablespoons chopped pecans
1 (8-ounce) package
  cornbread stuffing mix
¾ teaspoon sage
¼ teaspoon salt
¼ teaspoon pepper
1 cup chicken broth
6 skinless chicken breast
  halves with bone

Place all ingredients, except chicken, into a large slow-cooker; stir to combine. Place chicken on top and cook, covered, on low for 6 hours. Remove chicken breasts carefully, using a large spoon or spatula so that bones are not left in the stuffing. Place on a plate and serve with stuffing. Yield: 6 servings.

Per serving: Cal 379; Fat 8g; Prot 32g; Carb 43g; Chol 72mg; Sod 704mg; Dietary fiber 4g.

More of What's Cooking

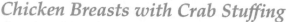

Chicken Breasts with Crab Stuffing

12 chicken breasts, skinned
  and deboned
Salt and pepper to taste
1 cup chopped onion
1 cup chopped celery
²/₃ cup butter or margarine,
  divided
1¼ cups dry white wine,
  divided
2 (7½-ounce) cans crab
  meat, drained and flaked
1 cup herb-seasoned stuffing
  mix
4 tablespoons flour
1 teaspoon paprika
2 (1.25-ounce) package
  Hollandaise sauce mix
1½ cups milk
1 cup shredded Swiss cheese

Pound chicken to flatten and sprinkle with salt and pepper. Cook onion and celery in 1 stick butter or margarine until transparent. Remove from heat; add 6 tablespoons wine, crab meat and stuffing. Mix well. Divide mixture among breasts; put some in the center of each breast, roll up and secure with toothpicks.

Combine flour and paprika; roll chicken in the mixture to coat. Place prepared breasts in 11x7-inch casseroles. Drizzle 2 tablespoons butter on top of each. Bake at 375° for 1 hour. Blend sauce mix and milk. Cook according to package directions, stirring until thick. Add cheese and remaining wine, stirring until cheese melts and is blended. To serve, pour sauce over chicken or have sauce on the side for guests to serve themselves. Yield: 12 servings.

The Gathering

Hawaiian Chicken

10 ounces breaded chicken
  tenders
1 (10-ounce) jar sweet and
  sour sauce
1 (8¾-ounce) can pineapple
  tidbits
1 (16-ounce) package frozen
  oriental vegetables

Prepare chicken tenders according to package directions. Place tenders in large skillet. Add sweet and sour sauce, pineapple, and vegetables. Cover and simmer 25 minutes or until vegetables are tender. Serve over rice.

More of the Four Ingredient Cookbook

Chicken and Dumplings

1 large chicken
Salt and pepper to taste

Water

Place the seasoned chicken in a large pot, adding enough water to cover. Bring to a boil. Cover pot, reduce the heat, and simmer the chicken until tender. Remove the chicken from the broth and cool. Reserve the broth. Bone the chicken, cut the meat into pieces, and set aside.

DUMPLINGS:

1½ teaspoons salt
3 teaspoons baking powder
6 tablespoons butter, melted

1¼ cups sweet milk, room
  temperature
3¾ cups flour

Mix all ingredients in order listed and divide the dough in half. Roll half the dough very thin on a well-floured surface. Cut the dough into short strips. Set aside. Roll out and cut the remaining dough. Drop the dumpling strips into the boiling chicken broth. Cover, reduce heat, and simmer for approximately 40 minutes. Add chicken pieces the last 15 minutes. Add thickening to the broth if needed.

The Cariker Hotel, Kountze.

Boardin' in the Thicket

Charcoal Dove

12 doves (mourning or
    white-winged)
8 ounces Italian salad
    dressing
1 teaspoon Worcestershire
    sauce or to taste

Seasoned salt
Lemon pepper seasoning
Jalapeño peppers
12 strips bacon

Fillet doves from breastbone and marinate in salad dressing and
Worcestershire sauce for 30 minutes to an hour. Sprinkle with
seasoned salt and lemon pepper. Wrap a whole breast (2 fillets)
around a thin strip of jalapeño, then wrap a slice of bacon
around the dove. Place on a skewer and cook over open coals
for 15 minutes or until bacon is cooked. Serves 4-6.

The Star of Texas Cookbook

Doves Alfred

*Mike Hughes, owner of the Broken Arrow Ranch in Ingram says, "I
don't know who Alfred is, but Hap Perry and his father, John,
guaranteed that Doves Alfred is the best dove recipe known!"*

12-16 doves, split down the
    back
¼ cup Burgundy wine
5 ounces currant jelly
¼ cup barbecue sauce
¼ cup orange juice

1 teaspoon orange rind, finely
    grated
1 stick butter
1 teaspoon arrowroot
Watercress and orange slices
    for garnish

In broiler pan, place doves, breasts down. In pan over medium
heat, combine well next 6 ingredients; add arrowroot. Pour over
birds; broil on top rack in oven for 10 minutes or until birds are
brown; baste several times. Turn over birds; brush well with
sauce; broil 10 minutes more or until crisp and brown; baste
often. Remove to hot platter; spoon sauce over doves; garnish.
Serves 6-8.

Great Flavors of Texas

Bacon-Wrapped Quail with Basil

These little birds are very tasty; however, they do not have much meat. For the hearty appetite I suggest two quail and for the light appetite just one.

4 quail, washed and dried
White wine Worcestershire
  sauce
Light salt to taste
Black pepper to taste

Lemon pepper to taste
12 fresh basil leaves
4 large parsley sprigs
4 slices smoked peppered
  bacon

Preheat grill to low. Take a sharp paring knife and flatten the quail by splitting the breast bone on the cavity side. Sprinkle each quail with Worcestershire, salt, pepper, and lemon pepper to taste. Place 3 basil leaves and one parsley sprig on each quail's breast and wrap with a bacon slice, securing the bacon with a toothpick. Grill quail (covered) to the degree of doneness you desire, approximately 20 minutes. Serves 4.

Per serving: Cal 436; Prot 60g; Carb 2.38g; Fat 19g; Chol 5.2mg; Fiber .09g; 39% Cal from Fat.

The 30-Minute Light Gourmet

Proud Bird with a Golden Taste

4-6 quail
3 tablespoons salt and pepper
1 cup flour
¼ cup butter or margarine
¼ cup onion

½ cup fresh mushrooms
1 tablespoon fresh parsley
½ cup white wine
½ cup whipping cream
Cooked rice

Dredge cleaned birds in flour mixed with seasoning. Sauté in butter until slightly browned. Remove birds. Sauté onion and mushrooms in butter. Add birds. Add wine. Cook 30 minutes. Add cream and blend well. Serve over white rice. Makes 4 servings.

The Wild Wild West

Breast of Pheasant with Fresh Mushrooms and Cognac

3 pheasant breasts
4 tablespoons safflower oil
1 cup flour
2 tablespoons unsalted
  margarine
1 pint fresh mushrooms,
  chopped

½ onion, chopped
3 tablespoons cognac
1 (10½-ounce) can
  mushroom soup
½ cup pine nuts
1 cup green grapes

With a sharp knife, remove the skin from the pheasant breasts and discard. Cut along the breast bone and remove the breast. Cut into 2 pieces. Heat the safflower oil in a heavy skillet; dust the pheasant breast with flour and sauté over low heat on both sides until brown. Remove the pheasant from the pan and keep warm. Discard the oil.

In the same pan, melt the margarine and sauté the mushrooms and onions. Add cognac and the mushroom soup and bring to a boil. Spoon over the pheasant breast and serve. Garnish with pine nuts and sliced green grapes. Serves 6.

Recipe by Chef Joe Mannke, Rotisserie for Beef and Bird, Houston.

Top Chefs in Texas

Wild Turkey in a T-Shirt

1 skinned wild turkey
Salt and pepper
1 onion, chopped
2 ribs chopped celery

1 old clean T-shirt
1 stick of butter, oleo or
  bacon drippings

Imagine our distress when we found our Thanksgiving wild turkey, brought home from the locker plant still wrapped, had been skinned rather than picked. The only thing we had to wrap the bare bird in was a clean old T-shirt.

The bird was salted, peppered and stuffed with the chopped onion and celery. The T-shirt was dampened and dipped in melted butter. We clothed the turkey in the T-shirt and cooked it in a 325° oven for 2½ hours. It was the best wild turkey every.

The New Texas Wild Game Cook Book

Whole Fried Wild Turkey, Cajun Style

1 (15-20-pound) wild turkey
5 gallons peanut oil
Salt, pepper, and red pepper
   to taste
3 tablespoons or more
   Tabasco

1 (16-ounce) bottle Italian
   dressing
5 tablespoons Worcestershire
   sauce

Sprinkle turkey liberally with salt, pepper, and red pepper, inside and out. Place in heavy-duty foil. Mix together Tabasco, Italian dressing, and Worcestershire sauce. With a large syringe, inject mixture into turkey, just under the skin. Carefully pat into place. Wrap turkey in foil and place in refrigerator several hours to marinate. Remove 30 minutes prior to cooking.

On a large outdoor burner, place a large pot with basket. Heat oil very hot (350°) and lower turkey in hot oil. Cook 3 minutes per pound. The turkey will be blackened and crispy on the outside and juicy and moist on the inside.

Note: Domestically raised turkey may be used as alternate meat choice.

Gathering of the Game

Southern Cornbread Stuffing

4 cups cornbread crumbs
8 cups lightly-packed, day-old
   bread crumbs
1½ teaspoons salt
¼ teaspoon pepper
Poultry seasoning (optional)
1½ cups (or less) boiling
   water

½ cup butter, melted
1 cup minced onion
1 cup diced celery
4 eggs, beaten
1 quart oysters, drained
   (optional)

Make cornbread (can be a day ahead). Break cornbread into small pieces and mix with bread crumbs, salt, pepper, and poultry seasoning. Add boiling water, melted butter, onion, and celery. Mix well. Mix eggs in well. Add oysters, mixing lightly so as not to break them. Makes enough dressing to stuff 1 medium-large turkey. This is a moist stuffing.

Houston Junior League Cookbook

Jalapeño Dressing

Family tradition at Thanksgiving—only in Texas! Mom always makes one pan of regular dressing for the weak at heart and one pan of jalapeño dressing.

1 bunch green onions, chopped
½ stalk celery with leaves, chopped
½ cup bacon drippings
1 cup water
8 cups crumbled cornbread
4 cups crumbled day-old bread

3½ cups chicken broth
1 cup jalapeño pepper juice
½ teaspoon salt
⅛ teaspoon black pepper
1-3 jalapeño peppers, chopped

Sauté onion and celery in bacon drippings. Add water and cook, covered, for about 7 minutes or until tender. Combine vegetables and liquid, breads, broth, and jalapeño juice. Season with salt and pepper. Add jalapeño peppers to taste. Add water to bread mixture as needed to achieve a very moist consistency. Spoon dressing into cavity of 20-pound turkey, placing extra dressing in greased casserole. Bake casserole at 350° for 30 minutes. Makes approximately 12 cups.

Per ½ cup serving: Cal 357; Prot 9.13g; Carb 52.8g; Fat 12g; Chol 38.4mg; Sod 926mg.

Changing Thymes

Cranberry Barbecue Sauce

Why not barbecue a holiday turkey?

1 (8-ounce) can jellied cranberry sauce
¼ cup firmly packed brown sugar
¼ cup prepared mustard

2 tablespoons fresh lemon juice
1 teaspoon Worcestershire sauce
⅓ teaspoon garlic powder

In a glass bowl, combine all ingredients and mix well. During the last hour of cooking, baste turkey with glaze every 15 minutes. Makes about 1½ cups.

Texas Barbecue

Seafood

Sailing is one of the many seashore recreations on beautiful South Padre Island,
the "Tropical Tip of Texas."

Pan-Fried Red Snapper with Sauce of Sweet Corn, Leek, Etc.

4 tablespoons peanut oil
4 (7-ounce) red snapper
 fillets, trimmed of skin and
 bones
Salt to taste

Sauce of Sweet Corn, Leek,
 Dallas Mozzarella, and
 Crabmeat
1 small bunch fresh chives,
 washed, dried, and cut into
 2-inch segments

Heat oil in a large skillet over medium heat. Season each fillet with salt. Pan-fry fillets on flesh side until a heavy crust forms, being careful not to burn them.

Turn fillets and cook just until no longer translucent. Allow no more than 5 minutes total cooking time for each ½ inch of thickness at the thickest part. Do not overcook. The fish should be very moist.

Spoon just enough Sauce to cover the bottom of each of four warm dinner plates. Place a red snapper fillet in the middle of each plate. Sprinkle sweet corn, leek, pepper, and crabmeat around each fillet, then sprinkle each serving with chive segments. Serve immediately.

SAUCE OF SWEET CORN, LEEK, DALLAS MOZZARELLA, AND CRABMEAT:

1 tablespoon corn oil
2 cups fresh sweet corn
 kernels
1 shallot, chopped
1 clove garlic, chopped
1 serrano chili, seeded and
 chopped
3 sprigs fresh cilantro
2 sprigs fresh thyme
2 cups chicken stock
½ cup heavy cream
1 ounce Dallas Mozzarella (or
 other fresh Mozzarella
 cheese)

Salt to taste
Lemon juice to taste
2 tablespoons unsalted butter
1 leek, white part only, cut
 into thin julienne strips
½ red bell pepper, seeds and
 membrane removed, cut into
 a fine dice
4 ounces jumbo lump
 crabmeat

Heat oil in a medium saucepan over medium heat. Sauté 1 cup

CONTINUED

corn kernels, shallot, garlic, and serrano chili for 3 minutes. Add cilantro, thyme, and chicken stock. Simmer for 20 minutes. Stir in cream and bring to a boil. Cook for about 15 minutes or until liquid is reduced by half, stirring occasionally.

Pour into a blender. Add Mozzarella and process until smooth. Strain through a fine sieve and season to taste with salt and lemon juice. Keep warm until ready to use.

Melt butter in a sauté pan over medium heat and add remaining 1 cup corn kernels, leek, and pepper. Sauté until vegetables soften. Add crabmeat and heat through. Keep warm until ready to use. Serves 4.

The Mansion on Turtle Creek Cookbook

Grilled Texas Tequila Tuna

Prepare ahead. Heat up outdoor grill!

¼ cup tequila
¼ cup red wine vinegar
2 tablespoons lime juice
1 tablespoon ground red
   chilies

2 cloves finely chopped garlic
1 finely chopped red bell
   pepper
2 pounds fresh tuna (4 steaks
   approximately ¾-inch thick)

Mix all ingredients together except tuna in a bowl. Place tuna in shallow dish. Pour marinade over. Refrigerate for 1 hour. Remove tuna from marinade and reserve liquid. Place tuna on grill over medium hot coals, turning once. Cook until done, approximately 6-7 minutes per side. Heat marinade to boiling in saucepan. Cook until bell pepper is tender. Serve over tuna. Serves 4.

Note: Alternative fish: swordfish and halibut.

Texas Sampler

South Padre Island hosts the Miss USA Pageants each year as well as world championship boxing matches. Dubbed the "Fireworks Capital of Texas," the island features fireworks over the bay every Friday at 9:15 PM from May 26 to September 15. Mexico is only 30 minutes away.

Red Snapper Veracruz

2 limes
1¾ - 2 pounds red snapper
  fillets
Salt

5 tablespoons olive oil
Fresh cilantro (coriander) for
  garnish

SAUCE VERACRUZ:

½ cup chopped onion
3 cloves garlic, crushed
4 tablespoons olive oil
3 large tomatoes, peeled,
  seeded, and chopped
1 large bay leaf
½ teaspoon oregano
12 green olives, cut in half
2 tablespoons capers

2 jalapeño peppers, seeded
  and cut in strips (fresh, if
  possible)
½ teaspoon salt
¼ teaspoon pepper
1 tablespoon fresh chopped
  cilantro (or ½ teaspoon
  dried)
1 tablespoon lime juice

Preheat oven to 325°. Squeeze lime juice over fish and set aside until ready to cook. To make the sauce, sauté onion and garlic in oil until soft. Stir in remaining ingredients. Season to taste. Cook over medium heat for 10 minutes or until some of the liquid has evaporated. Salt fillets and sauté in oil on both sides. Drain and remove to ovenproof casserole or platter. Cover with sauce and bake for 10-15 minutes. Garnish with fresh cilantro and serve. Serves 6.

The Star of Texas Cookbook

Peppered Fish with Creamy Dill Sauce

This is another good way to prepare fish. The fillets are particularly good when served on a bed of cooked rice with dill sauce spooned over the top.

4 fish fillets (snapper, flounder, or catfish)	2 tablespoons coarsely ground pepper
2 teaspoons olive oil, divided	Vegetable cooking spray

Brush the fish on both sides with 1 teaspoon olive oil; sprinkle with the pepper and gently press into the fillet. Cover and let stand for 15 minutes. Coat a large nonstick skillet with cooking spray. Add the remaining teaspoon of olive oil and place over medium heat. Add the fillets to the pan and cook for 3-5 minutes on each side, or until the fish flakes easily. Remove the fish to a serving plate. Spoon the warm Mustard Dill Sauce over the top of the fish and serve.

MUSTARD DILL SAUCE:

¼ cup no-fat yogurt	1 tablespoon Dijon mustard
¼ cup reduced-fat mayonnaise	1 teaspoon dried dill weed

Combine all the ingredients for the Mustard Dill Sauce and mix until smooth. Heat in the microwave for 40 seconds on High. About 5 grams of fat per serving. Serves 4.

New Tastes of Texas

Salmon Croquettes

This is an 1891 recipe.

One can of salmon. Turn into a vessel (not tin) for awhile before using, to "air." Use two-thirds as much rolled cracker crumbs as you have salmon. Butter the size of the yolk of an egg melted in one-half cup of water. Pepper, salt, and a few drops of lemon juice. Sift the rolled crackers, using coarser part to the salmon, finer to roll the croquettes in. After mixing ingredients thoroughly, mold, roll in beaten egg, then cracker crumbs. Fry in hot lard.

Seconds of A Pinch of This and A Handful of That

Orange Roughy with Cheese Crumb Topping

1 pound orange roughy fillets
½ tablespoon diet margarine
½ onion, finely chopped
½ teaspoon minced garlic
¾ cup Italian-flavored bread
  crumbs

¼ cup part-skim Mozzarella
  cheese, finely grated
1 teaspoon paprika
Pepper, to taste
Nonstick vegetable cooking
  spray

Preheat oven to 350°. Spray ovenproof dish with cooking spray; place fish in prepared dish. Melt margarine; add onion and garlic. Cook until onion is soft. Transfer to bowl and toss with bread crumbs, cheese, and paprika; season to taste with pepper. Spoon mixture evenly over fish. Bake until fish flakes and crumb topping is golden, about 15-20 minutes. Yield: 4 servings.

Per serving: Cal 173; Fat 4g; Prot 20g; Carb 14g; Chol 26mg; Sod 247mg; Dietary fiber 1g.

What's Cooking at the Cooper Clinic

Seafood Casserole for a Crowd

3 pounds shrimp, cooked and
  chopped
3 pounds crab meat (imitation
  or genuine crab)
2 cups finely chopped celery
1 large bell pepper, chopped
1 large onion, chopped

1 tablespoon Worcestershire
  sauce
2 cups (1 pint) mayonnaise
Dash of hot pepper sauce
2 cups bread crumbs
½ cup (1 stick) margarine or
  butter, melted

Combine shrimp, crab, celery, bell pepper, onion, and Worcestershire sauce; mix well. Spoon mixture into greased extra-large (18x14x3-inch) casserole dish.

Mix mayonnaise with dash of hot pepper sauce; mix bread crumbs with melted butter; combine mayonnaise and bread mixtures. Spoon over shrimp mixture. Bake at 350° for 30 minutes. Serves 30.

Coastal Cuisine

Linguine and Scallops

8 ounces scallops
Nonstick vegetable cooking
 spray
2 tablespoons diet margarine
1½ cups fresh sliced
 mushrooms
⅓ cup sliced green onions
½ teaspoon minced garlic

1 tablespoon Chablis or other
 dry white wine
Dash of cayenne pepper
 (optional)
7 ounces dried linguine
3 tablespoon Parmesan
 cheese
¼ cup fresh snipped parsley

Cut scallops into bite-size pieces. Rinse scallops in cold water; drain and set aside. Coat large skillet with cooking spray; add diet margarine and place over medium-high heat until margarine melts. Add mushrooms, green onions, and garlic; sauté 1 minute or until tender. Using a slotted spoon, remove vegetables from skillet; set aside. Add scallops, wine and cayenne pepper; bring mixture to a boil. Cover and reduce heat.

Simmer mixture 5-6 minutes or until scallops are done. If more liquid is needed, add 1-2 tablespoons more wine. Add vegetables and cook until heated. Cook linguine according to directions on package. Serve vegetables over linguine and sprinkle with Parmesan cheese and parsley. Yield: 4 servings.

Per serving (1 ½ cups): Cal 275; Fat 5g; Prot 18g; Carb 38g; Chol 25mg; Sod 261mg; Dietary fiber 2g.

What's Cooking at the Cooper Clinic

Shrimp 'N Pasta

5 pounds shrimp, unpeeled
¾ cup butter
½ cup vegetable oil
¼ cup olive oil
1 cup green onion, chopped
1 cup white onion, chopped
1½ tablespoons garlic, minced
½ cup parsley, chopped
2 teaspoons Konriko Creole Seasoning
2 teaspoons salt
1 teaspoon white pepper
¾ teaspoon cayenne
¾ teaspoon thyme
1½ teaspoons black pepper
¾ teaspoon oregano
¾ cup white wine
1 cup seafood stock
12-ounce fettuccine, cooked and drained

Peel shrimp and butterfly. Place in boiling salted water for 30 seconds, drain. Combine butter and oils in large skillet on medium heat. Add onions, garlic, and parsley; cook, stirring often, until onion is soft. Add seasonings, wine, stock, and shrimp. Cook on low heat for 5 minutes or until shrimp is done. Toss with fettuccine. Serves 8-10.

Best of Friends Two

Tequila-Lime Shrimp

½ stick margarine
2 tablespoons olive oil
2 garlic cloves, minced
1½ pounds medium shrimp, shelled, deveined
3 tablespoons tequila
1½ tablespoons lime juice
½ teaspoon salt
½ teaspoon chili powder
4 tablespoons coarsely chopped fresh cilantro
Hot cooked rice
Lime wedges for garnish

Pat shrimp dry with paper towels. Heat margarine and oil in a large skillet over medium heat. Add garlic and shrimp; cook about 2 minutes, stirring occasionally. Stir in tequila, lime juice, salt, and chili powder. Cook 2 minutes more or until most of liquid is evaporated and shrimp are pink and glazed. Add cilantro. Serve over hot cooked rice, garnished with lime wedges.

Southwest Ole!

Shrimp, Rice and Artichoke Casserole

Make ahead for a great dish.

1 medium onion, chopped	4 cups cooked rice
2 ribs celery, chopped	½ cup tomato sauce
3 cloves garlic	1 cup whipping cream
2 green bell peppers, chopped	¾ teaspoon cayenne pepper
2 bay leaves	Salt to taste
4 tablespoons butter	2 (14-ounce) cans artichoke
3 pounds shrimp, peeled,	hearts, drained and halved
deveined and boiled	

Preheat oven to 350°. Sauté onion, celery, garlic, bell peppers, and bay leaves in butter. Add cooked shrimp. Remove garlic. Add rice. Stir until hot. Add tomato sauce, cream, cayenne, salt, and artichokes. Stir well. Remove bay leaves.

Pour into a 9x13x2-inch glass baking dish. If casserole is not to be baked immediately, cover and refrigerate until ready to bake. Before baking, cover with cheese. Bake, covered, 30 minutes or until ingredients are thoroughly heated. Serves 6-8.

Necessities and Temptations

Lemon Barbecued Shrimp

This recipe using fresh gulf shrimp was contributed by Travis County Extension Office home economist Linda Waggoner.

2½ pounds unpeeled large	¼ cup soy sauce
shrimp	3 tablespoons minced fresh
½ cup fresh lemon juice	parsley
¼ cup reduced-calorie	3 tablespoons minced onion
Italian salad dressing	1 clove garlic, crushed
¼ cup water	½ teaspoon black pepper

Peel and devein shrimp, then place in a large shallow glass baking dish. Combine remaining ingredients in a jar, cover tightly, and shake vigorously. Pour ¾ of the mixture over shrimp, reserving remainder for later use. Cover shrimp and refrigerate for 4 hours.

Remove shrimp from marinade and thread onto skewers. Grill 5-6 inches from heat for 3-4 minutes per side, basting frequently with reserved marinade. Serves 6.

Texas Barbecue

Shrimp Bisque
(In Puff Pastry)

¼ cup grated onion
2 tablespoons grated green
   bell pepper
2 tablespoons butter or
   margarine
1 (10¾-ounce) can cream of
   potato soup
¾ cup light cream

½ cup grated sharp Cheddar
   cheese
2 teaspoons lemon juice
1½ cups shrimp, cooked
   and peeled or seafood of
   choice
1 (10-ounce) package frozen
   puff pastry shells

In a skillet, sauté onion and green pepper in butter. Blend in soup, cream, Cheddar cheese, lemon juice, and prepared seafood. Season to taste. This may be stored in refrigerator or frozen until serving. When ready to serve, prepare puff pastry shells according to package directions. Thaw and heat seafood mixture thoroughly; pour into baked pastry shells. Serves 4-6.

Amazing Graces

Albondigas De Camaron
(Egg and Shrimp Fritters)

4 eggs
¼ cup onion, minced
2 teaspoons salt
¼ teaspoon black pepper

1½ cups shrimp, cooked
   and chopped
2 tablespoons flour
Cooking oil

In large mixing bowl beat eggs; add onion, salt, black pepper, and shrimp. Mix well. Add flour to egg mixture and blend. This makes a batter. In deep skillet heat 1 inch cooking oil. Pour ¼ cup batter for each fritter into hot oil. Fry, a few at a time, till golden brown, about 1 minute on each side. Drain on paper towels. Serve hot with ranchero sauce, if desired. Serves 4-6. Makes 8-10 fritters.

South Texas Mexican Cook Book

Dee's Crawfish Etoufée
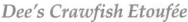

3 sticks margarine
1½ cups finely chopped onions
1 cup finely chopped celery
1 cup finely chopped green onions
1½ teaspoons garlic powder
6 tablespoons flour
1 (14-ounce) can stewed tomatoes

3 cups fish stock or chicken broth*
3 teaspoons salt
1½ teaspoons black pepper
¼ teaspoon cayenne
10 drops Tabasco
2 tablespoons Worcestershire sauce
2 pounds crawfish tails, drained

In a 5-quart pot, sauté in margarine the onion, celery, green onion, with garlic powder until vegetables are tender. Add flour, stirring constantly, for 3 minutes. Add tomatoes (mashed a little) plus juice from can. Continue cooking and stirring 5 minutes. Mixture will be golden brown. Blend in stock and seasonings and simmer, stirring occasionally for 10 minutes. Add crawfish and cook slowly for 20 minutes. Adjust seasonings. Serve over rice. Serves 6-8.

Note: This is good made ahead—flavors have a chance to blend. *You can use chicken broth but fish stock is better. Recipe follows.

FISH STOCK:

2 quarts water
1 large onion, quartered
½ teaspoon garlic powder
2 ribs celery

2 pounds shrimp heads and shells, crawfish heads, fish carcasses or other seafood shells

Put enough cold water to cover ingredients. Use large pot. Bring to boil, then simmer about 4 hours, adding water as needed to keep at least a quart at all times. Strain, cool and refrigerate. Freeze in containers if any is left.

Best of Friends

Buddy Holly is honored with a heroic size bronze statue as a lasting tribute to Lubbock's most famous son.

Texas Star Crabmeat Casserole

1 pound lump crabmeat
¼ cup lemon juice (juice of 3 lemons)
½ teaspoon salt
½ cup butter or margarine
2½ tablespoons all-purpose flour
1½ cups milk
½ teaspoon garlic salt
½ teaspoon celery salt

1 teaspoon parsley flakes
1 cup grated Cheddar cheese
2 tablespoons white wine (optional)
6 cups cooked wild rice or Uncle Ben's Wild Rice Mixture
1 (6-ounce) can sliced mushrooms, drained

Combine crabmeat, lemon juice, and salt in a medium bowl and refrigerate while preparing sauce.

Melt butter or margarine in a medium saucepan. Add flour; stir and cook for about 1 minute. Add milk slowly, stirring constantly, and cook until sauce thickens. Add seasonings, cheese, and wine (optional). Stir until cheese is melted and sauce is smooth. Drain crabmeat, add to sauce and heat until bubbly.

Layer cooked wild rice in bottom of a lightly oiled 2-quart casserole dish. Pour crabmeat and sauce over rice. Top with mushroom slices and bake at 350° for about 30 minutes or until lightly browned. Serve with a crisp green salad and crunchy rolls. Yield: 6 servings.

More Tastes & Tales

To Fry Oysters

Dry your oysters well, either in a colander or by spreading on a dry cloth. Take fine cornmeal and season well with salt and pepper; roll the oysters in the meal and fry at once in boiling lard while the meal is dry. Cook a light brown.

The First Texas Cook Book

Sopes Stuffed with Crabmeat

Sopes are silver dollar-sized, boat-shaped appetizers made from much the same dough as corn tortillas. They are indigenous to the Guadalajara region of Mexico, where they are eaten as street food. Typically, sopes are stuffed with cheese, salsa, chorizo, or some other meat, but they can also be fried and eaten plain.

2 cups masa harina	1 teaspoon baking powder
1¼ cups hot water	1 pound crabmeat, shell and
2 tablespoons lard or	cartilage removed
vegetable shortening	Vegetable oil, for frying
⅓ cup flour	1 cup Tomatillo-Jalapeño
½ teaspoon salt	Chutney (page 134)

In a mixing bowl, combine the masa harina with the hot water, cover, and let stand for 30 minutes. Add the lard or shortening, flour, salt, and baking powder to the masa harina mixture, and mix together thoroughly.

Divide the dough into 12 balls, then the 12 balls into 24, and the 24 into 48. Place the masa balls on a cookie sheet and cover with a damp towel or plastic wrap.

Lightly oil your fingers and flatten one of the sopes by patting it between the fingers of one hand and the palm of your other hand. Place about 2 teaspoons of crabmeat in the middle and enclose it with the masa dough; form into a boat or diamond shape. Repeat the procedure for the remaining sopes.

Pour enough oil into a large skillet to come ¼-inch up the sides, and heat until lightly smoking. Fry the sopes over medium-high heat for 2 minutes per side. Serve with the Tomatillo-Jalapeño Chutney. Makes 6-8 servings.

The New Texas Cuisine

Texas Blue Crab Cakes

Blue crabs get their name from the color of their shells and claws. They can be expensive, particularly away from the Gulf, but this recipe stretches a little of the succulent meat a long way.

1 egg, lightly beaten
2 tablespoons mayonnaise
2 teaspoons prepared Creole
  mustard
2 teaspoons prepared
  horseradish
2 teaspoons Worcestershire
  sauce
1½ teaspoons crab-boil
  seasoning, such as Zatarain's
1 teaspoon coarse-ground
  black pepper

¼ teaspoon salt
Several dashes of Tabasco or
  other hot pepper sauce
1 pound crabmeat, picked
  over to remove any shells
¾ cup saltine cracker
  crumbs (about 1½ ounces)
½ cup minced red bell
  pepper
3 tablespoons olive oil
1 tablespoon unsalted butter
Lemon wedges, for garnish

In a large bowl, stir together the egg, mayonnaise, mustard, horseradish, Worcestershire sauce, Old Bay seasoning, pepper, salt, and Tabasco. Gently mix in the crabmeat, cracker crumbs, and bell pepper. For the ideal combination of crisp exterior and creamy interior, form 8 patties ¾-inch thick.

Warm the oil and butter together over medium-high heat. Fry the crab cakes 5-7 minutes on each side, or until they are golden. Drain them.

Serve the cakes immediately. They are so flavorful that they require little more than a squeeze of lemon juice for accompaniment. Makes 8 crab cakes.

Texas Home Cooking

Located across the street from the Texas & Pacific Depot, the Grace Hotel was built in 1909 to serve as a rest stop for weary railway passengers. Today the restored and renovated Mission-style building serves as the home of the Museums of Abilene.

Meats

The Texas longhorns are the proud symbol of the University of Texas.

Honest-To-Goodness Chili

This is really great chili, not a hot one! Do not substitute tomato sauce for paste, or other substitutes, or it will taste differently. You will love this one.

3 garlic cloves, minced
2 tablespoons cooking oil
4 pounds round steak, ground
6 large onions, sliced
4 large green bell peppers
3 (1-pound) cans tomatoes
4 (1-pound) cans red kidney
  beans, drained

2 (6-ounce) cans tomato paste
¼ cup chili powder
1 teaspoon white vinegar
3 dashes cayenne pepper
3 whole cloves
1 bay leaf
Salt and pepper, to taste

Sauté garlic in oil till golden. Crumble ground meat in pieces and cook 10 minutes, breaking up to brown evenly. (Have butcher grind the meat just once or twice.) Pour off some of the fat into another skillet and cook sliced onions and green pepper till tender. Add to cooked ground round with tomatoes, beans, and the remaining ingredients. Cover; cook over low heat for 1 hour. If too dry, add more tomatoes. If thin, uncover and simmer longer. Serve with crackers, tacos, or other Mexican dishes of your choice. Serves 12-16, depending upon the extent of your menu.

The Mexican Collection

Soul Satisfying Chili

2 pounds beef round or chuck
  steak, cut into cubes
1 pound hamburger meat
3 tablespoons vegetable oil
2 medium onions, chopped
¼ cup flour
2-4 cloves garlic, chopped
½ (6-ounce) can tomato paste
3 cups canned tomatoes,
  chopped

5 cups beef broth
6 tablespoons powdered red
  chilies
2 teaspoons whole or ground
  cumin
1 teaspoon oregano
½ teaspoon black pepper
2 teaspoons salt
3 tablespoons cider vinegar

Heat oil in a large skillet and brown meat in it in 3 or 4 batches. As each batch is finished, transfer the meat to a large Dutch

CONTINUED

oven. Stir onions into skillet (making sure there are 2 table-spoons of fat left in it). Cover and cook over low heat for 5 minutes. Remove lid, raise heat, stir onions until light brown. Sprinkle flour over onions, stir for 1 minute, transfer to pot with beef.

Add all remaining ingredients to mixture, stir thoroughly and bring to a boil. Lower heat, cover and simmer for at least 1½ hours, stirring occasionally. Degrease before serving if necessary.

Note: This tastes even better the next day.

Canyon Echoes

Best-Ever Chili

9 pounds lean beef, chopped	1 tablespoon cumin
3 quarts water	1 tablespoon marjoram
3 (16-ounce) cans tomatoes	9 tablespoons paprika
6 medium onions, chopped	3 tablespoons salt
3 tablespoons sugar	1 tablespoon black pepper
1 tablespoon garlic powder	1 tablespoon cayenne pepper
10 tablespoons chili powder	6-12 tablespoons cornmeal

Brown beef lightly in large nonstick saucepan; drain. Add water, tomatoes, and onions. Simmer for 1 - 1½ hours. Add sugar, garlic powder, chili powder, cumin, marjoram, paprika, salt, black pepper, and cayenne pepper; mix well. Simmer for 45 minutes. Stir in cornmeal 1 tablespoon at a time, simmering until of desired consistency. Yield: 30 servings.

Approx Per Serving: Cal 325; Prot 27g; Carbo 10g: Fiber 2g; T Fat 20g; 55% Calories from Fat; Chol 89mg; Sod 818mg.

Gatherings

Chile con carne literally means "pepper with meat." Not an authentic Mexican dish, earliest accounts show it was sold on the square in San Antonio in the last decades of the nineteenth century. Lyndon Johnson suggested chili be named the state food of Texas—it now is.

White Lightning Chili

1½ cups dried navy beans
3 (14-ounce) cans chicken
  broth
¼ stick margarine
1 cup water
1 onion, chopped
1 clove garlic, minced
3 cups chopped, cooked
  chicken
1 (4-ounce) can chopped
  green chilies

½ teaspoon sweet basil
½ teaspoon white pepper
1½ teaspoons ground cumin
½ teaspoon dried oregano
⅛ teaspoon cayenne pepper
⅛ teaspoon ground cloves
6 (8-inch) flour tortillas
Grated Monterey Jack
  cheese
Commercial salsa (optional)

Sort and wash beans; place in a Dutch oven. Cover with water 2 inches above beans. Soak overnight. Drain beans. Add broth, margarine, water, onion, and garlic. Bring to a boil; reduce heat and cover. Simmer 2½ hours, stirring occasionally. With potato masher, mash beans several times so that about half of the beans are mashed. Add chicken, green chilies, basil, white pepper, cumin, oregano, cayenne pepper, and cloves. Bring to a boil; reduce heat and cover. Simmer another 30 minutes. With kitchen shears, make 4 cuts in each tortilla toward center, but not through center. Line serving bowls with tortillas, overlapping cut edges. Spoon in chili and top with cheese or salsa.

Southwest Ole!

Skillet Supper

Not fancy but fine.

1½ pounds lean ground
  meat
1 large onion, chopped
1 teaspoon seasoned salt
½ teaspoon salt

½ teaspoon pepper
1 can Rotel tomatoes and
  green chilies
½ cabbage, chopped
Soy sauce, optional

Brown ground meat and chopped onion in a large skillet. Season with seasoned salt, salt and pepper. Add Rotel tomatoes; stir and cover with cabbage. Cover with a tight fitting lid and cook on low heat until cabbage is tender. May season with soy sauce. Serve this with a salad and don't forget the cornbread.

More Calf Fries to Caviar

Mexican Mini Meat Loaves

1½ pounds ground beef
1 cup Pace Medium Picante
   Sauce, divided
½ cup crushed tortilla chips
   or corn chips
1 medium onion, chopped

1 egg
1½ teaspoons ground cumin
1 teaspoon salt
½ cup sharp Cheddar or
   Monterey Jack cheese,
   shredded

Combine ground beef, ¾ cup of picante sauce, chips, onion, egg, cumin, and salt. Shape to form 6-8 loaves. Place in 13x9x2-inch baking dish. Bake at 350° about 35 minutes, or to desired doneness. Spoon remaining picante sauce over meat loaves; sprinkle with cheese while hot. Cover with foil until serving time. Serve with more sauce, if desired.

Busy cooks with an eye on the clock will appreciate the convenience of these individual servings, which bake far faster than a standard meatloaf.

The Second Typically Texas Cookbook

Mexicana Good Stuff

Sure to please.

1 pound ground beef
1 small onion, chopped
½ cup green pepper,
   chopped
1 clove garlic, minced
1 tablespoon chili powder
1 teaspoon salt

1 can tomato sauce
½ cup milk
2 cups rice, cooked
1 cup Cheddar cheese, cubed
Flour tortillas
Hot sauce
Corn chips

Cook together ground beef, onion, green pepper, garlic, chili powder, and salt until meat is done and vegetables are tender. Stir in tomato sauce, milk, and rice. Heat thoroughly and fold in cubed cheese.

Roll in warmed flour tortillas and serve with hot sauce. Or may serve piled on top of corn chips, if desired.

More Calf Fries to Caviar

Burrito Bake

1 can refried beans	1 tomato, chopped
1 cup Bisquick	1 avocado, sliced
¼ cup water	1-2 cups shredded Cheddar
1 pound ground beef	cheese
1 small jar Pace Picante Sauce	Sour Cream

Combine refried beans, Bisquick and water and spread on a greased pie pan. Brown meat and spread on bean mixture; layer picante, tomato, avocado, and cheese on top of meat. Bake at 350° for 30 minutes. Remove from oven and spread sour cream on top.

M. D. Anderson Volunteers Cooking for Fun

Beef Burritos

(Rolled Sandwiches)

1 cup refried beans	1 cup Cheddar cheese, grated
8 (10-inch) flour tortillas	2 cups shredded lettuce
2 cups cooked beef, shredded	2 tomatoes, chopped

Spread 2 tablespoons beans on each tortilla, cover with ¼ cup beef. Top with cheese, lettuce and tomatoes. Fold one end of warm tortilla over filling; roll. To heat omit lettuce and tomatoes, wrap in foil and heat in preheated 350° oven for 15 minutes, or wrap loosely in plastic wrap and cook in microwave for 30 seconds.

Variation: Try beans and cheese. Cooked chicken. Ground beef with taco seasoning. Or eggs with sausage or bacon.

'Cross the Border

 Texas is the nation's largest producer of cattle, most of which are beef breeds, as opposed to the dairy varieties. The cattle industry actually began in Texas with long-horn cattle, which were driven by cattlemen to Kansas and Missouri for shipment by railroad.

Chilies Rellenos Con Carne
(Meat Stuffed Green Chilies)

1 (10-ounce) can green
   chilies, whole
²/₃ pound ground elk, deer,
   or moose
½ cup raw rice
½ (1.25-ounce) package taco
   seasoning

1 (8-ounce) can tomato sauce
1 (6-ounce) can vegetable
   juice
Dash paprika
½ cup picante sauce (hot or
   mild)
Grated cheese

In a casserole, place juice from green chilies. Split chilies and set aside. In a bowl, mix ground meat, rice, taco seasoning, and one-half can of tomato sauce. Stuff chilies with meat mixture. Secure each with a toothpick.

Place stuffed chilies in casserole with juices from chilies. Top each with additional tomato sauce. Add vegetable juice to pan. Sprinkle peppers with paprika and picante sauce on top and around peppers.

Bake at 350° for 50-55 minutes, basting frequently with pan juices. Top each chile with grated cheese and return to oven briefly to barely melt cheese. Serve hot, removing toothpicks. Yield: 8 Chilies Rellenos con Carne.

Note: Ground beef may be used as alternate meat choice.

Gathering of the Game

Chile Relleños Casserole

1 pound ground beef
½ cup chopped onion
½ teaspoon salt
½ teaspoon pepper
2 (4-ounce) cans green
  chilies, divided
2½ cups shredded sharp
  Cheddar cheese, divided

1½ cups milk
2 tablespoons flour
⅔ teaspoon salt
Pepper to taste
Hot sauce to taste
3 eggs, beaten

Cook beef, onion, salt and pepper in a skillet until the meat begins to brown. Drain. Spread 1 can of the green chilies over the bottom of a 9x13-inch baking dish. Sprinkle with ½ the cheese and top with all of the meat mixture. Add the remaining cheese and second can of chilies. Combine milk, flour, salt, pepper, hot sauce, and eggs. Pour over casserole and bake at 350° for 50 minutes or until knife inserted comes out clean. Cool 5 minutes. Cut in squares. May be frozen. Reheat while still frozen at 400° until heated through. Serves 4-6.

The Texas Experience

Sun Devil Surprise

1 pound ground beef
2 tablespoons soy sauce
2 tablespoons teriyaki sauce
Dash onion powder

Pepper
4 flour tortillas
Grated cheese
1 tablespoon picante sauce

Brown beef on high heat, drain, lower heat to medium. Mix in soy sauce, teriyaki sauce, onion powder, and pepper. Put mixture on a warm flour tortilla, top with cheese and picante sauce and eat it. Makes 4 servings, takes 15 minutes.

The College Cookbook

Lone Star Chicken-Fried Steak and Gravy

Fry chicken this way too!

2 pounds round steak, tenderized	Seasoned pepper
1¼ cups flour	2 eggs, slightly beaten
1 teaspoon salt	½ cup milk
	Oil

Trim steak and cut into 6-8 pieces. Combine flour, salt and pepper. Dredge all steak pieces in flour mixture until lightly coated. Combine eggs and milk. Dip steak into egg mixture and dredge again in flour, getting plenty of flour mashed into steak. Heat ½ inch of oil in a heavy skillet and fry steak pieces until golden brown.

CREAM GRAVY:

6-8 tablespoons pan grease or bacon drippings	3 cups milk
6 tablespoons flour	½ teaspoon salt
	¼ teaspoon pepper

To make gravy, remove steaks to warm oven, retaining drippings (bacon drippings make better gravy if you happen to have it). Add flour. Cook and stir until flour only begins to brown. Add milk and stir until thickened. Season with salt and pepper and serve in a bowl to cover steaks or mashed potatoes. This is a true Texas tradition!

A Little Taste of Texas

Barbara Harris' Chicken Fried Steak

2½ pounds round steak,
  tenderized and cut into 6
  equal pieces
2 cups buttermilk, in a pie
  plate

2 cups flour, in separate plate
Vegetable shortening, for
  frying

Dip each steak in buttermilk; dredge in flour; repeat process. Cook in deep fryer at 350° until golden brown, about 4-5 minutes. Serve immediately, drowned in wonderful creamy gravy! Serves 6.

Great Flavors of Texas

Ross's Favorite Chicken Fried Steak and Gravy

1 (16-ounce) (½-inch thick)
  top round steak, cut into 4
  equal serving pieces
½ cup lime juice
4 teaspoons "Ross's Special
  Seasoning," divided
2 teaspoons Worcestershire
  sauce, divided

2 egg whites at room
  temperature
¼ cup cornstarch
1 cup Grape Nuts
1 cup boiling water plus 2
  chicken bouillon cubes
Pam no-stick cooking spray
1 recipe Chicken Fried Gravy

One hour before cooking, dip each steak in lime juice. Sprinkle one side of each steak with ½ teaspoon of Ross's Special Seasoning and place seasoned-side-down on plate. Pour ½ teaspoon Worcestershire sauce on top of each steak and sprinkle each with ½ teaspoon of remaining seasoning. Marinate 1 hour; if marinating longer, refrigerate.

Beat egg whites until foamy; add cornstarch and beat until stiff. Spray a large skillet with Pam and heat until hot but not smoking. Dip steak into egg whites, then Grape Nuts; coat evenly.

Place steak carefully in skillet and brown on both sides, adding broth a little at a time to keep from burning. Cook to desired doneness, about 2-3 minutes per side. Serves 4.

Per Serving: Cal 307; Fat 4.3g; 13% Fat; Prot 37.5g; Carb 34.5g; Sod 697mg; Chol 93mg.

CONTINUED

CHICKEN FRIED GRAVY:

2 tablespoons defatted
   chicken broth
2 tablespoons Grape Nuts
   cereal plus 1 tablespoon flour
1 cup evaporated skim milk
2 tablespoons cornstarch plus
   3 tablespoons cold water to
   form a paste

2 tablespoons reduced fat
   cream of mushroom soup
Salt (optional) and pepper to
   taste

Sauté Grape Nuts and flour in broth until cereal is soft. Slowly add evaporated milk; stir well. Heat to a slow simmer; slowly stir in cornstarch mixture and cook until thick. Add soup and season to taste. Serve with chicken fried steak. Makes about 24 tablespoons (2 cups).

Per Serving: Cal 9; Fat 0.1g; 10% Fat; Prot 0.49g; Carb 1.55g; Sod 17.4mg; Chol .39mg.

The Lite Switch

Ross's Special Seasoning

¼ cup plus 1 teaspoon chili
   powder
½ cup plus 2 teaspoons salt
   or lite salt
¼ cup plus 1 teaspoon brown
   sugar

½ cup (less ½ teaspoon)
   cumin
1¼ teaspoons ginger
½ teaspoon plus ⅛ teaspoon
   mace
2½ teaspoons garlic powder

Mix all ingredients and use as a marinade for meats. Makes about 2 cups.

Per entire recipe: Cal 180; Fat 0; 0% Fat; Prot 0g; Carb 48g; Sod 3.9mg; Chol 0mg.

The Lite Switch

 The Marine Military Academy, located in Harlingen, boasts the original Iwo Jima Monument from which the Arlington, Virginia, statue was cast.

Swiss Steak

Back on the farm this was a good way to cook steak from range cattle which had not been fattened up for the kill. Since we are going to cut away all visible signs of fat, it is still a good way to cook the less tender cuts of steak.

2 pounds round steak, 1-inch thick	**1 medium onion, sliced**
¼ cup flour	**½ medium bell pepper, chopped**
½ teaspoon salt	**1 clove garlic**
½ teaspoon pepper	**1 cup canned tomatoes**
1 tablespoon vegetable oil	**¼ cup mushrooms, optional**

Cut away all visible signs of fat. Tenderize steak by pounding with a meat mallet. Dredge it in a mixture of the flour, salt, and pepper. Heat vegetable oil in nonstick skillet. Brown meat on both sides in vegetable oil. Add onion, garlic, and green pepper and cook until onion is clear. Add tomatoes and 1 cup of boiling water. Simmer, covered, for about 1 hour. Place steak on serving plate. Spoon sauce over top. Makes 8 servings.

Per serving: Cal 160; Fat 1g; Chol 53mg; Sat Fat 2g; Food exchanges 3 meat; 1 vegetable.

Low-Cal Country

Beef Burgundy

⅓ cup flour
2 teaspoons salt
½ teaspoon pepper
2 pounds round steak, cut in
   1-inch cubes
2 cloves garlic, minced
⅓ cup cooking oil
2 cans condensed beef broth
2 cups burgundy
½ teaspoon dillweed,
   crushed

½ teaspoon dried marjoram,
   crushed
2 (14-ounce) cans artichoke
   hearts, drained and quartered
3 cups fresh mushrooms,
   sliced
⅓ cup flour
½ cup water

In a bowl, combine flour, salt and pepper. Toss meat in mixture to coat. In a Dutch oven with hot oil, brown meat and garlic. Add broth, burgundy, dillweed, and marjoram. Simmer covered 1½ hours, stirring occasionally. Add artichoke hearts and mushrooms. Cook 10 minutes. Preheat oven to 400°.

In a separate bowl, combine remaining flour and water and mix well. Stir into beef mixture. (Freeze or refrigerate at this point, if desired.)

Place beef burgundy in oven and bake 30-40 minutes until heated thoroughly. Serve over buttered noodles. Yields 10 servings.

Celebrate San Antonio

Carne Con Papas
(Potato-Beef Hash)

3-4 medium potatoes, cubed
3 tablespoons cooking oil
1 tablespoon salt
1½ pounds chuck steak,
   cubed

1 teaspoon mixed spices
   (peppercorns and cumin)
2 cloves garlic
1 can whole tomatoes
3 cups water

Brown potatoes in oil and add salt. Add beef cubes to browned potatoes. Stir, cover, simmer for 20 minutes. Grind spices and garlic and add a little water to mortar. Add spices, tomatoes, and water to meat and potatoes. Simmer 20 minutes.

South Texas Mexican Cook Book

207

Red Raider Stew

1½ - 2 pounds lean stew meat
Flour
1 large onion, chopped
1 cup celery, chopped
1 large potato, cubed
1 large can ranch-style beans
2 cups boiling water
1 large can tomatoes
1 cup diced carrots

½ cup okra, sliced
1 small bell pepper, chopped
1 can whole kernel corn
2 tablespoons Worcestershire
  sauce
½ teaspoon salt
Garlic salt, chili powder, and
  cumin to taste

Dredge meat cubes in flour and brown in skillet with onions. Chop all vegetables, add to beef; cook until beef and vegetables are tender. Season to taste.

Raider Recipes

No Peek Stew

2 pounds stew meat
1 (10½-ounce) can cream of
  mushroom soup
1 (1.25-ounce) package onion
  soup mix
1 cup thinly sliced carrots
1 cup thinly sliced celery

¾ cup red wine
Marjoram, dash
Thyme, dash
Paprika, dash
Salt and pepper, dash
Minced parsley, dash

Combine all ingredients. Place in 3 to 5-quart baking dish. Cover. Bake at 300° for 3 hours. Don't peek! Yield: 6 servings.

Note: Good served with buttered noodles or rice.

Deep in the Heart

Siesta Roast N' Beans

Sleep while it cooks.

3-4 pound roast	1 onion, chopped
2 cups pinto beans, uncooked	1 can tomato sauce
1 can green chilies, chopped	Water
1 can tomatoes	Salt and pepper

Place roast in a large pan. Place pinto beans, green chilies, tomatoes, onion, and tomato sauce on top of roast. Cover entire contents with water. Place in 250° oven covered with lid. Cook at least 12 hours. (May cook longer). Season with salt and pepper. Serve with salad, cornbread, and a dessert for a complete meal.

'Cross the Border

Venison Roast

Take knife and insert bacon and garlic into roast. Make the following marinade:

1 medium carrot, grated	2 bay leaves
1 cup chopped onion	½ teaspoon salt
½ cup chopped parsley	½ teaspoon pepper
½ cup diced celery	6 whole cloves

Put half of the above mixture in baking pan. Place roast on the vegetables marinade and cover with the other half. Pour over this 2 cups of oil and 3 cups of dry white wine. Marinate for 2 days in the refrigerator, turning meat several times. Roast and baste with marinade at 350° until tender.

The New Texas Wild Game Cook Book

Beef and Brew Take Along

5 pounds sirloin tip roast	½ teaspoon salt
1 (12-ounce) can beef	½ teaspoon pepper
4 tablespoons flour	½ teaspoon onion salt

Place roast in large plastic bag and add beer. Close tightly and refrigerate at least 12 hours. When ready to prepare, preheat oven to 325°. Remove roast from plastic bag reserving beer marinade. Rub roast with flour, salt, pepper, and onion salt. Place in large roasting pan and add beer marinade to pan. Bake about 1½ hours or until meat thermometer reads 140°. Baste often with pan drippings.

WINE MARINADE:

½ cup salad oil	¼ teaspoon onion salt
¼ cup red wine vinegar	¼ teaspoon garlic salt
½ cup tomato purée	Pinch of pepper
½ cup sherry	½ cup prepared Marinara
¼ cup burgundy	sauce
½ teaspoon salt	

Combine ingredients for wine marinade. Mix well and set aside. Slice the cooled roast very thin. Place in large casserole and pour wine marinade over meat. Cover and refrigerate about 12 hours. Take to picnic in casserole and serve over pumpernickel bread. If desired, serve warm with wine marinade heated and poured over meat. Yield: 12 servings.

Celebrate San Antonio

Coke Roast

1 package dry onion soup mix	1 (12-ounce) regular coke
1 (12-ounce) jar chili sauce	1 beef brisket or roast

Mix soup, chili sauce and coke together. Pour over roast, cover and bake at 350° for 30 minutes per pound. (Do not use foil with this because of coke.)

More of the Four Ingredient Cookbook

Stuffed Tenderloin with Marsala Sauce

1 (10-ounce) package frozen
chopped spinach, thawed,
drained
2 tablespoons prepared
horseradish
½ cup crumbled blue cheese
¼ teaspoon pepper
8 tenderloin steaks
8 slices bacon

¼ cup olive oil
½ cup Marsala
½ cup dry red wine
1½ teaspoons finely
chopped garlic
¼ teaspoon hot pepper
sauce
1 tablespoon tomato paste
1 tablespoon water

Combine first 4 ingredients in bowl; mix well. Cut pocket in
each steak with sharp knife. Stuff with spinach mixture. Wrap
each with 1 slice bacon to close opening. Cook steaks on 1 side
in hot olive oil in skillet for 3 minutes for rare or for 5 minutes
for medium. Turn steaks. Cook for 3-5 minutes or until done to
taste. Remove to warm platter. Add wines, stirring for 30
seconds to deglaze skillet. Add garlic. Cook for 1 minute. Stir
in pepper sauce and mixture of tomato paste and water; reduce
heat. Cook for 1 minute, stirring constantly. Add steaks, turning to coat well. Place on platter; top with sauce. Garnish with
parsley. Yield: 8 servings.

Approx per serving: Cal 453; Prot 47g; Carbo 3g; Fiber 1g; T Fat 25g; Chol
138mg; Sod 308mg.

Texas Cookin' Lone Star Style

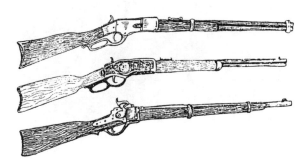

Grilled Beef Tenderloin with Creole Mustard Sauce

| 1 (3-4-pound) beef tenderloin | Creole seasoning |
| 3 tablespoons olive oil | Salt and pepper to taste |

Rub tenderloin with olive oil and season generously with the seasonings. Grill over hot coals for about 20-30 minutes, turning frequently. Transfer to a platter.

MUSTARD SAUCE:

½ cup finely chopped onion	¼ cup Creole or any grainy,
2 cloves garlic, minced	spicy mustard
2 tablespoons butter	¼ cup Worcestershire sauce
2 cups half-and-half	Freshly ground black pepper

Cook onion and garlic in the butter until translucent. Add half-and-half and cook until sauce is reduced by half. Add the mustard and Worcestershire sauce and season with black pepper to taste. Serve with sliced tenderloin. Serves 8-10.

Buffet on the Bayou

Lobster Stuffed Tenderloin

2 lobster tails, 4 ounces each
3-4 pounds whole beef
  tenderloin
1 tablespoon butter, melted

1½ teaspoons lemon juice
6 slices bacon, partially
  cooked

WINE SAUCE:
½ cup chopped green onion
½ cup butter
½ pound fresh mushrooms

½ cup dry white wine
⅛ teaspoon garlic salt

Place lobster tails in boiling salted water to cover. Return to boiling, reduce heat, and simmer for 5-7 minutes. Cut beef tenderloin lengthwise to within ½ inch of bottom to butterfly. Carefully remove lobster from shells. Cut in half lengthwise. Place lobster end to end, inside beef. Combine 1 tablespoon melted butter with lemon juice and drizzle on lobster. Close meat around lobster and tie roast with string at 1-inch intervals. Place on a rack in a shallow roasting pan. Roast at 425° for 25 minutes for rare. Lay partially cooked bacon slices on top and roast 5 minutes more. Meanwhile, in a saucepan, cook green onions in remaining butter; add mushrooms and sauté until tender. Add wine and garlic salt and heat through, stirring frequently. To serve, slice roast and spoon on wine sauce.
Serves 8.

Lone Star Legacy II

After many years of Spain and then Mexico's rule, some Texans demanded independence—and the Texas Revolution began, leading to the Battle of the Alamo. There on March 6, 1836, a small band of Texans held out for 13 days before falling to Mexico's forces. Among the casualties were non-Texans, Davy Crockett and Jim Bowie. That defeat inspired others to "Remember the Alamo" and win Texas independence.

Lone Star Sauerbraten

Best in the West.

1 (4-5-pound) beef roast (top
  or bottom)
1 tablespoon salt
Pepper, to taste
2 bottles Lone Star Beer
1 cup vinegar
1-2 cups water
1 onion, sliced
3 bay leaves

10 whole black peppercorns
2 tablespoons sugar (or Equal
  equivalent)
4 cloves
¼ teaspoon allspice
3 ounces slab bacon
Flour
6 gingersnaps, crushed
½ cup raisins

Rub beef with salt and pepper. Place in large, glass bowl. Heat beer, vinegar, water, onion, bay leaves, peppercorns, sugar, cloves, and allspice, but do not boil. Pour heated mixture over beef to partially cover. Cool, then cover with plastic wrap securely, and place in refrigerator. Turn beef once or twice each day for 7 days. Using iron pot (Dutch oven), cut up bacon and fry until soft. Remove. Add beef, which has been dredged lightly in flour; sear quickly on all sides. Lower heat to very low; add beer and vinegar mixture, including onion, and bacon. Simmer 3 hours, or until very tender. By this time, liquid should be cooked down. Remove beef; keep warm. Add crushed gingersnaps to thicken gravy. Add raisins and a little water, if necessary. Slice beef with electric knife or very sharp knife, as the meat will be soft. Serve with red cabbage and your favorite dumplings.

The Second Typically Texas Cookbook

The armadillo has long been associated with Texas, having emigrated from South America. Not too swift, it is more often seen dead as a road kill than alive. Once hunted for its meat, the armadillo is now more of a tourist attraction, and its "shell" (actually a super thick skin) is often fashioned into assorted baskets and gift items.

Babette's Carnitas

Use two forks to shred this deliciously moist, tender meat.

1 (3-4-pound) beef chuck roast
1 (7-ounce) can chopped green chilies
2 tablespoons chili powder
½ teaspoon oregano
⅓ teaspoon cumin
1 clove garlic, minced
Salt, to taste
Tortillas
Guacamole
Salsa

On a large piece of heavy-duty foil, place roast. In small bowl combine green chilies, chili powder, oregano, cumin, garlic, and salt. Spread mixture on top surface of the beef roast. Wrap in foil and seal securely. Place in ovenproof dish and bake for 3½ - 4 hours at 300°. Cook longer if necessary. (The meat should be so tender that it will fall apart.) For each serving, spoon meat into hot tortilla. Serve with guacamole and salsa. Yield: 4-6 servings.

More Calf Fries to Caviar

Cowboy Casserole

1½ pounds ground beef
4 tablespoons oil
2 stalks celery, cut into thin
    strips
1 slice green bell pepper
¾ cup chopped onion
1 cup uncooked rice
1 (28-ounce) can chopped
    tomatoes
2 teaspoons salt

2 teaspoons chili powder
½ teaspoon pepper
1 teaspoon Worcestershire
    sauce
Tabasco sauce to taste
1 cup chopped large black
    olives
8 ounces Monterey Jack
    cheese, sliced

Brown ground beef in 2 tablespoons oil in skillet; drain. Remove ground beef to 2-quart casserole. Add remaining 2 tablespoons oil, celery, green pepper, onion, and rice to skillet. Cook until rice is browned. Add undrained tomatoes, salt, chili powder, pepper, Worcestershire sauce, Tabasco sauce, and half the olives; mix well. Bring to a boil. Pour over ground beef. Bake, covered, at 325° for 1 hour. Layer remaining olives and cheese over baked layers. Broil for 5 minutes or until cheese is bubbly. Yield: 8 servings.

Approx Per Serving: Cal 487; Prot 26g; Carbo 26g; Fiber 3g; T Fat 33g; 59% Calories from Fat; Chol 82mg; Sod 1078mg.

Gatherings

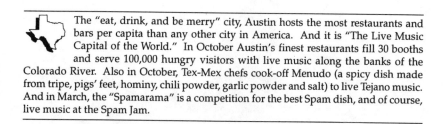

The "eat, drink, and be merry" city, Austin hosts the most restaurants and bars per capita than any other city in America. And it is "The Live Music Capital of the World." In October Austin's finest restaurants fill 30 booths and serve 100,000 hungry visitors with live music along the banks of the Colorado River. Also in October, Tex-Mex chefs cook-off Menudo (a spicy dish made from tripe, pigs' feet, hominy, chili powder, garlic powder and salt) to live Tejano music. And in March, the "Spamarama" is a competition for the best Spam dish, and of course, live music at the Spam Jam.

Ranch Hand Mexican Pie

Enough prepared mashed
  potatoes for 4 servings
1 egg, slightly beaten
¼ cup sliced green onions
  (with tops)
1 pound ground beef
½ cup chopped onion
1 (8-ounce) can tomato sauce
¼ cup sliced ripe olives

2-3 teaspoons chili powder (to
  taste)
¼ teaspoon salt
¼ teaspoon garlic powder
1 cup shredded Cheddar or
  Monterey Jack cheese
Garnish: sour cream, green
  bell pepper, tomato,
  avocado

Heat oven to 425°. Grease 9-inch pie plate. Place mashed potatoes in a bowl, stir in egg and green onions. Spread and press potato mixture evenly against bottom and side of pie plate. Bake 20-25 minutes or until light brown. Cook ground beef and chopped onion in 10-inch skillet, stirring occasionally, until beef is brown; drain thoroughly. Stir in remaining ingredients except cheese. Cover and cook over low heat 5 minutes, stirring occasionally. Spoon into shell; sprinkle with cheese. Bake 2-3 minutes or until cheese is melted. If desired, garnish with sour cream, green bell pepper, tomato, and avocado.

    Serves 4.

Down-Home Texas Cooking

A Cowboy's Pie

Wonderful after a cold snowy day's work.

STEW:

3 tablespoons salad oil, divided

2 pounds beef for stew, cut into 1-inch cubes

1 large onion, diced

1 (14.5-ounce) can beef broth

2 teaspoons Worcestershire sauce

½ cup water

1 teaspoon salt

¼ teaspoon ground black pepper

3 medium-sized sweet potatoes

1 medium-sized baking potato

1 tablespoon all-purpose flour

2 tablespoons water

1 (10-ounce) package frozen peas

1 (10-ounce) package frozen corn

1 egg, beaten

In a large pot, over medium-high heat, in 2 tablespoons of hot salad oil, cook beef chunks until well browned on all sides. Set aside in a bowl. Reduce heat to medium. In one more tablespoon hot salad oil, cook onion until almost tender, stirring occasionally. Stir in beef broth, Worcestershire sauce, ½ cup water, salt and pepper.

Return meat to pot. Over high heat, heat to boiling. Reduce heat to low. Cover and simmer 45 minutes. While meat is simmering, peel and cut sweet potatoes into 1-inch chunks. Cut, but do not peel, the baking potato into 1-inch chunks. When the meat is ready, add sweet potatoes and baking potatoes. Cook 20 minutes longer or until meat and vegetables are tender.

Skim fat from beef mixture. In a cup, stir 1 tablespoon flour and 2 tablespoons water until blended. Gradually stir flour mixture into beef mixture. Cook until mixture boils and is slightly thickened, stirring constantly. Stir in frozen vegetables, heat through. Spoon beef mixture into a 2-quart casserole. Place the pie crust loosely over beef mixture. Flute the edge gently around the casserole rim. Cut several slits in pie crust for steam to escape during baking. Brush crust with beaten egg. Bake in a preheated 425° oven for 15 minutes or until crust is golden brown.

CONTINUED

PIE CRUST:

1 cup flour, sifted
½ cup whole-wheat flour
Dash of salt

⅓ cup vegetable oil
3 tablespoons milk

Mix flours and salt. Pour oil and milk into measuring cup, but do not stir. Add to flour. Stir until mixed. Press into a smooth ball. Flatten and place between 2 sheets of wax paper. Roll out to a shape that matches the casserole pan the stew mixture will be placed in. Dough should be about 1 inch larger than pan. Makes 8 serving.

The Wild Wild West

Judy Barbour's Famous Wild Game Swiss Steak
All New Southwest Style!

2 pounds elk, deer, or moose
   steaks
4 tablespoons flour
Salt, pepper, garlic powder,
   and paprika to season
2 tablespoons oil

1½ (10-ounce) cans
   tomatoes with green chilies
½ cup each: celery, carrots,
   and onions, chopped
½ cup Cheddar or Monterey
   Jack cheese, grated (optional)

Mix together flour and seasonings. Pound into meat on each side. Reserve any leftover flour mixture. Brown meat in oil in a heavy skillet. Transfer meat to a large shallow baking dish. Blend reserved flour mixture in pan in drippings. Add tomatoes with green chilies, celery, carrots, and onion. Cook, stirring constantly until mixture boils. Pour over meat. Cover and bake for 1 hour at 350° or until meat is tender. Sprinkle cheese, if desired, over meat and let melt. Serves 4.

Note: Beef round or flank steak may be used as alternate meat choice.

Gathering of the Game

Marinated Flank Steak

Flank is the good-news, bad-news cut of beef. It can be as tough as John Wayne's boots, but if you know how to tame it, the meat has great flavor. We give you a choice of two marinades here, and then use a combination of quick cooking and thin slicing against the grain to make this steak purr. We recommend charcoal-grilling, but the steak can also be broiled.

2 flank steaks totaling about 2½ pounds

PEPPA MARINADE:

½ cup soy sauce
⅓ cup Pickapeppa or
  Texapeppa Sauce
¼ cup Worcestershire sauce
3 tablespoons dry red wine

3 tablespoons red wine
  vinegar
2 tablespoons dark brown
  sugar
2 garlic cloves, minced

RED-EYE MARINADE:

1 cup strong black coffee
½ cup tomato sauce
¼ cup unsalted butter
¼ cup Worcestershire sauce

1 tablespoon dark brown
  sugar
1 tablespoon coarse-ground
  black pepper

Place the steaks in 1 layer in a shallow nonreactive pan. Combine the ingredients for 1 of the 2 marinades, and pour the marinade over the steaks. Cover the pan, and refrigerate it at least 12 hours, preferably twice that long. Turn the meat occasionally during the marinating.

Fire up enough charcoal to form a single layer of coals beneath the meat, if you are grilling outdoors, or heat the broiler. Remove the steaks from the marinade, reserving the liquid if you used the Peppa version. Discard the red-eye marinade, which would become bitter if reheated.

Grill the meat uncovered over hot, ashen-gray coals for 4 to 5 minutes per side, or until the steaks are done to your taste. Broiling should take about the same amount of time. Let the meat rest 5 to 10 minutes before slicing it thin, across the grain. If you used the Peppa marinade, bring the liquid to a boil in a small saucepan, allowing it to reduce by about a third, a matter of just a few minutes. Spoon some of it over the sliced meat. Serve the meat immediately. Serves 6 to 8.

Texas Home Cooking

Brisket Rub

This recipe comes from Fritz's Capitol City Catering of Austin. When these people cook, they really cook. The following recipe makes enough rub for 21 briskets. Don't despair, though; the leftover rub stores well.

1 cup sugar
1 cup salt
½ cup chili powder

¼ cup garlic powder
½ cup black pepper

Combine all ingredients and store in a tightly covered container. Rub 2½ tablespoons of mixture onto brisket prior to cooking. Makes about 3½ cups.

Texas Barbecue

Bar-BQ Ranch Sauce

A lot of Texans eat their barbecue without a sauce, or with just meat juices laced with cayenne, but others prefer a robust sauce full of Southwestern seasonings.

1 tablespoon oil, preferably
  canola or corn
2 cups chopped onions
2-3 minced fresh jalapeños
2-3 minced fresh serranos
8 garlic cloves, minced
1 cup ketchup
¾ cup Worcestershire sauce
¾ cup strong black coffee

⅓ cup unsulphured dark
  molasses
¼ cup cider vinegar
¼ cup fresh lemon juice
¼ cup chili powder
2 tablespoons prepared
  yellow mustard
1½ teaspoons ground cumin
1½ teaspoons salt

In a saucepan, warm the oil over medium heat. Add the onions, chiles, and garlic, and sauté over medium heat until everything is softened. Mix in the remaining ingredients and bring the sauce to a simmer. Cover and cook for 30 to 40 minutes. Allow the sauce to cool briefly.

Strain the sauce and purée the solids in a food processor. Return the puréed mixture to the sauce, stirring thoroughly. Refrigerate the sauce overnight to allow the flavors to mingle and mellow.

Use the sauce warm or chilled. It keeps for weeks. Makes about 4 cups.

Smoke & Spice

Caldillo of Smoked Brisket with Green Chiles

At an altitude of nearly four thousand feet, El Paso gets darned cold in winter, and when it does, our attention turns to the kitchen, where a big pot of caldillo is soon simmering away. Caldillo means "little broth," and while it can be generically applied to any kind of stew, in El Paso it has come to mean a beef and green chili stew, one quickly concocted by using leftover beef (or sometimes pork or lamb).

12 long green chiles
3 tablespoons olive oil
4 cups coarsely chopped
   onion
1 tablespoon ground cumin
1 teaspoon dried oregano,
   crumbled
8 cups beef broth or chicken
   broth, homemade or canned
2½ pounds boiling potatoes,
   peeled and cut into ½-inch
   dice

2 cups canned crushed
   tomatoes with added purée
2 pounds smoked brisket or
   left-over pot roast of beef,
   pork, or lamb, trimmed and
   cut into ½-inch cubes
Salt to taste

In the open flame of a gas burner or under a preheated broiler, roast the long green chiles, turning them, until they are lightly but evenly charred. Steam the chiles in a paper bag, or in a bowl, covered with a plate, until cool. Rub away the burned peel. Stem and seed the chiles and coarsely chop them. There should be about 2 cups.

In a deep pot over low heat, warm the olive oil. Add the onions, cumin, and oregano, and cook, covered, stirring once or twice, for 15 minutes.

Add the broth, potatoes, tomatoes, and green chiles, and bring to a boil. Lower the heat and simmer, partially covered, stirring once or twice, for 30 minutes. Add the cubed brisket and continue to simmer until the potatoes and the meat are very tender and the stew is thick, about 15 minutes. Add salt to taste.

Serves 8.

Texas Border Cookbook

Black Jack Bar B Q Sauce and Ribs

"Bruce's Special"

BLACK JACK BAR B Q SAUCE:

¼ cup Del Monte Hot Chili
   Peppers, minced
1 cup strong black coffee
1 cup Worcestershire sauce
1 cup catsup
½ cup cider vinegar

½ cup brown sugar
3 tablespoons chili powder
2 teaspoons salt
2 cups onions, chopped
6 cloves garlic, minced

Stem and seed peppers; measure whole before chopping. Combine all ingredients and simmer for 25 minutes. Strain or purée. Refrigerate. Makes 5 cups.

RIBS:
5 pounds ribs
3 cups Black Jack Bar B Q Sauce

Place ribs in a flat pan or dish. Pour sauce over ribs, turning to coat all over. Pierce meat with a fork. Marinate for 8 hours, turning once. Remove ribs from marinade and brush off excess sauce. Broil or grill over coals for 10 minutes. Brush with marinade and cook for 4-5 minutes more. Heat some sauce and serve with ribs. (May be cooked covered in a 350° oven for 1½ hours.)

A Casually Catered Affair

Braggin'-Rights Brisket

The medieval alchemists who sought to turn base metals into gold, should have tried barbecuing a brisket on a wood-burning pit. The transformation of the meat is on the same magnitude of magic and much more successful.

8-pound to 12-pound
   packer-trimmed beef brisket

Bar-BQ Ranch Sauce,
   optional (recipe follows)

WILD WILLY'S NUMBER ONE-DERFUL RUB:

¾ cup paprika
¼ cup ground black pepper
¼ cup salt
¼ cup sugar

2 tablespoons chili powder
2 tablespoons garlic powder
2 tablespoons onion powder
2 teaspoons cayenne

BASIC BEER MOP:

12 ounces beer
½ cup cider vinegar
½ cup water
¼ cup oil, preferably canola
   or corn
½ medium onion, chopped

2 garlic cloves, minced
1 tablespoon Worcestershire
   sauce
1 tablespoon Wild Willy's
   Number One-derful Rub

The night before you plan to barbecue, combine the rub ingredients in a small bowl. Apply the rub evenly to the brisket, massaging it into every little pore, reserving at least 1 tablespoon of the rub. Place the brisket in a plastic bag and refrigerate it overnight.

Before you begin to barbecue, remove the brisket from the refrigerator. Let the brisket sit at room temperature for 45 minutes.

Prepare the smoker for barbecuing, bringing the temperature to 200°-220°.

In a saucepan, mix together the mop ingredients and warm over low heat.

Transfer the brisket to the coolest part of the smoker, fat side up, so the juices will help baste the meat. Cook the brisket until well-done, 1 - 1¼ hours per pound. Every hour or so, baste the blackening hunk with the mop.

When the meat is cooked, remove it from the smoker and let it sit at room temperature for 20 minutes. Then cut the fatty top

CONTINUED

section away from the leaner bottom portion. An easily identifiable layer of fat separates the two areas. Trim the excess fat from both pieces and slice them thinly against the grain. Watch what you're doing because the grain changes direction. If you wish, serve Bar-BQ Ranch Sauce, or other tomato-based barbecue sauce on the side. Serves 12-18.

Smoke & Spice

Texas Tech Barbecue Sauce

This recipe was recorded on the feed bin at the West end of the dairy barn there on the campus. It was used at all Aggie steak feeds back then. It was copied in 1948.

1 pint vinegar
1 quart cooking oil
16 ounces seasoned salt
27½ ounces lemon juice
1 teaspoon cinnamon
1 teaspoon cloves

45 ounces prepared mustard
2 teaspoons allspice
3 bottles Worcestershire
 sauce
1 teaspoon red pepper

Mix all ingredients together. Makes a large amount.

Raider Recipes

Michael Conner's "Black Magic" Barbecue Sauce

Mike is one of the chefs at Lake Austin Spa Resort and if he never invented another recipe (unlikely), his reputation would rest secure on the merits of this sweet, dark, smoky barbecue beauty.

½ small onion, finely diced
1 tablespoon vegetable oil
1 clove garlic, minced
¼ cup brown sugar
2 tablespoons blackstrap
  molasses
½ cup Creole mustard
2 tablespoons Worcestershire
  sauce

2 ounces dark beer
10 ounces catsup
1 teaspoon Tabasco sauce
½ teaspoon cayenne
1 tablespoon liquid smoke
½ cup cider vinegar

Caramelize onion over high heat with vegetable oil. Add garlic and brown sugar and reduce heat, stirring until sugar melts and darkens. Add all other ingredients and simmer, stirring occasionally, over low heat for 30 minutes. Serve as an accompaniment for smoked meats. Yield: 1 quart.

Lean Star Cuisine

Though Lyndon B. Johnson made barbecue quite famous in Texas with his huge political occasions, "barbacoa" actually came from Spain via the West Indies. "Barbecue" can refer to the food that is prepared, the grill it is cooked on, or the event at which it is served.

Martha Lou's Veal Chops in Wine

8 tablespoons butter
¼ cup flour
½ teaspoon salt
Pinch of pepper
½ teaspoon rosemary
1 teaspoon fresh chives, snipped
¾ cup red wine
1 (10½-ounce) can condensed beef bouillon
½ pound fresh mushrooms, sliced
2 tablespoons lemon juice
4 veal loin chops, 1¼-inch thick, excess fat trimmed, and each wiped with damp paper towel
1½ cups onion, sliced
1 clove garlic, minced

In saucepan, melt 4 tablespoons butter; remove from heat; stir in next 5 ingredients. Add enough wine to bouillon to make 2 cups. Gradually, stir wine mixture into flour mixture; stir occasionally; bring to boil; remove from heat. Separately, toss mushrooms with lemon juice; sauté in 1 tablespoon butter about 5 minutes; set aside. In skillet, heat 3 tablespoons butter; brown chops on both sides.

Move chops to side of skillet; add onion and garlic; sauté until golden; add ½-cup wine mixture and mushrooms; simmer, covered, over low heat, for 30 minutes or until chops are tender; add more wine mixture as needed. Place chops on platter; stir any remaining wine mixture into skillet; mix well; reheat; pour over chops. Sumptuously Elegant! Serves 4 divinely!

Great Flavors of Texas

Weiner Schnitzel
(Breaded Veal Cutlets)

Cut 2 pounds of veal steak, ½-inch thick, into serving pieces. Sprinkle with salt and pepper, dredge in cracker or bread crumbs, then dip in beaten egg, and again in the crumbs. Let stand for a few minutes, then fry, turning so both sides are browned and done. Sprinkle with lemon juice and garnish with a fried egg per each portion.

A Pinch of This and A Handful of That

Moussaka

Beautiful and delicious!

2 medium eggplants, cut into
  ¼-inch slices, ends removed
Salt
1 pound ground beef or lamb
1 tablespoon butter
1 onion, finely minced

1 green pepper, minced
½ cup tomatoes, chopped
½ cup fresh parsley, chopped
1 teaspoon allspice
2 teaspoons vegetable oil
Parsley to garnish

Sprinkle eggplant slices with salt and let stand 1 hour. In heavy skillet, brown meat in butter lightly. Add onion, green pepper, tomatoes, chopped parsley, and allspice. Mix well; simmer 5 minutes. Preheat oven to broil. With paper towels, dry eggplant; arrange in lightly oiled 11x16-inch pan. Brush with oil and broil slightly. Reduce oven heat to 350°. Arrange ⅓ of eggplant covering bottom of 3-quart casserole. Cover with ⅓ of meat mixture. Repeat layers until done. Bake 30-35 minutes. Garnish with parsley before serving. Serves 6.

Jubilee Cookbook

Tequila Marinated Pork Tenderloins

2 (1-pound) pork tenderloins
4 cloves garlic, thickly sliced

3 tablespoons fresh rosemary,
  chopped

MARINADE:
1 cup tequila
2 teaspoons salt
1½ cups vegetable oil

1 tablespoon black pepper
¼ cup fresh lime juice

Make several 1-inch deep slits in the tenderloins. Stuff the slits with garlic and rosemary. Combine the marinade ingredients and marinate the tenderloins 8-10 hours, or overnight, turning occasionally. Prepare charcoal grill. (Recommend adding some mesquite chips that have been soaked in water.) When coals are white hot, put the tenderloins on the grill and cook 15-20 minutes, turning to grill evenly. Serves 4-6.

Duck Creek Collection

Smart Pork Tender

Pork tenders are lean and tasty. This recipe is easy to prepare and tasty enough to use for special gatherings.

1½ pounds pork tender	1 tablespoon fresh ginger,
2 cloves of garlic	diced very fine
1 can crushed pineapple	¼ cup low-sodium soy sauce
Juice of 3 oranges	Salt and pepper to taste

Poke holes all over the pork tender with knife. Slice the garlic very thin and stuff into the holes. Combine remaining ingredients. Put meat in a glass dish. Spoon the mixture over the tender. Let marinate 2-6 hours. Preheat oven to 425°. Cook only 30 minutes and then remove the meat from the oven to see if it is pink inside. Don't overcook, as this lean cut of meat will dry out quickly. Serve with a green salad, steamed veggies, and some rice. Serves 4.

The College Cookbook

Three-Nut-Crusted Pork Tenderloin

This selection won the National Pork Producer's Council Award in 1988.

12 (3-ounce) mignons fresh
  pork tenderloin
Salt
Freshly cracked pepper
½ cup flour
3 eggs, lightly beaten
1 cup bread crumbs, toasted
1 cup All Bran flakes

½ cup finely chopped pecans
½ cup finely chopped
  hazelnuts
½ cup finely chopped
  macadamia nuts, toasted
⅓ cup olive oil
⅓ cup clarified butter

Season pork mignons with salt and freshly cracked pepper. Dust with flour and dip in beaten eggs. Combine bread crumbs, bran, and nuts. Coat pork in nut mixture and set aside. Heat large skillet; add olive oil and butter and sauté pork mignons until golden brown on all sides. Bake in 350° oven for about 5 minutes. Serve at once. Serves 6.

Cuisine Actuelle

Apricot Glazed Pork Chops

1 (20-ounce) can whole
  apricots, pitted
1 tablespoon bottled steak
  sauce

1 teaspoon salt
1 teaspoon whole cloves
6 pork chops

Drain syrup from apricots into saucepan; stir in steak sauce and salt. Heat to boiling. Cook uncovered for 15 minutes. Brush chops with syrup; arrange in baking dish. Stud apricots with cloves. Arrange around chops; brush with syrup. Add remaining syrup to baking dish. Bake at 400° for 25 minutes. Turn chops and bake for 30 minutes more.

Jubilee Cookbook

Pork Mandarin

This recipe came from a transplanted Texan who enjoys serving Texas food to friends in England.

1 pork tenderloin (1½ pounds)
2 tablespoons all-purpose flour
½ teaspoon salt
¼ teaspoon black pepper
3 tablespoons vegetable oil
2 medium onions, chopped

1 (11-ounce) can mandarin oranges
Grated rind and juice of 1 orange
1 cup water
1 chicken bouillon cube
1 green bell pepper, sliced

Coat tenderloin with flour seasoned with salt and pepper. Pour oil into a large skillet and heat. Add tenderloin and brown on all sides. Transfer to a 3-quart casserole dish. Add onions to oil and sauté until transparent. Spoon around meat.

Drain juice from mandarin oranges into a medium saucepan (reserve orange sections for later). Add grated orange rind and juice, water, bouillon cube, and green pepper slices. Simmer for 5 minutes. Pour over meat and onions, cover and bake at 350° for 1½ hours. Spread orange slices over top of tenderloin and return to oven for 15 minutes. Serve with rice or noodles. Yield: 4 servings.

More Tastes & Tales

Spicy Lamb Brochette

These are excellent served over couscous or rice pilaf. A yogurt dill sauce also offers a nice accompaniment.

2 pounds lamb tenders (or
   boned leg of lamb), cut into
   1-inch cubes
1 cup Spanish extra-virgin
   olive oil
2 tablespoons chopped garlic
¼ cup chopped parsley
1 teaspoon salt

1 teaspoon pepper
1 teaspoon crushed red
   pepper flakes
1 teaspoon dried oregano
1 teaspoon ground cumin
1 teaspoon paprika
Chopped parsley and
   rosemary sprigs

In a large bowl, combine olive oil, garlic, parsley, salt, pepper, red pepper flakes, oregano, cumin, and paprika. Add lamb cubes, cover, and marinate in the refrigerator for at least 12 hours.

Place lamb cubes on metal or bamboo skewers (soak bamboo skewers in water to prevent burning) and grill or broil to desired doneness (about 15 minutes). Serve on a platter, each brochette garnished with chopped parsley and a rosemary sprig. Serves 4-6.

Recipe from Barcelona's Mediterranean Cafe, San Antonio.

San Antonio Cuisine

Cakes

The Texas State Capitol at Austin is the largest state capitol in the US.

Sam Houston's Golden Spice Cake

7 egg yolks	1 teaspoon ground cloves
1 whole egg	2 teaspoons ground cinnamon
2 cups brown sugar	2 teaspoons ginger
1 cup sweet butter	1 nutmeg ground
1 cup molasses	A speck of cayenne pepper
1 teaspoon soda	1 teacup sour milk
5 cupfuls flour	2 cups raisins, optional

Beat eggs, sugar, and butter to a light batter before adding the molasses. Then add the molasses, soda, flour, spices, and milk. Beat it well together and bake in a moderate oven (350°, in 2 loaf pans about 35-45 minutes). If you use fruit, take 2 cupfuls of raisins, flour them well, and put them into the batter last.

Jane Long's Brazoria Inn

Old Fashioned Chocolate Fudge Cake

2 cups flour	1 cup oil
2 cups sugar	1 cup buttermilk
1½ teaspoons baking soda	2 eggs, beaten
¼ teaspoon salt	3 teaspoons vanilla
½ cup cocoa	¾ cup hot water

Sift flour, sugar, soda, salt, and cocoa. Add oil, buttermilk, eggs, vanilla, and hot water; mix well. Bake in greased 9x13-inch pan at 350° for 30-40 minutes.

ICING:

4 tablespoons cocoa	1 tablespoon vanilla
6 tablespoons milk	1 cup chopped pecans,
1 stick butter	optional
1 (1-pound) box powdered	
sugar	

Make a paste of cocoa and milk in a saucepan. Add butter and bring to a boil, stirring constantly. Remove from heat, and add powdered sugar and vanilla. Beat well; add pecans. Pour over still hot cake in baking pan.

Lone Star Legacy

Chocolate Amaretto Cake

Delicious and moist! A real winner!

BATTER:

1 (18½-ounce) box chocolate
   cake mix
1 (3¾-ounce) box instant
   chocolate pudding mix
2 (7-ounce) rolls or cans
   almond paste

4 eggs
½ cup vegetable oil
½ cup amaretto liqueur
½ cup water

Blend cake and pudding mix with almond paste. Add eggs, oil, Amaretto and water. Mix well. Pour into a greased and floured Bundt pan. Bake at 350° for 45-50 minutes. Cool and glaze.

GLAZE:

½ cup butter or margarine
½ cup sugar

½ cup amaretto liqueur
¼ cup water

Mix Glaze ingredients and bring to a boil. Boil 1 minute. Pour over the cake while Glaze is still hot. Be ready for rave reviews! Yield: 20 slices.

Cook 'em Horns: The Quickbook

Seduction Cake

1 (6-ounce) package
   semi-sweet chocolate chips
¾ cup chopped pecans
1 (18.5-ounce) box chocolate
   butter cake mix
4 eggs

½ cup oil
¼ cup water
1 teaspoon vanilla extract
1 (3½-ounce) box instant
   chocolate pudding
1 (8-ounce) carton sour cream

Coat chocolate chips and pecans in a spoon or two of dry cake mix. Mix remaining ingredients together and fold in chocolate chips and pecans. Pour into a greased and floured Bundt or tube pan. Bake at 350° for 50 minutes. Serves 16.

Lone Star Legacy II

Kahlua Cake

1 package Duncan Hines
Golden Butter Cake Mix
4 eggs
1 cup sour cream
1 (3¾-ounce) package
instant vanilla pudding

¾ cup Wesson oil
1 teaspoon vanilla
1 cup brown sugar, packed
⅓ cup (scant) Kahlua
¾ cup chopped pecans

Put cake mix in a large bowl; add eggs, one at a time, beating well. Add sour cream, pudding mix, oil, and vanilla; mix well. Divide batter in half; to one-half add brown sugar, Kahlua, and pecans. In a greased Bundt pan, place half of pecan mixture, then all of plain mixture, then remaining half of pecan mixture. Run knife through batter to marbleize slightly. Bake 1 hour and 15 minutes at 350°.

The Denton Woman's Club Cookbook

Applesauce Cake

2½ cups cake flour
2 cups sugar
1½ teaspoons baking soda
1½ teaspoons salt
¼ teaspoon baking powder
¾ teaspoon cinnamon
½ teaspoon cloves
½ teaspoon allspice

1½ cups applesauce
½ cup water
½ cup oil
2 eggs
1 cup raisins
½ cup chopped walnuts
Powdered sugar

Beat first 12 ingredients together. Add raisins and walnuts. Pour into a 13x9-inch greased and floured pan. Bake at 350° for 30 minutes. Cool. Sprinkle with powdered sugar. Yield: 16-20 servings.

Note: May be frozen. When adding raisins, toss lightly with flour so they do not sink to bottom of cake.

Wild About Texas

Hawaiian Dump Cake

And you don't even have to wear a lei to enjoy it.

1 (21-ounce) can cherry pie
  filling (apple is good, too)
1 (20-ounce) can crushed
  pineapple, undrained
1 (18½-ounce) box yellow
  cake mix

2 sticks margarine or butter,
  melted
1 (8-ounce) package shredded
  coconut
1 cup chopped pecans

In a 9x13-inch baking dish, layer the following ingredients, spreading each over the one it covers: pie filling, crushed pineapple, dry cake mix, margarine, coconut, and chopped pecans. Bake 1 hour in 350° oven. So good and so easy.

Cook 'em Horns: The Quickbook

Cake That Never Lasts

3 cups flour
1 teaspoon cinnamon
1 teaspoon soda
1 teaspoon salt
2 cups sugar
1¼ cups cooking oil

1 (8-ounce) can crushed
  pineapple with juice
1½ teaspoons vanilla
3 eggs
2 cups diced ripe bananas
1 cup chopped pecans

Sift together into a large mixing bowl the flour, cinnamon, soda, salt, and sugar, then add the cooking oil, pineapple, vanilla, eggs, bananas, and pecans. Mix all together but do not beat. Pour into 9-inch greased Bundt or tube pan. Bake at 350° for 1 hour and 20 minutes. Cool before removing from the pan.

Chuckwagon Recipes.

Angelina is the only county in Texas named for a woman. Angelina, a Hasinai Indian girl educated by the Franciscan Fathers, helped the Spanish re-establish the Mission San Francisco de los Tejas on the Neches River around 1716. She weiled such authority in her village and tribe that historians disagree that she was either a saint or a domineering woman. Nevertheless, she has a River and a national forest also named in her honor.

Mamie's Pineapple Orange Cake

Very moist and rich.

1 box lite yellow cake mix
1 large can lite mandarin
  oranges, undrained
½ cup each: unsweetened
  applesauce and Kraft Free
  Mayonnaise
1 cup Egg Beaters

1 large can unsweetened
  crushed pineapple, undrained
1 (3-ounce) package instant
  vanilla pudding mix
1 box Betty Crocker Fluffy
  White Frosting Mix, prepared

Mix together the first 4 ingredients. Spray 3 (9-inch round) cake pans with Pam and flour each. Divide batter between pans and bake at 325° for 20 minutes. Cool.

Mix pineapple with pudding mix. Refrigerate. When pudding is semi-set, mix in 1 cup prepared frosting. Chill until firm. Ice cake and serve. Serves 16.

Per Serving: Cal 215; Fat 1.5g; 7% Fat; Prot 5g; Carb 45g; Sod 377mg; Chol 0.

The Lite Switch

Esther's Blueberry Sour Cream Cake

½ cup butter or margarine
1 cup sugar
3 eggs
1 cup sour cream
1 teaspoon vanilla
2 cups sifted flour

1 teaspoon baking soda
1 teaspoon salt
2 cups blueberries
⅓ cup packed brown sugar
½ cup chopped nuts
½ teaspoon cinnamon

Cream butter and sugar together until fluffy. Add eggs, one at a time, beating well after each addition. Blend in sour cream and vanilla. Sift together flour, soda, and salt; add to creamed mixture, beating until smooth. Fold in blueberries. Spread one-third of batter into greased and floured Bundt pan. In a small bowl combine brown sugar, nuts, and cinnamon; spread half evenly over top of batter in the pan. Spread another third of batter evenly over nut mixture, then top with remaining nut mixture and then top with remaining batter. Bake at 350° 1 hour or until done. Cool cake in pan on wire rack. Sprinkle with powdered sugar before serving. Makes 12-16 servings.

The Blueberry Lover's Cookbook

Banana Cake with Sour Cream

2½ cups flour
2 teaspoons baking powder
1 teaspoon baking soda
¼ teaspoon salt
½ cup margarine
1½ cups sugar

3 whole eggs, beaten
1 teaspoon vanilla
1 cup sour cream
1 cup mashed ripe bananas
½ cup chopped nuts, pecans
   or walnuts

Sift flour, baking powder, soda, and salt. Cream margarine, sugar, and eggs; add vanilla. Add sour cream, bananas, and nuts, alternating with dry ingredients. Bake in 2 well-greased and floured 9-inch baking pans. Bake at 350° for 30-45 minutes, or until cake tests done. Frost with Butter Cream Frosting.

BUTTER CREAM FROSTING:

1½ sticks margarine,
   divided
3 tablespoons flour

¾ cup milk
¾ cup granulated sugar
⅓ teaspoon vanilla

In saucepan melt ½ stick of margarine. Slowly, add flour and milk over low heat. Cook to a pudding consistency and chill thoroughly in refrigerator. In a bowl, cream remaining 1 stick of margarine and gradually add sugar. Beat until sugar seems to dissolve. Add pudding mixture gradually, beating until fluffy. Add vanilla and continue to beat until light, about 1 minute.

The Second Typically Texas Cookbook

Super Buttermilk Cake

This cake is very light and of a sponge-cake consistency. It can be used as is, without the glaze, with a topping of fruit and whipped cream, or a dessert sauce. It is also delicious with just the glaze.

CAKE:

2 cups flour
½ teaspoon soda
½ teaspoon baking powder
Pinch salt
2 sticks margarine

2 cups sugar
4 large eggs
1 teaspoon pure vanilla
1 cup buttermilk

Sift dry ingredients together. Cream margarine with 2 cups sugar, vanilla, and eggs, one at a time. Beat until fluffy. Add sifted flour mixture alternately with buttermilk beginning and ending with flour. Pour into a greased and floured 13x9x2-inch baking dish. Bake in a preheated 350° oven for 40-45 minutes or until it tests done in center. Pour warm glaze over cooled cake in pan. This cake must be served from the pan.

GLAZE:

1 cup heavy cream or
  evaporated milk, not
  condensed

2½ tablespoons sugar

Heat the sugar and cream in a saucepan, stirring, until hot. Do not boil. Yield: 1 (13x9x2-inch) cake.

Note: Evaporated milk may be substituted for whipping cream if you want to cut calories.

Raleigh House Cookbook II

Comptroller of Public Accounts Lemon Gold Cake
This should be kept in a vault!

2 cups sifted Swans Down
  Cake Flour
2 teaspoons Calumet Baking
  Powder
½ cup butter or other
  shortening (I use half lard)
1 cup sugar

3 egg yolks, beaten until thick
  and lemon-colored
¾ cup milk
1 teaspoon vanilla, or ½
  teaspoon lemon extract (I use
  vanilla)

Sift flour once, measure, add baking powder, and sift together 3 times. Cream butter thoroughly, add sugar gradually, and cream together until light and fluffy. Add egg yolks and beat well. Add flour, alternately with milk, a small amount at a time. Beat after each addition until smooth. Add flavoring. Beat well. Bake in 2 greased 9-inch layer pans in moderate oven (375°) 25-30 minutes. Spread Luscious Lemon Frosting between layers and on top and sides of cake. Double recipe to make 3 (10-inch) layers.

LUSCIOUS LEMON FROSTING:

3 teaspoons grated orange
  rind
Dash of salt
3 tablespoons butter

3 cups confectioners' sugar
2 tablespoons lemon juice
1 tablespoon water

Add orange rind and salt to butter; cream well. Add part of sifted sugar gradually, blending after each addition. Combine lemon juice and water; add to creamed mixture, alternately with remaining sugar, until of right consistency to spread. Beat after each addition until smooth. Makes enough frosting to cover tops and sides of 2 (9-inch) layers. For a deeper yellow frosting, tint with yellow coloring.

Ma's in the Kitchen

 In 1925, Texas became the second state in the United States to have a woman governor. Miriam Ferguson served as governor of Texas for two terms.

Bride's Delight

1 cup butter	2½ cups flour, sifted
1½ cups sugar	½ teaspoon salt
1 egg plus 1 egg yolk	1 egg white
(save white)	2 teaspoons water
2 teaspoons almond extract	½ cup almonds, sliced

Cream butter, sugar, egg, egg yolk, and almond extract until fluffy. Add flour and salt. Press into two 8- or 9-inch round cake pans. Mix egg white with 2 teaspoons water and brush over cakes. Sprinkle with sliced almonds and lightly with sugar. Bake at 325° for 25-35 minutes (it should not brown). Serve cut in wedges either alone or with strawberries and whipped cream topping. Makes 12-16 servings.

Pass it On...

Blackberry Wine Cake

1 white cake mix	1 cup blackberry wine
1 (3-ounce) package	(Manischewitz)
blackberry gelatin	½ cup chopped pecans
4 eggs	(optional)
½ cup Crisco oil	

Blackberry Jello is hard to find; you may substitute black cherry or grape Jello. Combine cake mix and gelatin. Add eggs, oil, and wine. Beat with mixer on low speed until moistened, then on medium speed for 2 minutes, scraping bowl often. Grease and flour Bundt pan well. If using pecans, sprinkle in bottom of pan; pour in batter. Bake in preheated 325° oven for 45 minutes. When done, remove from oven and poke holes in cake; pour ½ of Glaze over hot cake while still in pan. Cool 30 minutes. Turn cake out of pan and cool. Add a little more powdered sugar to Glaze and pour over cake.

GLAZE:

1 cup powdered sugar	½ cup blackberry wine
1 cup butter	

Mix and bring to good boil. Drizzle over cake.

Feast of Goodness

Rum Cake

1 package yellow cake mix	½ cup water
1 small package instant	½ cup rum
vanilla pudding	½ cup chopped pecans
4 eggs	Glaze (recipe follows)
½ cup salad oil	

Mix first 6 ingredients about 2 minutes. Sprinkle pecans on bottom of greased tube pan or Bundt pan. Pour batter over nuts and bake at 325° about 1 hour. Remove from oven and pierce top thoroughly with handle of wooden spoon; immediately pour Glaze over top. Cool completely before removing from pan.

GLAZE:

1 stick butter	1 cup sugar
¼ cup water	1 ounce rum

Boil butter, sugar, and water for 1 minute. Remove from heat and add rum.

M. D. Anderson Volunteers Cooking for Fun

A Pioneer Birthday Cake

This recipe was used to make a birthday cake for a little Texas girl long ago when there was no flour to be had. Corn was ground on a hand mill. The meal was carefully emptied from one sack to another, and the fine meal dust clinging to the sack was carefully shaken out on a paper. The sack was again emptied and shaken, and this process was repeated laboriously, time after time, until two cups of meal dust was obtained. The rest of the ingredients were as follows:

One half cup of wild honey, one teaspoon of homemade soda, one wild turkey egg, one scant cup of sour milk, and a very small amount of butter, to all of which was added the two cups of meal dust.

The batter was poured into a skillet with a lid and placed over the open fire in the yard; the skillet lid was heaped with coals.

Seconds of A Pinch of This and A Handful of That

Black Russian Cake

1 Duncan Hines deep
  chocolate cake mix
½ cup salad oil
1 (4½-ounce) box instant
  chocolate pudding mix

4 eggs, room temperature
¾ cup strong coffee
¾ cup Kahlúa and Crème de
  Cacao, combined

Preheat oven to 350°. Combine cake mix, oil, pudding, eggs, coffee, Kahlúa and Crème de Cacao in a large bowl. Beat 4 minutes on medium speed until smooth. Spoon into a well-greased Bundt pan. Bake for 45-50 minutes. Cool slightly before removing from pan.

TOPPING:

1 cup powdered sugar, sifted
2 tablespoons strong coffee
2 tablespoons Kahlúa

2 tablespoons Crème de
  Cacao

Combine all ingredients, beating well until smooth. Pour topping over warm cake.

The Gathering

Chocolate Torte

If we had to pick the one most requested new recipe, this would be it. The prune purée serves to replace the fat, but unless you say something, no one will believe anything is missing from this rich, dark, densely chocolate cake. It freezes well.

2 cups flour	2 teaspoons vanilla
1 cup unsweetened cocoa powder	2 eggs, beaten
2 cups sugar	1 cup skim milk
2 teaspoons baking soda	½ teaspoon cinnamon
1 teaspoon baking powder	1 cup strong coffee
¼ teaspoon salt	Vegetable cooking spray
4 (2.5-ounce) jars baby food puréed prunes	Powdered sugar

Preheat oven to 350°. Sift together the flour, cocoa, sugar, baking soda, baking powder, and salt in a large mixing bowl. Add the prunes, vanilla, eggs, milk, and cinnamon, and stir just until blended. Stir coffee into the batter until blended. Pour the batter into 2 (9-inch) baking pans or springform pans that have been sprayed with vegetable spray.

Bake for 30-35 minutes, or until center tests done with a toothpick. Let the cakes cool in pans for 10 minutes. Invert onto a wire rack to cool. Sift powdered sugar over the top of the cakes before slicing. Yield: 12 servings per cake.

Per serving: Cal 141; Fat 1.25g.

Lean Star Cuisine

 In Bracketville, in the Southwest Texas Badlands, the cowboys still ride into the sunset at Alamo Village, the original movie set for John Wayne's epic "The Alamo" and the location for the blockbuster mini-series "Lonesome Dove." In nearby Seminole Canyon State Historical Park, you can see the ancient Indian legacy left behind in 10,000-year-old pictographs on the canyon walls.

Raspberry Walnut Torte

Tart, tangy, delicious.

1¼ cups flour, divided	2 eggs
⅓ cup powdered sugar	1 cup sugar
½ cup butter, softened	½ teaspoon baking powder
1 (10-ounce) package frozen	½ teaspoon salt
raspberries, thawed and	1 teaspoon vanilla
drained, reserving syrup	Whipped cream
¾ cup chopped walnuts	Raspberry Sauce

In a small mixing bowl, combine 1 cup flour, powdered sugar, and butter; blend well. Press into bottom of ungreased 9-inch square pan. Bake at 350° for 15 minutes. Cool.

Spread drained berries over crust; sprinkle with walnuts. With an electric mixer, combine eggs, sugar, remaining flour, baking powder, salt, and vanilla. Blend well at low speed. Pour over berries and nuts. Bake at 350° for 35-40 minutes until golden brown. Cool. Cut into squares, and serve with whipped cream and Raspberry Sauce. Yield: 9 servings.

RASPBERRY SAUCE:

½ cup sugar	Reserved raspberry syrup
2 tablespoons cornstarch	1 tablespoon lemon juice
½ cup water	

In small saucepan, combine first 4 ingredients; cook, stirring constantly, until thick and clear. Stir in lemon juice. Cool.

Homecoming

A Good Cake

One cup sweet milk, one cup butter, three cups sugar, five cups of flour, two teaspoons baking powder.

The First Texas Cook Book

Pecan Torte

4 eggs, well-beaten
1 pound brown sugar
1 cup flour
1½ teaspoons baking
    powder

1 cup pecans, chopped
1 teaspoon vanilla

Mix all ingredients, pour into two 9-inch well-greased and floured cake pans, and bake at 325° for 30-35 minutes. Cool completely before removing from pans. The layers will be thin.

FILLING:
1 tablespoon butter
2 teaspoons flour
1 cup whipped cream

5 teaspoons sugar
1 cup pecans, chopped

Melt butter in top of double boiler. Blend in flour, stir in whipped cream, and cook until thick. Cool. Add sugar and nuts. Spread mixture between layers of torte.

ICING:
2 cups sweetened whipped
    cream

½ cup pecans, chopped

Ice top and sides of torte with whipped cream and sprinkle top with chopped nuts.
The Harvey Houses, Southeast Texas.

Boardin' in the Thicket

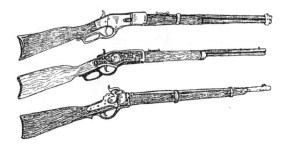

Heavenly Dessert Torte

6 egg whites
2 teaspoons vanilla
½ teaspoon cream of tartar
Dash salt

2 cups sugar
2 cups whipping cream
6 ounces or more crushed
    Heath bars

Combine egg whites, vanilla, cream of tartar, and salt. Beat to soft peaks. Gradually adding sugar; beat to stiff peaks. Cut 2 (9-inch) circles of brown paper. Place on a cookie sheet and cover with egg white mixture. Bake 1 hour at 275°. Let cool in oven.

Whip cream and combine with crushed Heath bars. Spread half of mixture on 1 meringue circle, top with second meringue circle, and cover with remaining half of whipped cream mixture. Chill in refrigerator at least 8 hours. Serves 10.

The Denton Woman's Club Cookbook

Apricot Cheesecake

CRUST:

¼ cup butter or margarine
2 tablespoons sugar

½ teaspoon vanilla
½ cup flour

Preheat oven to 375°. In large bowl beat margarine until soft. Gradually add sugar and beat until light and fluffy. Add vanilla. Stir in flour. Flour fingers and press dough on bottom of 9-inch ungreased springform pan. Bake until golden brown (about 8-10 minutes). Cool.

APRICOT FILLING:

¾ cup dried apricots
2 tablespoon sugar
½ cup water

2 tablespoon amaretto
1 teaspoon lemon juice

Bring to boil and cook for 5 minutes. Purée in blender. Cool to room temperature.

CREAM CHEESE FILLING:

²/₃ cup sugar
2 tablespoon flour
⅛ teaspoon salt
3 (8-ounce) packages cream
   cheese, room temperature

2 eggs, room temperature
¼ cup amaretto
1 tablespoon vanilla
1 cup whipping cream,
   unwhipped

Combine sugar, flour, and salt. Mix well. Add cream cheese with mixer at medium speed. Mix until smooth and well blended. Add eggs, amaretto, and vanilla. Mix until blended. Stir in cream. Pour all on crust. Drop Apricot Filling by teaspoonfuls into cream cheese mixture and press down until covered. Bake 1 hour. (Could take longer.) Run spatula around edges and cool for 1 hour. Remove rim. Refrigerate 4-5 hours before cutting. Can top with hot apricot preserves.

Feast of Goodness

Mary Lou's Cheesecake

1 box zwieback
½ cup sugar
¼ cup melted butter or
  margarine
1 teaspoon cinnamon
5 eggs
4 (8-ounce) packages cream
  cheese
1¼ cups sugar
1 teaspoon vanilla
½ teaspoon pineapple
  flavoring
1 pint sour cream
3 tablespoons sugar
½ teaspoon salt
½ teaspoon vanilla

Use steel blade of food processor. Crumble a layer of zwieback by hand into the work bowl. Start motor. Continue to crumble zwieback and drop it through the feeder tube until all is processed into fine crumbs. Drop in sugar, melted butter, and cinnamon. Process until well blended. Press crumbs firmly into a greased springform pan, covering bottom and sides.

Beat the eggs for 5 minutes in a large bowl; cut cream cheese in chunks and add to eggs; add 1¼ cups sugar, 1 teaspoon vanilla, and pineapple flavoring; beat until thoroughly blended and smooth. Pour into crust-lined pan. Bake 45 minutes to 1 hour at 325°. Combine sour cream, remaining sugar, salt, and remaining vanilla. Pour over warm cheesecake and return to oven for 5 minutes. Chill several hours before serving.

The Denton Woman's Club Cookbook

March Second Cheesecake

A dandy dessert for Texas Independence Day.

1 (8-ounce) package cream
  cheese, softened
⅓ cup sugar
1 cup sour cream
2 teaspoons vanilla
1 (8-ounce) container
  non-dairy whipped topping
1 prepared graham cracker
  crust
Fresh strawberries for garnish

Cream cheese until smooth; gradually beat in sugar. Blend in sour cream and vanilla. Fold in whipped topping, blending well. Spoon into crust and chill until set...at least 4 hours. Garnish with fresh strawberries, if desired.

Cook 'em Horns: The Quickbook

Pumpkin Cheesecake

3 (8-ounce) packages cream
  cheese
1½ cups sugar
1 cup brown sugar
¼ cup flour
1 teaspoon cinnamon
½ teaspoon nutmeg
½ teaspoon ginger
3 eggs
1 (16-ounce) can pumpkin
Graham cracker crumbs

Blend cheese, both sugars, flour, cinnamon, nutmeg, and ginger. Add eggs and beat until fluffy. Mix in pumpkin. Butter a springform pan, lightly coat the bottom of pan with graham cracker crumbs. Pour in batter. Bake for 1½ hours in 350° oven.

Hint: Two tablespoons of bourbon can give an extra flavor spark!

The Texas Experience

Mocha Angel Food Cake

A lovely, light, scrumptious cake!

1 tablespoon instant coffee
¼ cup warm water
1 Duncan Hines Angel Food
Cake Mix

1 teaspoon maple flavoring

Dissolve coffee in warm water and use this mixture as part of the liquid when preparing cake according to package directions. Fold in maple flavoring. Bake and cool as directed.

FROSTING:

3-4 tablespoons milk
1½ teaspoons instant coffee
¾ cup margarine or butter,
softened
Dash salt
1½ teaspoons maple
flavoring

3½ cups powdered sugar,
sifted
½ cup pecans or almonds,
roasted and chopped

Warm milk, add coffee and stir to dissolve. Set aside to cool. In a mixing bowl, cream margarine until fluffy. Add salt and maple flavoring. Beat sugar into margarine gradually along with milk mixture. Continue beating until light and fluffy. Spread on cooled cake and sprinkle with roasted nuts. This cake will be easier to slice on the second day. Yield: 10-12 servings.

Celebrate San Antonio

Angels' Food No. 1

Beat the whites of eleven eggs to a stiff froth, take one and a half tumblerfuls of powdered sugar, one tumblerful of flour and one teaspoonful of pure cream tartar. Sift well together, and mix with the eggs, flavor, and bake forty minutes in a moderate oven. Turn the pan upside down to cool. The pan must not be greased.

The First Texas Cook Book

Cookies and Candies

Big Tex greets three million visitors to the State Fair of Texas each year.

Cream Cheese Brownies

CREAM CHEESE BATTER:

2 tablespoons butter or
  margarine
1 (3-ounce) package cream
  cheese, softened

¼ cup sugar
1 egg
1 tablespoon flour
½ teaspoon vanilla

Blend butter and cream cheese. Gradually add sugar, beating well. Stir in egg, flour and vanilla. Set aside.

CHOCOLATE BATTER:

4 ounces German's sweet
  chocolate
2 eggs
¾ cup sugar
½ teaspoon baking powder
¼ teaspoon salt

3 tablespoons butter or
  margarine
½ cup flour
½ cup chopped nuts
1 teaspoon vanilla
¼ teaspoon almond extract

Preheat oven to 350°. Grease an 8- or 9-inch square pan. Melt chocolate and butter over very low heat. Set aside to cool.

Beat eggs until thick and light in color; slowly add sugar, beating well. Add baking powder, salt, and flour. Stir in melted chocolate mixture, nuts, vanilla, and almond extract. Spread about half of the chocolate batter in the pan. Add cheese mixture, spreading evenly. Top with spoonfuls of chocolate batter. Zigzag with a spatula to marble. Bake for 35-40 minutes. Yield: 16 squares.

The Kimbell Cookbook

Turtle Caramel Brownies

Tastes like chocolate turtle candy. Delicious!

1 (14-ounce) package
  caramels
⅓ cup evaporated milk
1 (18.25-ounce) box German
  chocolate cake mix

¾ cup butter, melted
1 cup chopped pecans
⅓ cup evaporated milk
1 (6-ounce) package
  chocolate chips

Preheat oven to 350°. Melt caramels and ⅓ cup evaporated milk in a heavy saucepan. Use low heat, stirring often. Keep warm. In a large bowl, mix remaining ingredients except chocolate chips. Press half the dough into a lightly greased and floured 13x9-inch pan. Bake for 6 minutes. Sprinkle with chocolate chips. Spread caramel mixture over chips. Using a spatula, spread remaining dough evenly over caramel. Bake 15-20 minutes more. Cool completely before cutting. Yield: 3 dozen.

Wild About Texas

Chocolate Brickle Brownies

1 cup butter
½ cup cocoa
4 eggs
2 cups sugar
1½ cups unbleached flour
⅛ teaspoon salt

1 teaspoon vanilla
1 cup pecans, chopped
½ cup semi-sweet chocolate
  chips
½ cup Heath Bits or Brickle
  chips or chopped Heath Bars

Preheat oven to 350°. Melt butter and dissolve cocoa in the butter and set aside. Beat eggs and sugar together until fluffy. Beat in flour, salt and vanilla. Add cocoa and butter. Stirring well add pecans, chocolate and brickle chips. Bake in a greased and floured 9x13-inch metal pan for 30 minutes or until done. Makes 2 dozen.

The Wild Wild West

Nell's Apricot Bars

1 Duncan Hines (only) Yellow
  Butter Recipe Cake Mix
1 cup flour mixed with cake
  mix
1½ sticks margarine,
  softened

1 cup chopped pecans
1 cup coconut
1 (10-12-ounce) jar apricot
  preserves

Cut butter into cake mix and flour. Add nuts and coconut. Mix well. Pat ⅓ mixture into a 9x13-inch ungreased pan. Spread apricot preserves over mixture. Crumble remaining mixture over preserves. Bake 1 hour at 325°.

Gingerbread...and all the trimmings

Praline Squares

2 eggs
2 cups light brown sugar
1 cup melted butter or
  margarine

1½ cups flour
1 teaspoon vanilla
1 cup chopped pecans

Beat eggs, blend with sugar and stir in butter. Add flour gradually. Add vanilla and pecans. Pour into a greased 8x12-inch pan. Bake at 350° for 40 minutes. Cool and cut into squares. Yield: 3 dozen.

Per serving: Cal 137; Fat 8g; Carb 16g; Prot 1g.

Diamonds in the Desert

Lonesome Cowboy Bars

1 cup sugar
1 cup corn syrup
1½ cups crunchy peanut
   butter

6 cups corn flakes
12 ounces butterscotch chips

Over a medium heat, bring the sugar and syrup to a boil. Stir in the peanut butter. Remove from heat and pour over the corn flakes. Mix well, then pack into a 9x13-inch cake pan that has been greased with margarine. In a double boiler over a low heat, melt the butterscotch chips. Spread evenly on top of the cereal mixture. Cool completely and cut into bars. Makes 30 bars.

The Wild Wild West

Raspberry-Filled White Chocolate Bars

1 cup butter
4 cups vanilla chips
4 eggs
1 cup sugar
2 cups flour

1 teaspoon salt
2 teaspoons almond extract
1 cup seedless raspberry fruit
   spread or preserves
½ cup sliced almonds

Melt butter in a small saucepan over low heat. Remove and add 2 cups of the vanilla chips. Let stand—*do not stir*. In a large bowl, beat eggs until foamy. Gradually add sugar, beating at high speed, until lemon colored. Stir in vanilla chip mixture. Add flour, salt, and almond extract and mix on low speed until just combined. Spread ½ of the batter into a greased and floured 9x13-inch pan. Bake at 325° for 15-20 minutes, or until golden brown.

Stir remaining 2 cups of vanilla chips into remaining batter and set aside. Melt raspberry jam in a saucepan and spread evenly over cooked batter. Gently spoon remaining batter over fruit. (Some fruit may show through.) Sprinkle with almonds. Bake at 325° an additional 30-35 minutes. Test for doneness. Let cool completely and cut into 1x1-inch squares. Makes 9½ dozen.

Buffet on the Bayou

Carmelitas

36 light caramels
5 tablespoons evaporated
  milk
1 cup flour
1 cup rolled oats
¾ cup brown sugar
½ teaspoon soda
¼ teaspoon salt
¾ cup melted butter
6 ounces chocolate chips
¾ cup chopped pecans

Preheat oven to 350°. In a small saucepan, heat caramels and evaporated milk until mixture is smooth and creamy. Remove from heat and set aside. In mixing bowl, combine flour, oats, brown sugar, soda, salt, and butter. Press half of mixture into greased 8x12-inch baking pan. Bake 10 minutes. Sprinkle chocolate chips and pecans over cooked oatmeal mixture. Cover with caramel mixture. Top with remaining oatmeal mixture. Return pan to oven. Bake for an additional 15 minutes. Cool in refrigerator for 2 hours before cutting. Cut into bars and store in refrigerator or at room temperature. Yield: 4 dozen 1½-inch bars.

Celebrate San Antonio

Jean's Blueberry Strudel

½ pound butter
2½ cups flour
1 cup sour cream
2 cups blueberry jam
6 tablespoons fine bread
  crumbs
¾ cup finely chopped nuts
¾ cup coconut flakes

In a food processor blend butter and flour together until like meal. Add sour cream and mix well. Divide dough into 4 pieces and form into rolls; refrigerate overnight. The next day, roll each roll into a thin rectangle, about 14x10 inches. Spread thinly with blueberry jam. Mix together bread crumbs, nuts, and coconut; sprinkle over jam. Roll up rectangle in jelly roll fashion. Bake on a shallow pan at 325° for 50-60 minutes. Cool; cut diagonally into cookies about 1 inch wide. Makes about 48 cookies.

The Blueberry Lover's Cookbook

Napoleons

This takes a little time but is well worth it. It will impress anyone!

3 sheets Pepperidge Farms Puff Pastry, thawed

CUSTARD:

1 cup flour	**1 quart milk**
1 cup sugar	**2 teaspoon vanilla**
6 egg yolks	**½ pint whipping cream**
½ cup cold milk	

Mix together flour, sugar, egg yolks, and ½ cup cold milk. Bring 1 quart milk and vanilla to a boil. Add other mixture to this and cook over medium heat for 3-4 minutes. Cool. Whip cream and fold into cooled mixture.

ICING:

3 egg whites	**¹⁄₁₆ teaspoon cream of tartar**
½ cup sugar	**½ teaspoon vanilla**
2 tablespoons white corn syrup	**¼ cup melted semi-sweet chocolate**

Mix all ingredients (except vanilla and chocolate) together and place over boiling water for about 6 minutes, stirring with finger until too hot to do so. Remove from heat. Beat vigorously with mixer until icing holds shape, about 10 minutes. Blend in vanilla.

Roll out puff pastry to about ⅛ inch thick and 12 inches long. Prick with fork. Bake on a baking sheet at 350° for about 15-20 minutes. To assemble, layer 1 sheet of baked pastry on a platter, add custard, repeat. Top with third layer and ice. Drizzle top with chocolate. Serves 12-16. Cut with a serrated knife.

Best of Friends Two

Billy Bob's Texas in Fort Worth is the largest honky tonk in the world. There are 10,000 square feet of dancin' room in the 100,000-square-feet building where there's live country western music every Friday and Saturday night.

Jean's Chocolate Cookies

Wonderful!

2 tablespoons margarine
1 (12-ounce) package
  semi-sweet chocolate chips
1 can sweetened condensed
  milk

1 cup flour
1 teaspoon vanilla
1 cup chopped pecans

Melt margarine and chocolate chips in a double boiler. Add milk and mix well. Remove from heat. Add flour and vanilla. Add nuts. Roll walnut size balls of dough and put on cookie sheet. Bake at 350° for 10 minutes.

Central Texas Style

Collin Street Bakery Chocolate Cluster Cookies

2¾ cups sugar
3 tablespoons bread flour
½ teaspoon cream of tartar
1½ squares bitter chocolate
½ square semi-sweet
  chocolate

6 large egg whites
2 teaspoons shortening
1½ teaspoons vanilla
2½ cups pecan pieces
Waxed paper and Pam

In large saucepan, combine first 3 ingredients; add next 4 ingredients; place pan in pan of water over medium heat. Heat until chocolate melts and sugar dissolves; stir often. Remove from heat; add vanilla and nuts; mix well. Line cookie sheets with waxed paper; spray paper with Pam; drop batter by teaspoonfuls onto paper. Bake at 365° for 15-20 minutes. Do *not* overcook; cookies are done when soft in center. Wonderful! (Collen Street Bakers is in Corsicana.) Yields 4 dozen 2½-inch cookies!!

Great Flavors of Texas

Cow patties, cow pies, and meadow muffins usually do not refer to food at all, but are nicknames for cow dung. When dried, they are referred to as cow chips.

The World's Best Sugar Cookies!

1 cup Wesson oil
1 cup butter, softened
1 cup confectioners' sugar
1 cup granulated sugar
2 eggs
1 teaspoon vanilla

4 cups unsifted flour
1 teaspoon baking soda
1 teaspoon cream of tartar
½ teaspoon salt
Granulated sugar

Beat Wesson oil and butter. Add confectioners' sugar and granulated sugar and beat well. Beat in eggs and vanilla. Sift flour, soda, cream of tartar, and salt. Stir into sugar mixture. Mix well. Chill at least 2 hours. Roll into balls and roll them in granulated sugar. Place on ungreased cookie sheet and flatten with bottom of glass dipped in sugar also. Don't flatten too thin. Bake at 375° for approximately 10 minutes (depends on your oven) until light brown at edges. Makes approximately 5 dozen.

A Casually Catered Affair

Texas Cow Patties

2 cups margarine, softened
2 cups sugar
2 cups firmly-packed brown
    sugar
4 eggs
2 teaspoons vanilla
2 cups quick-cooking oats
2 cups corn flakes

4 cups all-purpose flour
2 teaspoons baking powder
2 teaspoons baking soda
1 (6-ounce) package
    semi-sweet chocolate morsels
2 cups chopped broken
    pecans

Cream margarine, sugar, and brown sugar together until light and fluffy. Add eggs, 1 at a time, beating well after each addition. Stir in vanilla. Add oats and corn flakes to creamed mixture, mixing thoroughly. Sift flour, baking powder, and baking soda together. Gradually add to creamed mixture, beating slowly to mix. Stir in chocolate morsels and pecans. Drop by rounded tablespoons onto greased cookie sheets.

Bake on top rack of oven at 325° for 17 minutes. Cool on wore rack. Makes 2 dozen.

Per serving: Cal 470; Prot 5.68g; Carb 57.4g; Fat 25.5g; Chol 35.3mg; Sod 286.

Changing Thymes

"Can't Stop" Cookies

Everyone loves these cookies.

2 cups sugar	½ teaspoon salt
2 cups butter or margarine	2 teaspoons soda
3 cups flour	4 cups corn flakes
2 teaspoons cream of tartar	1 cup chopped pecans

Cream sugar and butter. Add dry ingredients. Then, fold in corn flakes and nuts. Roll into balls and bake at 350° for 10-15 minutes.

The Second Typically Texas Cookbook

Extra Special Chocolate Chip Cookies

²/₃ cup butter	2 teaspoons baking soda
²/₃ cup shortening	1 teaspoon baking powder
1 cup brown sugar	1 (12-ounce) bag chocolate
1 cup white sugar	chips
2 teaspoons vanilla	1 (12-ounce) bag Reese's
2 eggs, slightly beaten	peanut butter chips
3 or 4 cups flour	½ cup pecans
1 teaspoon salt	

Cream butter and shortening. Add sugars; cream until sugar begins to dissolve. Add vanilla, and eggs. Stir together 1 cup flour, salt, baking soda, and baking powder. Add to butter mixture. Keep adding flour until dough looks dry (approximately 3½ cups). Stir in chips and nuts. Bake 10 minutes at 350° on ungreased cookie sheets. Makes 6-8 dozen depending on how much dough you eat.

Decades of Mason County Cooking

The Grand 1894 Opera House on Galveston Island has been designated the official Opera House of the State of Texas. The only theatre of its kind in Texas, it features double curved balconies and no seat farther than 70 feet from a stage that was once the largest in the state.

Texas Ranger Cookies

1 stick margarine	½ teaspoon baking powder
½ cup shortening	½ teaspoon salt
1 cup sugar	1 teaspoon vanilla
1 cup brown sugar	2 cups oatmeal, quick cooking
2 eggs	2 cups rice crispies
2 cups flour	1 cup pecans
1 teaspoons soda	1 cup coconut

Cream together margarine, shortening, sugars, and eggs. Sift together the flour, soda, baking powder, and salt. Gradually add to the creamed mixture. Add the vanilla. Stir in the oats, rice crispies, pecans, and coconut. With a large spoon, portion out the dough. Roll into small balls and flatten on cookie sheet. Bake in a preheated 375° oven for 8 minutes.

The Authorized Texas Ranger Cookbook

Orange-Oatmeal Cookies

2 cups flour	2 eggs
1 teaspoon baking soda	2 cups quick-cooking rolled
¾ teaspoon salt	oats
½ teaspoon cinnamon	⅓ cup orange juice
⅛ teaspoon allspice	1 cup raisins
1 cup shortening	½ cup chopped pecans
½ cup sugar	2 teaspoons grated orange
½ cup packed light brown	rind
sugar	

Sift flour, baking soda, salt, cinnamon, and allspice together. Cream shortening, sugar, and brown sugar in mixer bowl until smooth. Add eggs, beating until light and fluffy. Stir in oats. Add sifted dry ingredients alternately with orange juice, beating well after each addition. Stir in raisins, pecans, and orange rind. Drop by teaspoonfuls onto greased cookie sheets. Bake at 350° for 10-15 minutes or until golden brown. Yield: 48 servings.

Approx Per Serving: Cal 111; Prot 2g; Carbo 14g; Fiber 1g; T Fat 6g; 44% Calories from Fat; Chol 9mg; Sod 55mg.

Gatherings

Captain Crunch Cookies

1 cup Captain Crunch cereal	1½ cups Health Valley Fat
2 cups Rice Krispies cereal	Free Granola
2 cups thin pretzels, broken	4 cup miniature marshmallows
into 1-inch pieces	Pam no-stick cooking spray

Combine first 4 ingredients. Melt marshmallows in microwave-save dish coated with Pam. Add cereal mixture; mix well. Drop on sprayed wax paper by spoonfuls, or spread into dish. Serves 48.

Per Serving: Cal 22; Fat 0.1g; 4% Fat; Prot 0.45g; Carb 4.5g; Sod 63mg; Chol 0.

The Lite Switch

Praline Cookies

1½ cups light brown sugar	1½ cups flour
½ cup butter or margarine,	1½ teaspoons baking
softened	powder
1 egg	½ teaspoon salt
1 teaspoon vanilla	

Heat oven to 350°. Grease cookie sheets. In large mixer bowl, cream brown sugar and butter until fluffy. Add egg and vanilla; beat well. Add flour and baking powder and salt (sift first). Place on cookie sheet by rounded teaspoonfuls about 2 inches apart. Bake for 12-16 minutes. Cool 1 minutes and remove from pan.

FROSTING:

1 cup light brown sugar	1 cup powdered sugar
½ cup half-and-half cream	½ cup chopped pecans

In small saucepan, combine 1 cup brown sugar with half-and-half. Bring to boil for 2 minutes, stirring all along. Add powdered sugar and blend till smooth. Place ½ teaspoon of chopped pecans on each cookie and drizzle with frosting. These are GREAT! Makes 30-36 cookies.

The Mexican Collection

Mrs. Lyndon Johnson's Sand Tarts

These are the real McCoy. Light and tasty—you'll see why LBJ loved them.

½ pound butter	3 cups flour
4 tablespoons powdered sugar	1 cup pecans, chopped
2 tablespoons water	2 teaspoons vanilla

Blend butter and sugar; add other ingredients. Roll with the hand to finger size and turn into half moons. Bake about 25 minutes in 350° oven. Roll in powdered sugar.

Ma's in the Kitchen

Italian Cookies

2¾ cups sugar	Juice of ½ orange
2½ cups melted Crisco,	11¾ cups flour
(melt then measure)	¼ teaspoon salt
6 eggs	6 teaspoons baking powder
½ cup milk	2 teaspoons baking soda
7 teaspoons vanilla	(level)
Juice of ½ lemon	2 pounds sesame seed

Put sugar in warm, melted shortening, then add eggs, milk, vanilla, and juices. Work into sifted flour, salt, baking powder, and soda. Work into a smooth dough. It will be rather firm. Roll with palm of hand and roll in sesame seed. Cut dough at an angle. Place on ungreased cookie sheet and bake at 350° for 10-15 minutes.

Note: This recipe makes a lot; may be cut in half.

From Cajun Roots to Texas Boots

Ritz Cracker Cookies

Bet you can't eat just one!!!

1 (14-ounce) can Eagle Brand
    Milk
1 cup dates, chopped

1 cup pecans, chopped
1½ sleeves of Ritz crackers

FROSTING:
1 (3-ounce) package cream
    cheese, softened
⅓ cup margarine

1½ cups powdered sugar
1 teaspoon vanilla

Preheat oven to 325°. Cook and stir over medium heat, the milk and dates, until very, very thick. Stir constantly to prevent scorching. Remove and add pecans, stirring well. Immediately spread on Ritz crackers. Place on cookie sheet and bake 6-8 minutes. Remove and cool completely.

Prepare frosting mix, mixing until very smooth. When crackers are completely cooled, frost and then store in refrigerator. Yields about 5 dozen.

Potluck on the Pedernales Second Helping

Goof Balls

1 bag large marshmallows
2 packages caramel candy
1 cup butter or margarine
1 (14-ounce) can sweetened
    condensed milk

1 (10-ounce) box Rice
    Krispies cereal

Cut marshmallows in half and freeze. Melt caramels, butter, and milk in double boiler. Dip marshmallows in caramel mixture and roll in Rice Krispies cereal. Refrigerate to set. Yield: 4-5 dozen.

Potluck on the Pedernales

Mexican Fudge

5 cups sugar (total)
1 large can milk
1 cup oleo
1 cup Eagle Brand milk

1 pint marshmallow whip
2 teaspoons vanilla
4 cups pecans

Mix 4 cups sugar, can of milk, oleo, and Eagle Brand milk together; bring to a boil over medium-low heat. While cooking, pour 1 cup sugar in a heavy skillet; brown and when it's bubbling all over, cook ½ minute. Do not burn. Pour browned sugar syrup into first mixture and cook to soft-ball stage. Remove from heat and add 1 pint marshmallow whip. Beat 5 minutes on high speed with mixer, then place in cold water. Beat for 5 more minutes. Add vanilla and pecans; beat until dull. Pour on greased platter or pans. Makes a lot.

Chuckwagon Recipes

Easy Pralines

1 package butterscotch
   pudding mix (not instant)
1 cup sugar
½ cup brown sugar

½ cup evaporated milk
1 tablespoon butter
1½ cups pecan halves

Mix butterscotch pudding mix, sugar, brown sugar, milk, and butter in a heavy 1½-quart saucepan. Cook and stir to a full, all-over boil, then boil slowly 3-5 minutes until mixture reaches soft-ball stage. Take off heat. Stir in pecans. Beat until mixture begins to thicken, but still looks shiny.

Drop tablespoonfuls of mixture quickly onto waxed paper to form 3 inch pralines. If mixture thickens and starts to lose its shine, add a few drops of milk before dropping more pralines. Let pralines stand until firm. Makes about 18.

Chuckwagon Recipes

Patience

3 cups sugar
1 cup milk
¼ cup butter

1 cup pecans, broken
12 or more marshmallows

Combine 2 cups of the sugar, and the milk and butter in a saucepan. Cook over low heat, stirring only until sugar is dissolved. Melt the remaining 1 cup of sugar in a skillet, without stirring, until lightly browned. Mix very gradually into the first mixture. Continue to cook to 238°, or until a few drops in cold water forms a soft ball.

Beat until candy is creamy and loses its gloss. Mix in pecans. Pour into a greased pan, the bottom of which has been covered with marshmallows. Cut into squares.

Down-Home Texas Cooking

Candied Orange Peel

My mother always made this for Christmas.

4 navel oranges
2½ cups sugar, reserving
  ½ cup for dipping

1 cup water
¼ cup light corn syrup

Remove orange peel in about ⅓-inch strips with a sharp knife, leaving some of the white on the orange. Cut into 3-inch lengths. Put in a large, heavy saucepan and cover with cold water. Bring to a boil and boil 3 minutes. Drain, and repeat the procedure 3 times in all, discarding the water each time and replacing it with fresh. Drain peel after last boiling and set is aside in a bowl.

Rinse out the saucepan and combine 2 cups of the sugar, water, and syrup in it. Place over medium heat and cook, stirring, until sugar dissolves. Add orange peel, turning heat to simmer, and cook gently until peel is translucent, about 30 minutes. Cool in syrup about 45 minutes, then lift out each strip with a fork, draining over edge of pan, and roll in the reserved ½ cup sugar. Place on waxed paper to firm up.

Raleigh House Cookbook

Pies and Desserts

The Old Courthouse. Granbury.

Raleigh House Buttermilk Pie

This pie was a popular dessert at Raleigh House. Many of my customers bought several for their freezers. They freeze well.

1 stick margarine, melted	Dash nutmeg
2 cups sugar	1 teaspoon vanilla
3 eggs	1 (9- or 10-inch) unbaked pie
3 rounded tablespoons flour	shell
1 cup buttermilk	

Mix melted margarine and sugar in mixer, beat well. Add eggs, one at a time, alternating with flour, beating after each addition. Add buttermilk, nutmeg, and vanilla. Mix again and pour into pie shell. Bake on the lower rack of a 375° oven for 30-35 minutes or until edges are firm but center is still a little trembly. This pie is good hot or cold. We always heated it in the microwave before serving. Yield: 6-8 servings.

Raleigh House Cookbook

Buttermilk Pecan Pie

1½ cups sugar	½ cup buttermilk
1 tablespoon flour	1 teaspoon vanilla
4 tablespoons unmelted	1 cup chopped pecans
margarine	1 (9-inch) unbaked pie shell
4 eggs	

Combine sugar, flour, and margarine in a bowl. Mix with electric mixer on low speed. Add eggs, 1 at a time, mixing well. Add buttermilk and vanilla. Mix well. Stir in pecans. Pour into pie shell. Bake in preheated 325° oven about 1 hour until light brown and middle is set.

The Authorized Texas Ranger Cookbook

Chocolate Pecan Pie

3 eggs, slightly beaten
1 cup corn syrup
4 ounces German sweet
  chocolate, melted, cooled
⅓ cup sugar

2 tablespoons melted butter
1 teaspoon vanilla extract
1½ cups pecan halves
1 unbaked 9-inch pie shell

Combine eggs, corn syrup, chocolate, sugar, butter, and vanilla in bowl; mix well. Stir in pecans. Spoon into pie shell. Bake at 350° for 50 minutes to 1 hour or until set. Cool on wire rack. Yield: 8 servings.

Approx per serving: Cal 539; Prot 6g; Carbo 61g; Fiber 2g; T Fat 33g; Chol 88mg; Sod 209mg.

Texas Cookin' Lone Star Style

Mother's Pecan Tassies

1 (3-ounce) package cream
  cheese

½ cup butter or oleo
1 cup flour

Let cheese and butter soften; blend. Stir in flour. Chill 1 hour. Shape into 2 dozen 1-inch balls; place in tea-sized muffin tins (ungreased). Press dough against bottom and up around sides.

FILLING:
1 egg
¾ cup sugar
1 tablespoon soft butter

Dash of salt
⅔ cup broken pecans
1 teaspoon vanilla

Beat together egg, sugar, butter, vanilla, and salt until smooth. Divide half of pecans among pastry cups and add egg mixture with teaspoon. Top with remaining pecan pieces. Bake at 325° for 25 minutes or until filling is set. Cool and remove from pans.

Note: These may be stored for several days in refrigerator or frozen in single layers in container.

From Cajun Roots to Texas Boots

Prodigal Pecan Pie

Nothing finishes a barbecue meal better than a sinfully rich pecan pie. This recipe is heavily influenced by John Thorne, editor of the wonderful Simple Cooking *newsletter, who came up with the method for making the filling so lusciously dense.*

1 cup dark brown sugar	½ teaspoon vanilla extract
²/₃ cup cane syrup,	½ teaspoon salt
preferably, or ⅓ cup light	4 eggs
corn syrup and ⅓ cup dark	2-3 tablespoons half-and-half
unsulphured molasses	2 generous cups pecan pieces
4 tablespoons butter	1 unbaked 9-inch pie crust
3 tablespoons dark rum	Pecan halves

Preheat the oven to 350°. In a large heavy saucepan, combine the brown sugar, syrup, butter, rum, vanilla, and salt. Heat to the boiling point, stirring frequently. Boil for 1 minute, stirring constantly. Remove the pan from the heat and let the mixture cool.

In a bowl, beat the eggs with the half-and-half until light and frothy. Mix the eggs into the cooled syrup, beating until well incorporated. Stir in the pecans. Pour the filling into the pie crust. Top with a layer of pecan halves.

Bake for 45-50 minutes, until a toothpick inserted into the center comes out clean. Serve warm or at room temperature. Serves 6-8.

Smoke & Spice

The International Apple Festival is held in Medina each summer, featuring every imaginable apple creation from pies to pizzas. You'll know you're in Medina when you see the big apple—a 20-foot high stone sculpture of an apple in the city park.

Three-Layer Raisin Pecan Pie

A luscious dessert that raisin lovers will enjoy.

1 cup seedless raisins,
  chopped
½ cup chopped pecans
1 cup sour cream
1 cup sugar
2 eggs, beaten
½ teaspoon cinnamon
¼ teaspoon cloves

¼ teaspoon salt
1 tablespoon butter
1 (3-ounce) package cream
  cheese, softened
½ cup sifted powdered sugar
1 cup whipping cream
1 (9-inch) pie shell, baked

In a saucepan, pour in raisins, pecans, sour cream, sugar, eggs, spices, and salt. Bring to a boil, then cook over reduced heat until thickened, stirring constantly. Add butter and cool completely. Blend cream cheese and powdered sugar together. Whip cream and fold into cheese mixture. Spread half of the cheese mixture in the pie shell. Add the raisin mixture and then top with remaining cheese combination.

The Second Typically Texas Cookbook

Sour Cream Apple Pie

This has to be the best apple pie ever.

1 cup sugar
2 tablespoons flour
1 egg, slightly beaten
1 cup sour cream
1 teaspoon vanilla
¼ teaspoon salt

5 cups pared, cored and diced
  apples
1 (9-inch) unbaked pie shell
½ cup sugar
5 tablespoons flour
¼ cup butter

Mix the sugar and flour. Add the egg, sour cream, vanilla, and salt. Beat until smooth. Add the diced apples and pour into the pie shell. Bake at 350° for 30 minutes. Mix the remaining sugar, flour, and butter to resemble crumbs. Cover the pie with crumbs and bake for 15 minutes longer. Serves 6 happy apple pie lovers. Can top with cheese or ice cream, your choice...I like mine plain.

Collectibles III

Turtle Creek Pie

When a guest couldn't make a choice between pecan pie and apple pie, Robert Zielinski, our pastry chef, created this recipe. It is the best of two possible worlds, combining my two favorite desserts.

3 extra large eggs
1 cup sugar
1 cup dark corn syrup
2 tablespoons unsalted butter,
  melted
1 teaspoon pure vanilla
  extract

4 Granny Smith apples,
  peeled, cored, and sliced thin
1 (10-inch) flan ring, lined
  with All-Purpose Pastry,
  unbaked (page 275)
½ cup pecan pieces

Preheat oven to 350°. Combine eggs and sugar, mixing until sugar is dissolved. Stir in corn syrup, butter, and vanilla. Strain through a fine sieve and set aside.

Place a layer of apple slices in one direction on the bottom of the All-Purpose Pastry shell to form a circle around the outside edge of the shell. Place a second layer inside the first in the opposite direction to form a concentric circle.

Slowly and carefully so as not to disturb slices, pour filling over apples. Sprinkle pecans around outer edge of apples.

Bake in preheated 350° oven for 1 hour. Shield edge with a ring of foil if it begins to get too brown. Return pie to oven and bake for an additional 20-25 minutes or until the filling is set. Let cool slightly before cutting. Makes 1 (10-inch) pie.

The Mansion on Turtle Creek Cookbook

Apple Meringue

Stew six apples, and while hot, put in a piece of butter the size of an egg. When cold add a cup of cracker crumbs, the yelks of three eggs, one cup of sweet milk, and sugar to taste. Bake in a large plate, with an under crust. When done, beat the whites of the eggs with a cup of sugar to a stiff froth, pour on top the pie and brown.

The First Texas Cook Book

All-Purpose Pastry

3 cups all-purpose flour
1 teaspoon salt
3 tablespoons sugar
1 cup very cold unsalted
  butter, cut into pieces

2 extra large egg yolks,
  lightly beaten
¼ cup ice water

Combine flour, salt, and sugar. Cut in butter with a knife or pastry blender until mixture resembles coarse meal. Gradually add egg yolks and ice water until a firm ball is formed. Do not overwork dough.

Seal the dough in plastic wrap and chill for at least 30 minutes before rolling out.

When chilled, roll out to about ⅛-inch thickness on a lightly floured surface either 2 inches larger than pan into which it will be fitted or cut into desired size or shape. When fitted into pan, trim edges and finish as directed. Yield: Enough for 1 double-crust pie.

The Mansion on Turtle Creek Cookbook

Texas Pie

This is another of Aunt Jo's recipes—lots of sugar, but it's really good! We cut stars out of the extra pastry trimming for a Texas-style garnish on top of each slice!

3 cups sugar
½ cup flour
3 eggs, beaten

1½ cups milk
½ cup butter (not margarine)
1 (unbaked (9-inch) pie shell

Combine sugar and flour. Add beaten eggs. In saucepan, heat milk and butter over low heat until butter is melted. Slowly add butter-milk mixture to the sugar-egg mixture, blending well with whisk.

Pour into unbaked pie shell, and bake in a preheated 350° oven for approximately 1 hour, or until knife inserted in center comes out clean. Cool and serve each slice garnished with whipped cream and a pastry star.

The Peach Tree Tea Room Cookbook

Royal Hawaiian Pie with Blueberries

1 (15-ounce) can crushed
   pineapple
3 tablespoons cornstarch
½ cup sugar
1⅓ cups coconut
½ cup pecan pieces

2 bananas
1 (9-inch) baked pie shell
1 cup blueberries
Whipped cream or whipped
   topping
2 tablespoons chopped pecans

Drain pineapple, reserving juice; add enough water to drained juice to make 1 cup. Dissolve cornstarch in ½ cup juice. Stir into remaining juice and combine with sugar, pineapple, coconut, and pecan pieces. Cook, stirring, over medium heat until thickened. Cool. Slice bananas evenly into bottom of pie shell; cover with blueberries. Pour pineapple filling over top. Top with whipped cream and sprinkle with chopped pecans. Chill thoroughly before serving. Makes 8 servings.

The Blueberry Lover's Cookbook

Banana Cream Pie

3 tablespoons cornstarch
1⅔ cups water
1 (14-ounce) can Eagle Brand
   Sweetened Condensed Milk
3 egg yolks, beaten
2 tablespoons margarine or
   butter

1 teaspoon vanilla
3 medium bananas, sliced and
   dipped in lemon juice and
   drained
1 (9-inch) baked pastry shell
1 small container whipped
   cream

In heavy saucepan, dissolve cornstarch in water; stir in sweetened condensed milk and egg yolks. Cook and stir until thickened and bubbly. Remove from heat; add margarine and vanilla. Cool slightly.

Arrange 2 bananas on bottom of prepared pastry shell. Pour filling over bananas; cover. Chill 4 hours or until set. Spread top with whipped cream; garnish with remaining banana slices. Refrigerate leftovers.

Raider Recipes

Sawdust Pie

This special pie is Apple Annie's most requested and loved recipe.

1½ cups sugar
1½ cups sweetened flaked
  coconut
1½ cups chopped pecans
1½ cups graham cracker
  crumbs

7 egg whites
1 teaspoon vanilla extract
1 (10-inch) unbaked pie shell
1 large banana, sliced thinly
Sweetened whipped cream
  and chopped pecans

Preheat oven to 350°. In a large mixing bowl, combine sugar, coconut, pecans, graham cracker crumbs, egg whites, and vanilla. Stir until blended. Pour mixture into pie shell and bake for about 30-35 minutes. Cool to room temperature.

Arrange banana slices over top of pie, then cover with whipped cream and sprinkle with pecans. Refrigerate until ready to serve. Serves 8.

Recipe from Apple Annie's Tea Room & Bakery, San Antonio.

San Antonio Cuisine

Grammy's Chocolate Pie

1½ cups sugar
¼ cup flour
½ cup cocoa
Dash of salt
3 egg yolks

2 cups milk
1 tablespoon vanilla
1 (9-inch) pie crust, baked
  and cooled

Mix dry ingredients. Add egg yolks and milk. Cook over medium-high heat, stirring constantly, until thick and bubbly. Take off heat and add vanilla. Stir. Pour into the baked pie crust.

MERINGUE:
3 egg whites   6 tablespoons sugar

Beat egg whites until stiff. Fold in sugar. Put meringue on pie filling and brown in 375° oven. Serves 6-8.

Central Texas Style

Chocolate Cloud

3 egg whites
1 teaspoon vanilla
1 teaspoon baking powder
¾ cup sugar
1 (4-ounce) package German
  sweet chocolate, grated

1 cup Ritz cracker crumbs
½ cup chopped pecans
1 cup whipping cream
2 tablespoons sugar
1 teaspoon vanilla

Beat egg whites and vanilla to soft peaks. Combine baking powder and sugar and gradually add to white, beating until stiff peaks form. Reserve 2 tablespoons chocolate and add remaining chocolate with crackers and pecans to egg white mixture. Spread in a 9-inch pie plate. Bake at 350° for 25 minutes. Cool thoroughly. Whip cream with sugar and vanilla and spread on top of pie. Garnish with reserved chocolate. Refrigerate at least 8 hours. Serves 8.

Lone Star Legacy

The Chocolate Pie

CRUST:

3 egg whites
Pinch salt
1 teaspoon vanilla
½ teaspoon almond extract
1 cup sugar

1 teaspoon baking powder
¾ cup minced pecans
½ cup saltine cracker
  crumbs

Beat egg whites, salt, vanilla, and almond until soft peaks form, gradually adding sugar. Beat until stiff. Mix together baking powder, pecans, and crumbs. Fold into egg white mixture. Grease a 10-inch pie plate and spread mixture to make a crust. Bake at 300° for 40 minutes.

FILLING:

1 cup sugar
⅓ cup cocoa
⅓ cup flour
3 egg yolks
1¾ cups milk
1 teaspoon vanilla

½ teaspoon almond extract
2 tablespoons softened butter
1 cup whipping cream,
  whipped with 1 tablespoon
  powdered sugar and ½
  teaspoon almond extract

Mix in double boiler sugar, cocoa, flour, yolks, and milk. Cook over medium heat until thick. Remove from heat; add flavorings and butter; blend well. Pour into baked shell. Cool. Top with whipped cream. Serves 8-10.

Best of Friends Two

20 Pie Crusts

5 pounds flour
2½ teaspoons salt

3 pounds Crisco
2 - 2½ cups Sprite

Mix flour and salt; cut in shortening until it looks like small peas. Add Sprite gradually; will be slightly sticky. Let rest one hour then form into 20 balls or 16 balls for large crusts and freeze. Thaw one hour before needed.

Potluck on the Pedernales

Legendary Delta Chocolate Pie
Divinely silky texture and flavor.

CRUST:

18 graham crackers,
crumbled (1½ cups)

½ cup butter, melted

FILLING:

1½ cups butter (no
substitutes)

2¼ cups sugar

3 squares unsweetened
chocolate, melted

3 teaspoons vanilla

6 eggs

1 pint whipped cream

Pecans or almonds for top of
whipped cream

Combine crust ingredients and press into 2 (9-inch) pans. Let set. With electric mixer, beat butter until fluffy; add sugar, and continue to beat. Add melted chocolate and vanilla; continue to beat. Add eggs one at a time, beating 3 minutes after each. Pour over crust; chill and top with whipped cream. Sprinkle with nuts and finely shaved sweet chocolate. Chill thoroughly. Makes 10-12 servings.

Pass it On...

Fresh Strawberry Pie

3 pints fresh strawberries

1 cup sugar

½ cup boiling water

3 tablespoons cornstarch

3-4 drops red food coloring

1 (9-inch) pie shell, baked

1 pint whipped whipping
cream

Mash enough strawberries to make 1 cup. Combine mashed strawberries with sugar and cornstarch and add ½ cup boiling water. Cook over medium heat, stirring constantly until thick. Add food coloring. Place glaze in refrigerator to cool. Wash remaining berries, slice to desired pieces, and place in baked pie shell. When ready to serve, pour cooled glaze over sliced berries and top with whipped cream.

Feast of Goodness

Fresh Peach Jubilee Pie

PASTRY:

1 heaping cup of flour
4 tablespoons powdered sugar

½ cup margarine, softened

Mix with pastry blender. Work into a soft ball by hand. Press into a 9-inch pie plate. Prick well. Bake at 350° until lightly brown, about 10 minutes. Set aside to cool.

FILLING:

1 cup sugar
3 tablespoons cornstarch
¾ cup water
3 tablespoons peach gelatin
½ teaspoon cinnamon
¼ teaspoon nutmeg

1 teaspoon almond extract
4 large peaches, peeled, sliced (add 1 teaspoon fruit protector to prevent discoloration)

Combine sugar, cornstarch, and water; cook over medium heat until thick and clear. Remove from heat; add gelatin, spices and almond extract. When cool, add peaches.

TOPPING:

2½ cups whipped cream or whipped topping

¼ cup sugar
1 cup sour cream

Add sugar to topping and gently fold in sour cream. To assemble pie, spoon ½ of filling into cooled pastry shell. Spread 2/3 of topping mixture over filling. Then gently spoon remaining filling over topping layer. With remaining topping mixture swirl a spoonful on each serving and top either with a maraschino cherry or peach slice, if desired. Freeze for 2 hours or until firm. Serves 6-8.

Jubilee Cookbook

Old Fashioned Peach Cobbler

This is the very popular peach cobbler that Peggy Cox introduced to our customers when she was Tea Room manager. It's an incredible crowd pleaser—Enjoy!

FRUIT MIXTURE:

6 tablespoons tapioca
6 or 7 cups fresh
  Fredericksburg peaches,
  sliced

1 cup sugar
¼ teaspoon cinnamon
¼ teaspoon nutmeg

COBBLER DOUGH:

½ cup butter, softened
1 cup sugar
2 cups flour

1½ cups milk
2 teaspoons baking powder
1 teaspoon salt

COBBLER TOPPING:

1½ cups sugar
2 tablespoons cornstarch
Cinnamon

Nutmeg
½ cup boiling water

Preheat oven to 375°. In a mixing bowl, combine all ingredients to make Fruit Mixture. Mix thoroughly. Pour the Fruit Mixture into a buttered 9x13-inch baking dish.

In a bowl, mix thoroughly all ingredients for Cobbler Dough. Spread over Fruit Mixture.

In a medium mixing bowl, stir together dry Cobbler Topping ingredients. Sprinkle evenly over the Cobbler Dough layer. Pour boiling water evenly over the cobbler. Bake for 1 hour and 20 minutes or until inserted knife comes out clean and the top has a golden crust. Serves 15.

The Peach Tree Family Cookbook

The prime-time soap, Dallas, which ran from 1978 to 1991, was set in Texas but primarily filmed in California. Southfork, the Ewing family mansion, is a real Texas home near Dallas, and many exterior shots were filmed there. Some of the filming was done in Dallas skyscrapers. Opening credits unscrolled over Texas fields, cattle and oil wells.

Creamy Lemon Pie

1 (8-ounce) package cream
  cheese, softened
1 can sweetened condensed
  milk

¼ cup lemon juice
1 can lemon pie filling
1 (9-inch) graham cracker pie
  crust

In mixing bowl, combine cream cheese, sweetened condensed milk and lemon juice. Beat until mixture is smooth. Fold in lemon pie filling. Pour into pie crust. Refrigerate several hours before serving.

I Cook - You Clean

Apricot Fried Pies

1 pound dried apricots
1½ cups sugar
Dash of salt

½ teaspoon nutmeg
¼ cup butter
1 teaspoon lemon juice

Soak apricots overnight. Cover apricots with water and bring to a boil; reduce heat and simmer, uncovered, 30 minutes. Drain some juice if needed. Add sugar, salt, nutmeg, butter, and lemon juice. Make Pie Crust and put 1-2 tablespoons of fruit on pie crust and fry in hot shortening.

Note: Might need to mash apricots after cooking if still pretty lumpy.

PIE CRUST FOR FRIED PIES:
3 cups flour
1 cup butter flavor shortening
1 teaspoon salt

1 egg slightly beaten (then
  water to make ¾ cup)

Mix flour, shortening, and salt, a little at a time. Mix in egg-water mixture. Make into a ball and wrap in Saran Wrap. Chill. Roll into dollar-size balls, then roll between waxed paper the size of a 3-pound shortening can lid. Put 1-2 tablespoons of fruit mixture on 1 side, leaving 1 inch space on the outside to seal. Moisten around outside; fold over and press edges with fingers. Crimp with a fork dipped in flour to seal. Cook in hot shortening about 375°. Cook on each side until golden brown. Drain on paper towels and cover with paper towels and cloth to keep from collecting moisture.

Chuckwagon Recipes

Margarita Pie

1 (8-ounce) package cream
  cheese, softened
2 packages Holland House
  Margarita Mix

½ - ¾ cup sugar
1 (8-ounce) carton Cool Whip
1 graham cracker crust

Cream the cream cheese until fluffy. Add margarita mix and sugar and beat until smooth. Add Cool Whip and mix. Freeze in graham cracker crust until ready to serve.

More of the Four Ingredient Cookbook

Divine Lime Pie

MERINGUE SHELL:
4 egg whites
¼ teaspoon cream of tartar

1 cup sugar

Preheat oven to 275°. Generously butter a 9-inch pie plate. In a small mixing bowl, beat egg whites and cream of tartar until foamy. Beat in sugar very slowly, 1 tablespoon at a time, until stiff and glossy, about 10 minutes. Pile into pie pan, pushing up around the sides. Bake for 1 hour. Turn off oven, leaving pie in the oven with the door closed for 1 hour. Remove from oven and let cool.

FILLING:
4 egg yolks
¼ teaspoon salt
½ cup sugar
⅓ cup fresh lime juice (2-3
  limes)

1 cup chilled whipping cream
1 tablespoon grated fresh
  lime peel
Whipped cream and lime peel
  for garnish

Beat egg yolks until light and lemon-colored. Stir in salt, sugar, and lime juice. Cook over medium heat, stirring constantly, until mixture thickens, about 5 minutes. Cool completely. In a chilled bowl, beat cream until stiff. Fold in filling mixture and grated peel. Pile into meringue shell and chill at least 4 hours. Garnish with whipped cream and lime peel twists. Serves 8.

The Star of Texas Cookbook

Angel Pie

2 egg whites
⅛ teaspoon salt
⅛ teaspoon cream of tartar
½ cup sugar
1½ teaspoons vanilla,
   divided

½ cup finely chopped pecans
Margarine
1 (4-ounce) package German
   sweet chocolate
3 tablespoons hot water
1 cup whipping cream

In a large mixing bowl, beat egg whites until foamy; add salt and cream of tartar. Beat until stiff peaks form. Fold in sugar, ½ teaspoon of the vanilla, and chopped pecans. Grease an 8-inch pie plate with margarine. Turn meringue mixture into pie plate, making a nest-like shell and building sides up above edge of plate. Bake in a slow oven at 300° for 1 hour 15 minutes or until shell seems crunchy. Cool.

Melt chocolate in top of double boiler. Add 3 tablespoons hot water; blend and set aside to cool. Meanwhile, beat whipping cream until stiff peaks form in a medium mixing bowl. Add the remaining 1 teaspoon of vanilla to cooled chocolate mixture; fold into whipped cream. Turn into meringue shell. Chill. Makes 8 small or 6 medium slices.

Amazing Graces

Crustless Chocolate Fudge Pie

2 large eggs	½ cup margarine
1 cup sugar	1 square unsweetened
½ cup flour	chocolate
1 teaspoon vanilla	½ cup pecans

Mix together eggs, sugar, flour, and vanilla. Melt margarine and chocolate. Add to first mixture, stirring well. Pour mixture into a buttered 8-inch pie plate. Top with pecans or mix pecans into batter. Bake at 350° for 25 minutes. Yield: 6-8 servings.

Wild About Texas

Blueberry Crumble

1 (13-ounce) box wild	⅔ cup chopped pecans
blueberry muffin mix	1 (16-ounce) can blueberry
⅓ cup sugar	pie filling
½ teaspoon cinnamon	¼ cup sugar
½ stick margarine, melted	1 teaspoon cinnamon

In a bowl, combine the muffin mix, sugar, cinnamon, and melted margarine. Stir and mix until crumbly. Add pecans and mix. Set aside. Pour the blueberry pie filling into a Pam-sprayed 9x13-inch glass baking dish. Pour the can of drained blueberries that comes in the mix over the top of pie filling. Sprinkle the sugar and cinnamon over top. Then crumble, with your hands, the muffin mixture over the top of the pie filling. Bake at 350° for 35 minutes. To serve, hot or room temperature, top with a dip of vanilla ice cream. Serves 8.

I Cook - You Clean

 The Texas Legislature financed the construction of the State Capitol in Austin in 1888 by trading three million acres of land in the Panhandle to the contractor with the best bid. The largest in the US, the Texas State Capitol has 400 rooms and 18 acres of floor space.

Ruth's Chris Bread Pudding

This fragrant bread pudding needs no additional sauce, as generous amounts of butter, half-and-half, and spices make it moist and flavorful.

1¼ cups sugar
½ cup firmly packed light
  brown sugar
⅓ teaspoon ground nutmeg
1½ teaspoons ground
  cinnamon
6 eggs, beaten
1 tablespoon vanilla extract
1 tablespoon bourbon
Pinch of salt

2 cups milk
1 pint half-and-half
½ cup raisins
½ apple, peeled, cored, and
  diced
½ pound French bread, cut
  into ½-inch cubes and
  toasted
Vanilla ice cream

Preheat oven to 350°. Combine sugars and divide in half. Add nutmeg, cinnamon, eggs, vanilla, bourbon, and salt to one of the sugar mixtures. In a saucepan, combine milk, half-and-half, and butter with other sugar mixture. Bring to a boil, then remove from heat.

Whisk a small amount of hot mixture into egg mixture, then add egg mixture along with raisins and apples to heated mixture. Add toasted bread cubes and let stand until soaked through to the center.

Pour mixture into 2 buttered 10x3x3-inch loaf pans or 1 buttered 9x13-inch pan. Bake until just set (about 30-45 minutes), then serve warm with vanilla ice cream. Serves 12-16.

Recipe from Ruth's Chris Steak House, San Antonio.

San Antonio Cuisine

Banana Pudding

My sister Millie took this banana pudding to the church supper, and the twenty-nine-year-old preacher, who had never had a reason to think about cholesterol or calories, just raved about the banana pudding. He insisted that his wife get the recipe, oblivious to the fact that the original old-fashioned country-cooking recipe had been changed into a diet dish.

2 egg whites
¼ cup egg substitute
½ cup sugar
12 packets Sweet One
¼ cup cornstarch
1 (12-ounce) can evaporated
   skim milk

½ cup fresh skim milk
1 teaspoon vanilla extract
10 graham crackers (double)
3 ripe bananas

Using an electric beater or hand beater, mix egg whites and egg substitute with sugar and sugar substitute. Mix the cornstarch with a small portion of the evaporated skim milk until smooth. Then add the rest of the canned milk and the regular skim milk. Blend the milk mixture with the egg and sugar mixture. Cook in saucepan over medium heat until mixture thickens. Add vanilla extract.

Line a 9x12-inch glass baking dish with 5 of the graham crackers. Add a layer of sliced bananas (about 1½ bananas). Pour half of the pudding mixture over the bananas; repeat a second layer. Make this up a few hours before serving and cool in the refrigerator. Makes 8 servings.

Per Serving: Cal 219; Fat 2g; Chol 2mg; Sat Fat 0.5g. Food Exchanges: 1 meat; 1 bread; ½ fruit; ½ milk.

Low-Cal Country

Caramel Bread Pudding

This recipe is from an old cookbook of my mother's. It is the fluffiest bread pudding I have ever eaten.

¾ cup light brown sugar,
    packed
3 slices buttered white, raisin
    or whole wheat bread, cut
    into ½-inch squares
3 large eggs

1 cup milk
Dash salt
½ teaspoon vanilla
Ice cream, whipped cream, or
    plain cream

Generously butter inside of double boiler top; pour in brown sugar; then add bread squares. Beat eggs with milk, salt, and vanilla; pour over bread; do not stir. Cook over boiling water, 1 hour. Serve warm with or without a pitcher of cream. Yield: 4 servings.

Variation: For chocolate pudding, melt 1 square chocolate in buttered double boiler top. Stir in brown sugar and ¼ cup milk. Cook over boiling water until sugar dissolves, then add rest of ingredients and remaining ¾ cup milk. Do not stir. Cook as in caramel recipe.

Raleigh House Cookbook II

Ricotta Almond Flan

1½ cups slivered almonds
1 (15-ounce) carton ricotta
    cheese
¾ cup sugar
6 large eggs, beaten

Grated zest of 2 large oranges
¼ cup dark rum
1 teaspoon vanilla extract
½ teaspoon nutmeg

Spread almonds on a baking sheet and bake at 300° until lightly browned, about 10 minutes. Remove from oven and cool. Increase oven temperature to 325°.

Grind almonds fine in a food processor, then blend in ricotta, sugar, eggs, orange zest, rum, vanilla, and nutmeg. Butter a deep pie dish, pour in ricotta mixture, and bake for 30-35 minutes or until center of flan is set. Cool before cutting into wedges. Serves 10.

The Mozzarella Company, Dallas.

Dallas Cuisine

Death By Chocolate

A beautiful dessert, and rated off the chart by our testers.

1 (9-ounce) box Jello
   Chocolate Mousse Mix
2 cups whipping cream,
   whipped
1 teaspoon vanilla

¼ cup sugar
1 pan brownies (homemade or
   bakery purchased)
¼ cup Kahlua liqueur
3 Skor candy bars, crushed

Prepare mousse only from box mix, and refrigerate. (Save the crumb mixture for another use.) Add vanilla and sugar to whipped cream. Soak brownies in Kahlua. Assemble in a glass trifle or fruit bowl. Using ½ of each ingredient at a time, layer in the following order: brownies, mousse, whipped cream, candy bars. Repeat layers. Refrigerate. Yield: 10-12 servings.

Homecoming

Pan Chocolate Eclairs

1 (16-ounce) package graham
   crackers, divided
2 (3-ounce) packages instant
   vanilla pudding

3½ cups milk
1 (8-ounce) carton whipped
   topping

Butter the bottom of a 9x13-inch cake pan and line with graham crackers, trying to fit right to the edges. Mix the pudding with milk and beat at medium speed for 2 minutes. Fold in whipped topping and pour half the pudding mixture over the crackers. Place a second layer of whole graham crackers over the pudding and pour the remaining pudding on top. Place a third and final layer of graham crackers on top and cover with plastic wrap. Refrigerate for 2 hours.

FROSTING:

¼ cup cocoa or 1 (1-ounce)
   square unsweetened
   chocolate, melted
2 teaspoons white corn syrup
2 teaspoons vanilla extract

2 tablespoons margarine,
   softened
1½ cups powdered sugar
3 tablespoons milk

Beat all frosting ingredients together until smooth and spread over cooled cake. Cover and refrigerate for 24 hours. Serves 16.

Lone Star Legacy II

Chocolate Velvet Mousse Cake

This recipe is from a special customer who loves the dessert, but prefers that someone else make it.

1 pound semi-sweet chocolate	6 tablespoons confectioners'
2 whole eggs	sugar
4 egg yolks	1 cup egg white
2 cups heavy cream	¼ cup grated white chocolate

Melt semi-sweet chocolate in double-boiler over simmering water. Cool slightly. Add whole eggs and yolks and mix thoroughly. Whip cream with sugar until stiff. Whip egg whites to medium-stiff peaks. Gently fold whipped cream and egg whites alternately into melted chocolate mixture.

CRUST:

1 (9-ounce) box chocolate	½ cup butter, melted
wafers	

Crush chocolate wafers in food processor. Add melted butter and combine. Press crust mixture into bottom of a 10-inch spring-form pan. Top with chocolate mousse. Refrigerate for 2 hours. Top with grated white chocolate. Serves 10-12.

Cafe Matthew, Fort Worth.

Note: Substitute egg substitutes for whole eggs, 4 cups Cool Whip, ¼ cup margarine, and use only ⅛ cup white chocolate.

Fort Worth is Cooking!

291

Apple-Blueberry Stir-Fry

2 tablespoons sugar
1 teaspoon cinnamon
¼ teaspoon nutmeg
Juice and grated peel of 2
  large oranges

4 tart green apples
1½ tablespoons margarine
2 cups blueberries
6 tablespoons low-calorie
  whipped topping (optional)

In a small bowl, mix sugar, cinnamon, and nutmeg; set aside. In a large bowl, mix orange juice and peel. Peel, core and thinly slice apples; toss with juice. Place a wok or skillet over medium heat; when wok is hot, add margarine.

When margarine is melted, add sugar mixture and cook, stirring constantly for about 1 minute. Add apple mixture to wok and stir-fry until apples are soft (about 3 minutes); bring to boil, and boil for 1 minute. Add blueberries and stir-fry until sauce is thickened; serve hot. Top with whipped topping if desired. Yield: 6 servings.

Per serving: Cal 145; Fat 4g; Prot 1g; Carb 30g; Chol 0mg; Sod 37mg; Dietary fiber 3g.

What's Cooking at the Cooper Clinic

Banana Split Chimichangas

8 ounces bittersweet
chocolate, chopped into
small pieces
6 tablespoons unsalted butter
1 cup heavy cream
4 (6-inch) flour tortillas
1 ripe banana, peeled and
quartered lengthwise

½ cup chopped macadamia
nuts
1 pint vanilla ice cream
1 egg, beaten
2-3 cups vegetable oil
Powdered sugar

Combine chocolate, butter, and cream in the top of a double boiler over simmering, not boiling water. Stir occasionally until all ingredients are melted and well combined. Set aside and allow to cool.

Heat a skillet or griddle over medium-high heat. (Do not grease.) Place tortillas over heat to soften enough to become pliable. Remove from heat and arrange 1 piece of banana, about ¼ cup cooled chocolate mixture, 2 tablespoons nuts, and 2 tablespoons ice cream off center on each tortilla.

Brush inside edges of tortillas with beaten egg. Fold top edge of tortilla about a quarter of the way over filling. Repeat with bottom edge. Starting with the unfolded edge closest to the filling, roll into a shape like an egg roll. Freeze for several hours or overnight. Keep frozen until ready to serve.

Just before serving, heat oil in a skillet or deep-fryer to 400°. Place tortilla rolls in hot oil until golden brown on all sides, about 3 minutes. Dust with powdered sugar and serve immediately. Serves 4.

Laurel's, Sheraton Park Central Hotel, Dallas.

Dallas Cuisine

Seven Hill Country art galleries linked by bluebonnet-lined highways sponsor the Highland Lakes Bluebonnet Trail each April. Beautiful Austin hosts the 6th highest number of artists per capita in the U.S.

Tortilla Fruit Rollups

The perfect ending to a Mexican dinner!

1 (21-ounce) can strawberry
    fruit pie filling
8-10 flour tortillas
Butter
2 cups water

1½ cups sugar
¾ cup margarine
1 teaspoon almond flavoring
Ice cream

Open and set aside the strawberry pie filling. Prepare flour tortillas by softening in butter in small skillet, or heat in microwave, if not fresh enough to roll. Place fruit filling in middle of each tortilla and roll like an enchilada. Place seam down in 13x9x2-inch baking dish.

Mix water, sugar, and margarine in saucepan. Bring to a boil and add almond flavoring. Pour mixture over filled tortillas. Place in refrigerator and let soak 1-24 hours. Baste with sugar mixture before and during baking. Bake in a preheated 350° oven for 20-25 minutes or until hot and slightly browned. Extra special touch—serve with ice cream!

'Cross the Border

Cream Puffs with Lemon Curd

The food processor makes this a snap!

CREAM PUFF:

1 cup water	1 cup flour
½ cup butter, cut into	½ teaspoon salt
chunks	4 eggs

Heat water and butter on high heat until water boils and butter melts. Add flour and salt all at once; stir over heat until ball of dough is formed and excess moisture has evaporated. Turn into food processor bowl with steel blade. Add eggs all at once and process until smooth. Drop dough by tablespoonsful onto baking sheet. Bake for 10 minutes at 400°, then at 350° for 25 minutes. Let stay in turned-off oven for 10 more minutes. Let cool, slice off tops and fill. Makes about 10 large puffs or 40 small.

LEMON CURD:

⅓ cup lemon juice	¼ cup cornstarch
1 cup sugar	3 eggs
¼ cup butter	

Process all ingredients together with steel blade. Cook over medium heat on top of range until thickened. Process again until smooth. Refrigerate until ready to use. The puffs can also be filled with tuna salad, egg salad, or chicken salad for a "new" sandwich.

Delicioso!

 Texas has far more farms than any other state—180,644—on an awesome 130 million acres of farm land. Agriculture was the leading industry for more than 100 years, but since the forties, the oil and gas industry has generated more income. Texas still leads the nation in cotton production.

Apple Dumpling Delight

PASTRY MIX:

2¼ cups flour
¾ teaspoon salt

¾ cup shortening
7-8 teaspoons ice water

Sift flour and salt together; cut in shortening with pastry blender. Sprinkle 1 teaspoon of water over mixture. Gently toss with fork. Repeat until all is moistened. Form into a ball. Roll on lightly floured surface. Cut into 6 squares.

FILLING:

6 medium tart apples
½ cup sugar
1½ teaspoons cinnamon

1 tablespoon butter or
   margarine

Preheat oven to 350°. Pare and core apples. Place an apple on each pastry square. Mix sugar and cinnamon together. Fill each apple with cinnamon mixture; dot with butter. Moisten points of pastry; bring points together over tops. Seal well. Place 2 inches apart in a 13x9-inch baking pan; place in refrigerator while preparing topping.

TOPPING:

1 cup sugar
¼ teaspoon cinnamon
2 cups water

4 tablespoons butter or
   margarine

Mix all ingredients together in saucepan. Boil for 3 minutes. Pour hot syrup around the chilled dumplings; bake 30-35 minutes. Serve warm with whipped cream, if desired. Serves 6.

Some Like it Hot

Dee's Baked Alaska

This is very easy and quick and can be made several days ahead of time and kept in freezer. Everyone, all ages, loves it!

SAUCE:

3 tablespoons cornstarch
3 tablespoons Chocolate-
  Raspberry liqueur

1½ cups Hershey's
  chocolate syrup

Combine cornstarch and liqueur in saucepan; stir in chocolate syrup. Cook, stirring constantly, until mixture thickens and bubbles 3 minutes. Remove from heat and cool *completely*.

1 baked 10-inch pie shell,
  cooled
½ gallon vanilla ice cream
Chopped cherries, optional
Chopped nuts, optional

4 egg whites
¼ teaspoon cream of tartar
¼ teaspoon salt
½ cup sugar
½ teaspoon almond flavoring

*Drizzle several spoonfuls of sauce into bottom of pie shell. Scoop ice cream with a large serving spoon—make a layer over sauce, drizzle more sauce and nuts and/or cherries, if desired. Continue layers ending with ice cream. Smooth ice cream, making a higher mound in the center. Freeze while making meringue.

Beat egg whites with cream of tartar and salt until foamy and double in volume. Beat in sugar, gradually, until meringue forms stiff peaks. Add almond flavoring. Frost ice cream with meringue, sealing to pastry edge. Make swirls. Freeze until serving time. Bake at 475° for 3 minutes or until meringue is touched with brown.

Heat remaining sauce. Cut into wedges, drizzle with sauce and serve.

*You usually have sauce left—if not, it only takes a minute to make more.

Best of Friends

Floating Islands

A family member recalls being intrigued and charmed as a child by such an exotic name.

3 egg whites	2 tablespoons cornstarch
3 cups milk	4 ounces grated chocolate
½ cup sugar	3 egg yolks
⅛ teaspoon salt	1 teaspoon vanilla

Beat egg whites to a froth. Drop by the teaspoonful in boiling sweet milk. When done place on a plate. Combine sugar, salt, and cornstarch in top of double boiler. Add milk, stir in chocolate and boil 8-10 minutes. Remove from fire and stir, adding egg yolks beaten well. Place again over fire and stir, but do not let boil. Add vanilla. Put in shallow dish and slip the islands on the cream.

Perfectly Splendid

Toffee Cream Surprise

1 cup buttermilk	1 (10-ounce) jar maraschino
1 (3-ounce) package French	cherries, drained and cut in
vanilla instant pudding	halves
1 (12-ounce) carton Cool	1 cup chopped pecans
Whip	1 cup miniature marshmallows
1 (12-ounce) package	
Keebler's Toffee Toppers	
Fudge Covered Shortbread	
Cookies	

In a mixing bowl, combine buttermilk and vanilla pudding. Beat with a whisk until thoroughly mixed. Fold in Cool Whip. *Lightly* crumble cookies with the knife blade of food processor. Don't pulverize cookies; you may have to break a few cookies up by hand. Leave some cookies in chunks. Fold cookies, cherries, pecans, and marshmallows into pudding mixture. Refrigerate in covered bowl and serve in individual sherbets. Best served same day. Serves 12.

I Cook - You Clean

Aunt Sadie's Frozen Eggnog Dessert

Aunt Sadie always kept several trays ready in her freezer and served in crystal champagne glasses with homemade cookies. A wonderful dessert any time of year.

4 eggs, separated
½ cup sugar
4 tablespoons whiskey

½ pint whipping cream
Nutmeg

Combine egg yolks, sugar, and whiskey in top of double boiler. Beat and cook until slightly thickened, about 3-5 minutes. Remove from heat; add to well-beaten egg whites; beat well and add whipping cream. Beat until well blended. Pour into 2 ice cube trays and freeze.

Lone Star Legacy

Pecos Cantaloupe Ice Cream

1½ cups sugar
Pinch of salt
3 eggs, well beaten
1 (14-ounce) can condensed milk
1 (13-ounce) can evaporated milk

1 quart milk
1 large, ripe cantaloupe, puréed in blender
Ice cream salt

Add sugar and salt to eggs; stir in milks; add cantaloupe; put in ice cream freezer; cover; pack with ice and salt; freeze until firm. Another *Great Flavor of Texas!* Yields 1 gallon.

Great Flavors of Texas

Butter Pecan Ice Cream

A food authority once claimed that Texans consume almost all the butter pecan ice cream made in the country. If you try this recipe, you'll understand why.

¼ cup unsalted butter	1 cup whipping cream
1 cup chopped pecans	¾ cup sugar
5 egg yolks	1 tablespoon vanilla
1 pint half-and-half	

Melt the butter in a small skillet over medium heat. Add the pecans, and cook until the nuts are coated with the butter and lightly crisped.

Strain the excess butter into the top of a double boiler. Add the egg yolks, half-and-half, whipping cream, sugar, and vanilla. Set the pan over its water bath. Warm the custard mixture over medium-low heat, whisking until the mixture is well blended. Continue heating, frequently stirring up from the bottom, until the mixture thickens. (Make sure it does not come to a boil; the egg yolks should poach, not scramble.) This process takes about 15 minutes. Remove the pan from the heat and pour the custard through a strainer into a bowl. Chill it thoroughly.

Transfer the custard to an ice cream maker, and process it according to the manufacturer's directions. After churning, stir in the pecans, and place the ice cream in the freezer until serving time.

This ice cream is best eaten within several days. Makes about 1 quart.

Texas Home Cooking

African Queen

Baudouin's own creation has become a Le Chardonnay classic.

CARAMEL SAUCE:

2 tablespoons sugar	1 teaspoon vanilla
1 teaspoon water	2 cups heavy cream

Cook sugar and water in heavy saucepan over low heat until mixture turns a rich golden color. In another saucepan, bring cream and vanilla to a boil. Add to sugar and cook, stirring constantly with a whisk, until smooth. Let cool.

2 bananas	4 large strawberries
16 sheets phyllo pastry	20 orange wedges
Melted butter	4 mint leaves
Sugar	4 scoops vanilla ice cream

Peel bananas and cut in half lengthwise. Brush one sheet phyllo with melted butter. Sprinkle with sugar. Repeat 3 times, stacking the sheets. Wrap one banana half in the pastry, refrigerate, and repeat with remaining banana halves. Bake wrapped bananas on sheet pan in preheated 375° oven until golden and crisp. To serve, place caramel sauce on half of each plate. Decorate the other half with fruit garnishes. Place cooked banana on sauce and top with ice cream. Serve immediately. Serves 4.
Le Chardonnay, Fort Worth.

Note: Spray butter-flavor Pam on pastry sheets, and substitute evaporated skim milk and low-fat ice cream.

Fort Worth is Cooking!

Ken's Banana Nut Ice Cream

3 eggs, beaten	1 can Eagle Brand milk
2 cups sugar	1 cup chopped pecans
1 tablespoon vanilla	1 pint half-and-half
3 bananas, mashed	Sweet milk

Blend all the above and add sweet milk to make 1 gallon; freeze.

Chuckwagon Recipes

Ruggles' Chocolate Parfait

Ruggles Grill, Houston, Chef/owner Bruce Molzan got inspiration for this layered, chocolate-on-chocolate dessert on a trip to Paris, where he worked in the kitchens of some of its most celebrated restaurants. "This is my absolute favorite chocolate dessert," says the CIA honors graduate.

CHOCOLATE CAKE:

1 cup cocoa	1 cup butter
2¾ cups all-purpose flour	2½ cups granulated sugar
2 teaspoons baking soda	4 eggs
½ teaspoon salt	1½ teaspoons vanilla
½ teaspoon baking powder	2 cups water

Preheat oven to 350°. In a mixing bowl, sift together the cocoa, flour, baking soda, salt, and baking powder. In a separate bowl, using an electric mixer, cream the butter with the sugar, eggs, and vanilla. Combine the two mixtures alternately in a third bowl, adding the water. Pour into a greased jelly roll pan and bake for 25-30 minutes. Cool and reserve.

MOUSSE MIXTURE:

1 pound semi-sweet chocolate, coarsely chopped	2 cups heavy cream, lightly whipped
4 ounces unsalted butter	

Melt the chopped semi-sweet chocolate with the butter over medium-low heat. Fold in the lightly whipped cream; reserve.

1½ ounces Chambord	Almond Brittle (recipe
1½ ounces simple syrup	follows)
(equal parts sugar and water)	Raspberry, mango, and
1 pint raspberries	chocolate sauce, optional
2 ounces shaved white	garnish
chocolate	
2 ounces shaved semi-sweet	
chocolate	

Take four circular tin molds, 2 inches deep and 3 inches in diameter (they are kind of like deep biscuit cutters), and line with parchment paper. (Bruce Molzan found these molds in Paris, but says that you can also use PVC piping material.)

CONTINUED

Place a layer of chocolate cake at bottom of each mold. Drizzle each layer of cake with Chambord and some of the simple syrup. Place raspberries on top of cake. Divide the chocolate mousse evenly on top of each mold and pack down. Chop up leftover chocolate cake into cubes and sprinkle on top of chocolate mixture. Sprinkle white and semi-sweet chocolate shavings over each dessert and refrigerator for 2 hours. Unmold and top with chopped Almond Brittle. Serve at room temperature.
Serves 4.

ALMOND BRITTLE:

1 cup granulated sugar	½ cup chopped almonds

Over medium heat, cook sugar until brown but not burned. Add almonds and continue cooking about 5 minutes more. Pour mixture into buttered sheet pan. Let cool and chop into small pieces.

Top Chefs in Texas

Barbecued Bananas Flambé

4 ripe unpeeled bananas
2 tablespoons dark brown
  sugar

6 tablespoons dark rum

Grill bananas over warm coals for 10 minutes on each side. Cut into halves lengthwise. Place on serving plates. Sprinkle with brown sugar and rum. Ignite and serve immediately. Yield: 8 servings.

Approx Per Serving: Cal 89; Prot 1g; Carbo 17g; Fiber 1g; T Fat 1g; 3% Calories from Fat; Chol 0mg; Sod 2mg.

Gatherings

Chambord Melba Sauce

Place fresh, poached or frozen peaches in tall stemmed glasses, add vanilla ice cream and top with this sauce.

1 (10-ounce) package frozen
  raspberries
½ cup currant jelly
¼ cup sugar

1 teaspoon cornstarch
⅓ cup Chambord liqueur
½ teaspoon fresh lemon
  juice

Combine the raspberries, currant jelly, sugar, and cornstarch in a saucepan. Stir over moderate heat until boiling. Then simmer gently for 10 minutes. Remove from heat and add the Chambord and lemon juice. Strain and chill before serving.

Raleigh House Cookbook II

Fruit Carousel

A delightful party dessert!

Make sauce first and have ready to cover fruit as soon as it is arranged to prevent darkening. Have chilled.

SAUCE:

¾ cup sugar	¼ cup lemon juice
¾ cup water	4 tablespoons cornstarch
1 cup orange juice	⅛ teaspoon salt

Mix and cook until thick and clear. Chill. Spread over fruit. You will probably have some left over. This makes a large amount.

CRUST:

1 package refrigerator sugar cookie dough	½ cup sugar
1 (8-ounce) package cream cheese	1 teaspoon vanilla

Slice cookie dough thin and press on pizza pan. Bake according to directions on package. Let cool. Cream together cream cheese, sugar and vanilla. Spread on crust. Chill.

FRUIT:

Strawberries, halved	Grapes, halved
Bananas, sliced	2 peaches, sliced
2 cups mandarin oranges, well drained	1 (8-ounce) can chunk pineapple well drained

Slice fruit and arrange in circles completely around the pan. Cover with sauce. Yield: 8 servings.

Variation: Make this to suit your own taste. Use any kind of fruits you like. A dollop of whipped topping is also good.

More Calf Fries to Caviar

Paisano Pete is a popular photo subject in Fort Stockton. At 20 feet long and 11 feet tall, Pete is probably the world's largest roadrunner.

Bread Pudding with Whiskey Sauce

1 (1-pound) loaf French bread
1 quart milk
3 eggs
2 cups sugar
2 tablespoons vanilla
1 cup raisins
1 cup peeled, chopped, fresh apple
3 tablespoons melted margarine

Preheat oven to 350°. Break bread into chunks and soak in milk for about 15 minutes. Crush with hands until well mixed. Combine and beat well eggs, sugar, vanilla, and fruit. Pour these ingredients over the soaked bread and stir them lightly with a fork until well blended. Pour the margarine into two 1-quart casseroles. Pour the bread pudding into the two casseroles. Bake at 350° for 1 hour. Allow to cool. Serve with whiskey sauce.

WHISKEY SAUCE:
1 stick margarine or butter
1 cup sugar
2 tablespoons water
1 egg, beaten
Whiskey to taste

Put margarine, sugar and water in top of double boiler and cook until sugar is dissolved. Add egg and whip quickly so that egg does not curdle. Cook for 1 minute to insure egg is well done, stirring constantly. Cool. Add whiskey. The pudding and sauce taste best at room temperature. Serves 10-12.

From Generation to Generation

Index

Ride 'em, cowboy! Pecos is the home of the world's first rodeo.

INDEX

INDEX

INDEX

INDEX

INDEX

Catalog
of
Contributing
Cookbooks

Dotting the landscape throughout much of Texas, these pump jacks—called donkey heads—rhymically dig deep for that rich black Texas gold.

CATALOG
of
CONTRIBUTING COOKBOOKS

All recipes in this book have been selected from the Texas cookbooks shown on the following pages. Individuals who wish to obtain a copy of any particular book may do so by sending a check or money order to the address listed. Prices are subject to change. Please note the postage and handling charges that are required. State residents add tax only when requested. Retailers are invited to call or write to same address for discount information.

AMAZING GRACES

The Texas Conference United Methodist Ministers' Spouses Assn.
12955 Memorial Drive
Houston, TX 77079   903-538-2492

From the parsonages of the Texas Conference, a sampling of delicious dishes as varied as the areas from which they come. The common ingredient is the Amazing Grace that gives the greatest flavor to each recipe and to each of the stories that are sprinkled throughout this little book.

$14.95 Retail price
$ 1.23 Tax for Texas residents
$ 2.50 Postage and handling
Make check payable to Texas Conference Ministers Spouses
ISBN 0-9636854-0-6

THE AUTHORIZED TEXAS RANGER COOKBOOK

Johnny and Cheryl Harris
P. O. Box 191
Hamilton, TX 76531   800-657-9019

More than just a cookbook, it's a wonderful and unique mix of history, old photographs, mouthwatering recipes, and stories of legendary Texas Rangers and their wives and friends. You will enjoy reading the book as much as cooking from it! 222 pages. 350 recipes. Hardcover concealed wire binding.

$18.95 Retail price
$ 1.47 Tax for Texas residents
$ 3.50 Postage and handling
Make check payable to Harris Farms Publishing Co.
ISBN 0-9641614-0-0

BEST OF FRIENDS and
BEST OF FRIENDS TWO
by Dee Reiser and Teresa Dormer
2614 S. Strathford Lane
Kingwood, TX 77345   713-361-5881 or 358-4208

Our recipes offer gourmet taste with a minimum of extra effort. Entertaining friends is a way of life for us, and sharing these recipes keeps our circle of friends growing.

$ 9.95 Retail price each
$ .72 Tax for Texas residents
$ 1.50 Postage and handling
Make check payable to Best of Friends
ISBN 0-9615950-5-1, 0-9615950-4-3

THE BLUEBERRY LOVER'S COOKBOOK
Muriel C. Pelham
P.O. Box 66
Village Mills, TX 77663   409-834-2882

A treasured collection of 435 delicious blueberry recipes in every imaginable use! This attractive hard-covered book with over 200 pages of recipes and helpful information is a *must* for every blueberry lover and collector. Tabbed category dividers and a recipe index make it easy to find specific recipes.

$14.00 Retail price
$ .88 Tax for Texas residents
$ 2.50 Postage and handling
Make check payable to Muriel Pelham

BOARDIN' IN THE THICKET
REMINISCENCES AND RECIPES OF EARLY BIG
THICKET BOARDING HOUSES
by Wanda A. Landrey
University of North Texas Press
P. O. Box 13856
Denton, TX 76203   817-565-2142

Wanda Landrey, descendant of one of the pioneering boarding house families, searched the Big Thicket to find survivors of the boarding house era and to collect their stories and recipes into this 216-page hardbound book, with 102 recipes and stories from 12 boarding houses, including 44 black-and-white photos from that era.

$19.95 Retail price
$ 1.65 Tax for Texas residents
$ 4.00 Postage and handling
Make check payable to UNT Press
ISBN 0-929398-07-6

BUFFET ON THE BAYOU

Houston Junior Forum
820 Marston
Houston, TX 77019   713-526-4797

Buffet on the Bayou offers over 460 triple-tested recipes reflecting the multicultural diversity of the Gulf Coast region in a beautifully designed hardback book. Its bright pink cover depicts a stunning view of the Houston skyline as seen from Buffalo Bayou. It is filled with historical, and sometimes hysterical, Houston highlights and tidbits.

$17.95 Retail price
$ 4.50 Postage and handling
Make check payable to *Buffet on the Bayou*
ISBN 09637270-0-1

CANYON ECHOES: RECIPES & REMEMBRANCES FROM PRAIRIE DOG PETE

P.O. Box 1286
Clarendon, TX 79226   800-658-9752

This 191-page cookbook is as colorful as a Southwestern sunset and contains a range of recipes spanning the spectrum from frontier campfires to microwave ovens. The narrator, Prairie Dog Pete, shares the secrets and unique history of West Texas cooking. A feast for every table.

$12.50 Retail price
$ .97 Tax for Texas residents
$ 2.00 Postage and handling
Make check payable to *Canyon Echoes*
ISBN 0-9645176-0-4

A CASUALLY CATERED AFFAIR

OR WHO FORGOT THE CHOCOLATE CAKE?
by Carole Curlee
3806 68th Street
Lubbock, TX 79413   806-795-0982

A "must-have." A solid cooking/entertaining guide for new brides, students away from home, experienced cooks who want tried, well-loved recipes! Top favorites from 30 years as a caterer, wedding consultant, food stylist, class instructor. Collection includes Mexican, crowd-sized, family, and entertainment favorites! 16th year, 11th printing, 428 recipes, plastic cover.

$17.99 Retail price
$ 1.41 Tax for Texas residents
$ 3.25 Postage and handling
Make check payable to Carole Curlee
ISBN 0-9645657-0-6

CELEBRATE SAN ANTONIO

San Antonio Junior Forum
P. O. Box 791186
San Antonio, TX 78279-1186   210-545-2187

San Antonio presents *Celebrate San Antonio*, a cookbook unlike any other on your shelves, it contains the tastes and sights of San Antonio's many diverse cultures, along with the festive, formal and easy-going lifestyles that make this city unique. Laced with stories, traditions and explanations, you'll like reading the book as much as cooking from it.

$19.95 Retail price
$ 3.50 Postage and handling
Make check payable to San Antonio Junior Forum
ISBN 0-9616917-0-0

CENTRAL TEXAS STYLE

Junior Service League of Killeen, Inc.
P. O. Box 1106
Killeen, TX 76540   817-554-5414

Central Texas Style is a unique collection of recipes from a unique collection of women who love Central Texas. Recipes include some from unusual, exotic and faraway places. *Style* is packed with old family recipes handed down from proud Central Texas pioneers. Above all, *Central Texas Style* is casual, easy, warm, hospitable and *delicious!*

$12.95 Retail price
$ 1.07 Tax for Texas residents
$ 3.00 Postage and handling
Make check payable to Junior Service League of Killeen, Inc.

CHANGING THYMES

Austin Junior Forum Publications
P. O. Box 26628
Austin, TX 78755-0628   512-835-9233

Changing Thymes is a collection of 490 wonderful recipes, ranging from light to indulgent. Each recipe includes its own nutritional analysis. There are eight separate food sections, including Pasta, Rice, and On the Grill, which reflects today's changing eating preferences—light, easy, and quick.

$17.95 Retail price
$ 2.50 Postage and handling
Make check payable to Austin Junior Forum Publications
ISBN 0-9607152-2-3

CHUCKWAGON RECIPES AND OTHERS
by Sue Cunningham and Jean Cates
P. O. Box 22
Hartley, TX 79044   806-365-4596 or 806-374-9733

Not just another cookbook, it has not only recipes, but stories and Western art. If you're tired of ordinary cookbooks and want to get into "cowboy cuisine," the book is cheap, the art is good, and it's fun to read even if you don't cook. Spiral bound, paperback, 120 pages and over 300 recipes.

$13.50 Retail price
$ 2.00 Postage and handling
Make check payable to Sue Cunningham
ISBN 0-9645414-0-8

COASTAL CUISINE, TEXAS STYLE
Junior Service League of Brazosport
P. O. Box 163
Lake Jackson, TX 77566   409-297-9113

From a crossroads of cultures comes a dazzling variety of cuisine served up by the Junior Service League of Brazosport. *Coastal Cuisine, Texas Style* celebrates its ties to the Deep South and to the Old West in this 286-page treasury of over 500 family tested favorites from the "Cradle of Texas History."

$16.95 Retail price
$ 1.40 Tax for Texas residents
$ 3.00 Postage and handling
Make check payable to Junior Service League of Brazosport
ISBN 0-9637804-0-9

COLLECTIBLES III
by Mary Pittman
Rt. 2 Box 76
Van Alstyne, TX 75495   903-433-2665

Collectibles III, gathered by Mary Pittman, has been created as an extension to *Collectibles II* for the busy gourmet...the housewife and mother, the volunteer, the career girl, the bachelor... anyone who likes to eat well and to entertain.

$10.00 Retail price
$ 1.50 Postage and handling
Make check payable to Mary Pittman

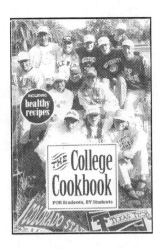

THE COLLEGE COOKBOOK FOR STUDENTS BY STUDENTS

Nancy S. Levicki
7714 Woodway
Houston, TX 77063   713-780-1268

Does "Macho Fettucine" sound familiar? Probably not, but it is a favorite recipe in *The College Cookbook*. Students from across the country contributed over 200 easy-to-prepare favorite recipes. With over 22,000 copies sold, *The College Cookbook For Students By Students* is a hit! This new expanded edition includes healthy, lower fat recipes.

$12.95 Retail price
$ 1.06 Tax for Texas residents
$ 2.50 Postage and handling
Make check payable to NJL Interests
ISBN 0-9631318-2-6

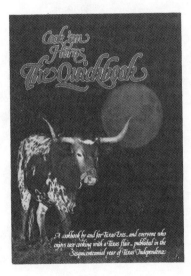

COOK 'EM HORNS: THE QUICKBOOK

The Ex-Students' Association
P. O. Box 7278
Austin, TX 78713   800-594-3935 or 512-471-8089

Cook 'em Horns: The Quickbook, contains the best of "quick" recipes submitted by alumni of The University of Texas from many parts of the world. The dishes are unusual enough for the gourmet, but easy enough for the beginner, proving that time-consuming recipes are no longer necessary to create exciting dishes. 192 pages, 7¾ x 10½.

$15.95 Retail price
$ 1.28 Tax for Texas residents
$ 3.25 Postage and handling
Make check payable to The Ex-Students' Assoication
ISBN 0-9635002-1-X

'CROSS THE BORDER

Janel Franklin and Sue Vaughn
1012 N. 9th Street
Lamesa, TX 79331   806-872-8667

The most sizzling, zesty, taste-tempting Southwestern recipes available. We have added our special touch: easy-to-find ingredients, simple-to-follow instructions, short-on-cooking methods, but always long on flavor! 132 pages.

$ 8.95 Retail price
$ .84 Tax for Texas residents
$ 2.00 Postage and handling
Make check payable to Jan-Su
ISBN 0-9610956-2-8

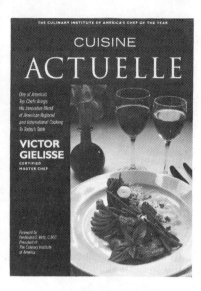

CUISINE ACTUELLE

by Victor Gielisse
Taylor Publishing Company
1550 W. Mockingbird Lane
Dallas, TX 75235   800-759-8120

An innovative blend of regional and international cuisine by one of America's top chefs. Gielisse brings the sumptuous realm of "today's cuisine" into the home with an emphasis on serving familiar food in unfamiliar ways. Over 150 exciting recipes and a 16-page full-color insert to aid in presentation.

$21.95 Retail price
$ 1.70 Tax for Texas residents
$ 3.00 Postage and handling
Make check payable to Taylor Publishing Company
ISBN 0-87833-786-5

DALLAS COWBOYS WIVES' FAMILY COOKBOOK AND PHOTO ALBUM
SUPER BOWL EDITION

Happy Hill Farm Academy/Home
Star Route, Box 56
Granbury, TX 76048   817-897-4822

This Super Bowl Edition cookbook, compiled by the Dallas Cowboys' wives, features favorite Cowboy recipes, candid family pictures, and behind-the-scenes information about the players and their families. All proceeds go directly to the Scholarship Fund at Happy Hill Farm Academy/Home.

$12.95 Retail price
$ 4.00 Postage and handling
Make check payable to Happy Hill Farm Academy/
Home
ISBN 0-9634855-1-2

DALLAS CUISINE

Compiled and Edited by
DOTTY GRIFFITH

Two Lane Press, Inc.
4245 Walnut
Kansas City, MO 64111   816-531-3119

Dotty Griffith, the Lifestyle Editor of the *Dallas Morning News*, offers a terrific selection of 130 recipes from "Roast Pork Loin with Pecan-Sage Butter" offered by Blue Mesa Grill, to Laurel's "Banana Split Chimichangas." Famed Dallas restaurants like The Mansion on Turtle Creek and The French Room are but two of the more than 50 outstanding restaurants featured in this volume.

$14.95 Retail price
$ 3.75 Postage and handling
Make check payable to Two Lane Press
ISBN 1-878686-06-2

DECADES OF MASON COUNTY COOKING

Riata Service Organization
P. O. Drawer S
Mason, TX 76856   915/347-5589

Riata Service organization, always active in encouraging education, promoting culture, and advancing the welfare of Mason County and its citizens, salutes the generations (from 1927) who have graciously contributed to our cookbooks, adding their culinary legacies to our community's heritage. Proceeds will benefit many endeavors, as well as restoring the Historical Building into a museum. Hardcover, 424 pages.

$15.00 Retail price
$ 2.00 Postage and handling
Make check payable to Riata Cookbook Fund

DEEP IN THE HEART

Dallas Junior Forum
800 E. Campbell Rd., Ste. 199
Richardson, TX 75081   214-680-5244

Over 500 tempting recipes, helpful hints, and decidedly Texas artwork, a tribute to kitchens all over the big state that's big on hospitality. Hard cover, comb binding and color throughout. All profits are donated to local charities. Over 100,000 copies in print. 300 pages.

$16.95 Retail price
$ 3.00 Postage and handling
Make check payable to Deep In The Heart
ISBN 0-9617187-0-6

¡DELICIOSO!

The Junior League of Corpus Christi, Inc.
P.O. Box 837
Corpus Christi, TX 78403   800-884-3315

!Delicioso! You're going to think so! With its bright and unusual folk art cover, !Delicioso! reflects the diversity of cultures that have blended together to produce a South Texas style of cooking. Over 800 carefully selected recipes with special sections on Mexican Food, Seafood, Quick and Easy Gourmet and Wild Game.

$18.95 Retail price
$ 4.00 Postage and handling
Make check payable to Junior League of Corpus Christi
ISBN 0-969144-0-4

THE DENTON WOMAN'S CLUB COOKBOOK

Denton Woman's Club
P. O. Box 2584
Denton, TX 76202   817-382-9597 or 382-8954

More than 1200 recipes from the talented hostesses of a town known for its hospitality and two Miss Americas. Old and new favorites, innovative originals, easy-to-follow instructions, menu suggestions, special food processor and microwave sections, and a comprehensive index. A frequently heard comment: "If I could have only one cookbook, this would be my choice."

$17.95 Retail price
$ 2.50 Postage and handling
Make check payable to *The Denton Woman's Club Cookbook*

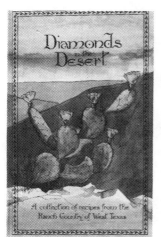

DIAMONDS IN THE DESERT

Ozona Woman's League
P. O. Box 1552
Ozona, TX 76943   915-392-2492

Diamonds in the Desert offers an eclectic array of 620 unique, imaginative recipes reflecting the gracious traditions of West Texas ranch country. Also included are calorie counts, nutritional summaries and an easy-to-use cross-referenced index. Lovely pen and ink drawings provide a delightful insight into the Texas ranchland charm of Crockett County.

$14.95 Retail price
$ .93 Tax for Texas residents
$ 2.00 Postage and handling
Make check payable to Ozona Woman's League
ISBN 0-9618029-0-1

DOWN-HOME TEXAS COOKING

by James Stroman
Gulf Publishing Company
P.O. Box 2608
Houston, TX 77252-2608   713-520-4444

Down-Home Texas Cooking shows there's no place like home when it comes to hearty, satisfying meals. This genuine taste of Texas includes 186 pages of tasty recipes for family favorites from every region of the state, including spicy Creole cuisine, flavorful Tex-Mex offerings, classic Texas fare, and delectable Gulf Coast seafood.

$12.95 Retail price
$ 1.47 Tax for Texas residents
$ 4.95 Postage and handling
Make check payable to Gulf Publishing Company
ISBN 0-88415-183-2

DUCK CREEK COLLECTION

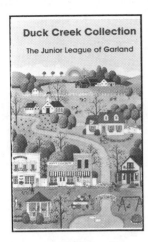

Junior League of Garland
700 A Main Street
Garland, TX 75040   214-272-9160

Good hosts on the lookout for recipes and new ideas for entertaining, will welcome this book to their collection. It is filled with a pleasurable selection of recipes that will entertain and delight. So invite a few friends over for delicious recipes from the Junior League of Garland's *Duck Creek Collection*. Proceeds benefit the agencies of the Junior League.

$10.00 Retail price
$ .83 Tax for Texas residents
$ 2.50 Postage and handling
Make check payable to Junior League of Garland

EATS: A FOLK HISTORY OF TEXAS FOODS

Ernestine Sewell Linck and Joyce Gibson Roach
c/o TCU Press, TCU Box 298300
Fort Worth, TX 76129   817-921-7822

With 400 recipes, *Eats* is as much history as it is cookbook, tracing Texas foods from Poke Sallet and Vinegar Pie to Barbecue, back to the immigrants who settled various areas. The book is also filled with quotes from travelers, pioneers, cooks and critics, along with jokes, an occasional verse or song or poetry, and sayings of folk wisdom.

$12.95 Retail price paper
$ 1.06 Tax for Texas residents
$ 4.00 Postage and handling .75 each additional
Make check payable to TCU Press
ISBN 0-87565-035-X

FEAST OF GOODNESS

Gruver United Methodist Women
Box 977
Grover, TX 79040   806-733-2156

Feast of Goodness, produced in 1994, contains about 250 delicious recipes gathered throughout the community. In a loose-leaf notebook with extra heavy paper, additional recipes may be added easily. Gruver may be very small, but cooking remains a very special art to most of its citizens.

$14.95 Retail price
$ 1.00 Postage and handling
Make check payable to Gruver UMW

THE FIRST TEXAS COOKBOOK

Eakin Press
P.O. Drawer 90159
Austin, TX 78709-0159   800-880-8642

A handsome reprint of the 1883 original of recipes from great-grandmother's kitchen collected by the ladies of the First Presbyterian Church of Houston. Original Texana with colorful words and phrases (such as yelk, instead of yolk), but also no-non-sense recipes for today's cooks.

$14.95 Retail price
$ .93 Tax for Texas residents
$ 1.50 Postage and handling
Make check payable to Eakin Press
ISBN 0-89015-518-6

FORT WORTH IS COOKING!

by Renie Steves
1406 Thomas Place
Fort Worth, TX 76107   817-732-4758

Fort Worth is Cooking! is for affluent diners who eat out regularly and also enjoy cooking at home. Twenty-two of Fort Worth's favorite restaurants, with editorial information, recipes, nutritional analysis and recipe modifications, signature dishes, wine and food pairing. Eight color photographs of owners and chefs are included in 120 pages.

$16.95 Retail price
$ 1.31 Tax for Texas residents
$ 2.00 Postage and handling
Make check payable to Cuisine Concepts
ISBN 0-9635470-1-1

THE FOUR INGREDIENT COOKBOOK
and MORE OF THE FOUR INGREDIENT COOKBOOK

Coffee and Cale
P. O. Box 2121
Kerrville, TX 78029   800-757-0838 / 210-895-5538

These simple recipes are great for those times when you don't feel like cooking, but you have to any-way! You will be amazed at what you can easily create in your kitchen with *Four Ingredients*. Over 200 recipes in each book using four ingredients (and sometimes less). Great time savers.

$ 9.95 Retail price each book
$ 1.00 Tax for Texas residents
$ 2.95 Postage and handling each book
Make check payable to Coffee and Cale
ISBN 0-9628550-06, 0-9628550-1-4

FROM CAJUN ROOTS TO TEXAS BOOTS

by Cookie Brisbin
P. O. Box 1108
Marfa, TX 79843-1108   915-729-3358

This 80-page cookbook is a collection of 250 recipes, including helpful cooking hints, gathered over the past 25 years from family and friends from the piney woods of North Louisiana to the mountains of Far West Texas.

$ 9.32 Retail price
$ .68 Tax for Texas residents
$ 2.75 Postage and handling
Make check payable to Cookie Brisbin

FROM GENERATION TO GENERATION

Sisterhood of Temple Emanu-El
8500 Hillcrest
Dallas, TX 75225   214-706-0000

From Generation to Generation, the award-winning cookbook from the Sisterhood of Temple Emanu-El in Dallas is a must for all who love to cook...and eat! The beautiful 330-page 4-color volume contains over 400 sumptious recipes and delightful paintings and illustrations along with useful tips and entertaining stories.

$16.95 Retail price
$ 1.40 Tax for Texas residents
$ 2.50 Postage and handling
Make check payable to Sisterhood of Temple Emanu-El
ISBN 0-9635036-0-X

THE GATHERING

The Blue Bird Circle
615 West Alabama
Houston, TX 77006   713-528-5607 or 528-0470

The washable hardback cover that lies flat has beautiful original artwork. 219 pages of 500 triple-tested recipes for both novice and gourmet cooks, including an outstanding party section and an excellent wild game section. Proceeds benefit The Blue Bird Circle Clinic for Pediatric Neurology in Houston's Texas Medical Center.

$12.95 Retail price
$ 1.04 Tax for Texas residents
$ 2.00 Postage and handling
Make check payable to The Blue Bird Circle
ISBN 0-9617897-0-0

GATHERING OF THE GAME
by Judy Barbour
2515 Carrington
Bay City, TX 77414   409-245-9322

A new and exciting, comprehensive and dynamic wild game, game birds and fish cookbook. *Gathering of the Game* is an invaluable resource that will enhance your enjoyment of preparing your bounty of the great outdoors—beautiful green cover with original art of game; gold-stamped. 140 pages, 115 recipes.

$15.95 Retail price
$ 1.16 Tax for Texas residents
$ 1.75 Postage and handling
Make check payable to Judy Barbour Books
ISBN 0-9611746-9-2

GATHERINGS
A WEST TEXAS COLLECTION OF RECIPES
Caprock Girl Scout Council
2567 74th
Lubbock, TX 79423   806-745-2855

From the ranches of Dickens, Bailey, Cockran and Parmer and the farms of Motley, Briscoe and Crosby Counties, our Girl Scout families have searched through mama's cookbooks to pick the best of their treasured recipes. Long remembered Sunday dinners in Garza, Castro, Swisher, Hale, Floyd, Lubbock, Hockley, and Lamb Counties have resulted in these one-of-a kind delights.

$12.95 Retail price
$ 1.00 Tax for Texas residents
$ 2.75 Postage and handling
Make check payable to Caprock Girl Scout Council

GINGERBREAD...and all the trimmings

Waxahachie Junior Service League, Inc.
P. O. Box 294
Waxahachie, TX 75165   214-937-2290

Just as our fine old homes in Waxahachie have all the trimmings, so does our cookbook. Historic Waxahachie homes are highlighted in each section and will guide you through the 258 pages and over 1,000 wonderfully tried and tested recipes. The next best thing to this cookbook would be joining a member for dinner in Waxahachie!

$15.95 Retail price
$ 2.50 Postage and handling
Make check to Waxahachie Junior Service League
ISBN 0-9623576-0-X

GOURMET GRAINS, BEANS, & RICE
by Dotty Griffith
Taylor Publishing Company
1550 W. Mockingbird Lane
Dallas, TX 75235   800-759-8120

Delicious recipes for healthful living. Includes tips on how to use kidney beans in fresh ways and how to incorporate meatless meals into the diet without giving up meat altogether. More than 200 recipes and a 16-page full-color insert.

$17.95 Retail price
$ 1.39 Tax for Texas residents
$ 3.00 Postage and handling
Make check payable to Taylor Publishing Company
ISBN 0-87833-785-7

GREAT FLAVORS OF TEXAS
Southern Flavors, Inc.
P. O. Box 922
Pine Bluff, AR 71613   800-874-5725

Great Flavors of Texas is a celebration of the distinctiveness and diversity of the Texas cooking experience. It provides very definite flavors of Texas to the non-native, and is a marvelous memento for the Texas native and visitor of the wonderful times and grand food that Texas offers!! We invite you to savor and enjoy!!!

$11.50 Retail price (includes postage,
        handling and tax)
Make check payable to Southern Flavors, Inc.
ISBN 0-9618137-2-5

GREAT TASTES OF TEXAS
by Barbara C. Jones
1901 South Shore Drive
Bonham, TX 75418   903-583-2832

Make Texas cooking quick and easy with this mini-cookbook full of zest and flavor. Recipes for taste-tempting treats. It's small, but big on flavor and fun!

$ 4.95 Retail price
$ .37 Tax for Texas residents
$ 1.75 Postage and handling
Make check payable to BCJ Publications
ISBN 0-9630404-5-6

HOMECOMING
SPECIAL FOODS, SPECIAL MEMORIES
Baylor Alumni Association
700 S. University Parks Dive, 2nd floor
P.O. Box 97116
Waco, TX 76706   1-800-BAYLORU

A collection of over 400 twice-tested recipes, interspersed with entertaining stories and quotes, *Homecoming* offers the best from the kitchens of Baylor alumni and friends. From quick and easy dishes to Grandma's favorites to current food trends— each recipe has that "something extra," in a book of more than 300 pages.

$16.95 Retail price
$ 1.40 Tax for Texas residents
$ 2.00 Postage and handling
Make check payable to B.A.S.E.
ISBN 0-9640969-0-0

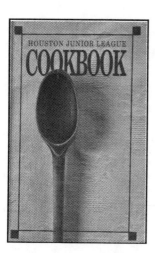

HOUSTON JUNIOR LEAGUE COOKBOOK
Junior League of Houston, Inc.
1811 Briar Oaks Lane
Houston, TX 77027   713-627-COOK

With more than 100,000 copies sold since its debut in 1968, *The Houston Junior League Cookbook* has long been a favorite not only of Houston cooks, but with cookbook aficionados around the country. The book features straightforward, easy-to-follow recipes, using ingredients found in most refrigerators and pantry shelves. A beautiful gift.

$14.95 Retail price
$ 1.23 Tax for Texas residents
$ 2.81 Postage and handling
Make check to The Junior League of Houston, Inc.
ISBN 0-9632421-0-5

I COOK - YOU CLEAN
by Barbara C. Jones
1901 South Shore Drive
Bonham, TX 75418   903-583-2832

I Cook - You Clean is cooking made easy with delicious results. It is practical and designed for everyday use—using "ready" foods and seasonings you already have in your pantry. Great menus for special occasions.

$11.95 Retail price
$ .89 Tax for Texas residents
$ 3.00 Postage and handling
Make check payable to BCJ Publications
ISBN 0-9630405-0-5

JANE LONG'S BRAZORIA INN
AN EARLY TEXAS COOKBOOK

Coldwater Press
9806 Coldwater Circle
Dallas, TX 75228   214-328-7612

The story of Texas' fight for representative government and religious freedom unfolds dramatically while you read the "receipts" for Stephen Fuller Austin's favorite Brazos River Catfish or General Sam Houston's Spice Cake. A look at pioneer life over the shoulder of a *courageous pioneer woman—the "Mother of Texas"*—who saw it all.

$ 9.95 Retail price
$ .83 Tax for Texas residents
$ 2.20 Postage and handling
Make check payable to Coldwater Press
ISBN 1-880384-02-7

THE JUBILEE OF OUR MANY BLESSINGS COOKBOOK

United Methodist Women of
Highland Park United Methodist Church
3705 Marquette
Dallas, TX 75225   214-368-4497

A collectible heritage cookbook of treasured and favorite recipes for your enjoyment and health. Celebrating the 75th anniversary of Highland Park United Methodist Church and the food and customs that unite us. A joyful mingling of our best efforts as cooks and keepers of the hearth and home.

$14.95 Retail price
$ 3.50 Postage and handling
Make check payable to Dallas Bethlehem Center, 4410 Leland, Dallas, TX 75215

THE KIMBELL COOKBOOK

by Shelby Schafer
3333 Camp Bowie Blvd.
Ft. Worth, TX 76107   817-332-8451

A collection of recipes from The Buffet Restaurant in The Kimbell Art Museum. After testing, tasting, writing, and rewriting, here are some of the most popular appetizers, soups, salads, and desserts offered.

$14.95 Retail price
$ 1.25 Tax for Texas residents
$ 4.00 Postage and handling
Make check payable to The Kimbell Art Museum
ISBN 0-912804-23-8

LEAN STAR CUISINE
by Terry Conlan
Lake Austin Spa Resort
1705 Quinlan Park Road
Austin, TX 78732   512-266-2444 or 800-847-5637

Delicious lowfat Southwestern cooking from the kitchen of Lake Austin Spa Resort. Whether it's BBQ, Cajun, or Tex-Mex; Appetizers, Entrees, or Desserts, you'll find healthy, inspired interpretations of your regional favorites. It's the whole (and wholesome) enchilada! 275 pages and 200 recipes with calories and fat grams listed for each.

$ 19.95 Retail price
$ 1.45 Tax for Texas residents
$ 3.00 Postage and handling
Make check payable to Lake Austin Spa Resort
ISBN 0-9619476-1-6

THE LITE SWITCH
LOW FAT COOKBOOK & HEALTH GUIDE
by June McLean Jeter
P.O. Box 121242
Arlington, TX 76012   800-6LOWFAT

Over 600 delicious low-fat, low cholesterol recipes, most with 5 grams of fat or less. No guess work—planned menus complete with grocery shopping list provided. Step-by-step instruction on fat grams and making substitutions, as well as tips on getting started, eating right, staying committed, and not feeling deprived!

$ 19.95 Retail price
$ 1.55 Tax for Texas residents
$ 3.00 Postage and handling $1 each additional book
Make check payable to *The Lite Switch*
ISBN 0-9634783-0-3

A LITTLE TASTE OF TEXAS
by Barbara C. Jones
1901 South Shore Drive
Bonham, TX 75418   903-583-2832

A Little Taste of Texas is a star-studded mini collection of recipes big on flavor and loaded with sure-fire winners. Top-notch recipes with clearly written instructions and great ideas for family eating or entertaining friends.

$ 6.95 Retail price
$ .52 Tax for Texas residents
$ 1.75 Postage and handling
Make check payable to BCJ Publications

LONE STAR LEGACY and LONE STAR LEGACY II

Austin Junior Forum Publications
P. O. Box 26628
Austin, TX 78755-0628   512-835-9233

An edible geography lesson of regional foods from the Rio Grande Valley to the High Plains. As the first Texas cookbook selected for the Walter S. McIlhenny Community Cookbook Hall of Fame, collectors testify to the value of Lone Star Legacy. Lone Star Legacy II was created in celebration of the Texas Sesquicentennial, and is further testimony of superb Mexican, French, German and typical Texas "ranch" recipes.

$17.95 Retail price each book
$ 2.50 Postage and handling each book
Make check payable to Austin Junior Forum Pub.
ISBN 0-9607152-0-7, 0-9607152-1-5

LOW-CAL COUNTRY

by Louise Dillow
Corona Publishing
P.O. Drawer 12407
San Antonio, TX 78212   210-341-7525

A chatty sequel to Mrs. Blackwell's Heart-of-Texas Cookbook that concentrates on taking the calories and cholesterol out of hearty country cooking.

$13.95 Retail price
$ 1.08 Tax for Texas residents
$ 2.00 Postage and handling
Make check payable to Corona Publishing Co.
ISBN 0-931722-91-2

M.D. ANDERSON VOLUNTEERS COOKING FOR FUN

M.D. Anderson Volunteer Service
1515 Holcombe Blvd. - 115
Houston, TX 77030   713-792-7180

Approximately 550 recipes in a 256-page hardback book. Includes healthy eating recipes from hospital dietitions plus four milkshake-type drinks specially for patients on chemotherapy. Re;cipes from professional chefs plus one from Barbara Bush. Proceeds benefit the Volunteer Endowment for Patient Support at the cancer center.

$15.00 Retail price
$ 3.00 Postage and handling
Make check to M.D. Anderson Cancer Center VEPS
ISBN 0-963031-0-3

THE MANSION ON TURTLE CREEK COOKBOOK

by Dean Fearing
2821 Turtle Creek Blvd.
Dallas 75219-4802   214-559-2100

One of America's most important and innovative chefs, Dean Fearing shares his imaginative, daring, yet relaxed approach to superb cooking in this beautiful cookbook. In it, Chef Fearing offers an eating experience that you must taste to believe—bold yet subtle in flavor, vividly appealing in presentation, and absolutely, utterly delicious.

$27.50 Retail price
$ 2.13 Tax for Texas residents
$ 3.00 Postage and handling
Make check payable to Dean Fearing
ISBN 0-8021-1397-4

MA'S IN THE KITCHEN

THE RECIPES AND HISTORY OF GOVERNOR MIRIAM A. FERGUSON

by Carl R. McQueary and May Nelson Paulissen
Eakin Press
P.O. Box 90159
Austin, TX 78709-0159   800-880-8642

A delicious look at one of the Lone Star State's most remarkable women. More than 200 of Miriam's kitchen tested, down-home recipes. The authors dish up Texas history along with these delightful dishes. Family album photographs, helpful hints, and amazing facts from Ma herself.

$16.95 Retail price
$ 1.06 Tax for Texas residents
$ 1.50 Postage and handling
Make check payable to Eakin Press
ISBN 0-89015-953-X

THE MEXICAN COLLECTION

by Carole Curlee
3806 68th Street
Lubbock, TX 79413   806-795-0982

Come share a fiesta of flavors from San Antonio, Houston, Austin, and Lubbock to Santa Fe, California, and Arizona! 288 exciting recipes from appetizers to desserts...great dips...extraordinary fajita marinades, charts, "how-to's," "Lite" Mexican food tips. A special caterer's collection—a "must have!" Third printing. Plastic cover.

$17.99 Retail price
$ 1.41 Tax for Texas residents
$ 3.25 Postage and handling
Make check payable to Carole Curlee
ISBN 0-9645657-1-4

MORE CALF FRIES TO CAVIAR

Janel Franklin and Sue Vaughn
1012 N. 9th Street
Lamesa, TX 79331   806-872-8667

Do you like good food but...don't know how to cook...don't like to cook...don't have time to cook...just too tired to cook?? Then try these quick, easy and delicious recipes. Too tired? Then just read our fun captions. 300 pages.

$14.95 Retail price
$ 1.35 Tax for Texas residents
$ 2.50 Postage and handling
Make check payable to Jan-Su

MORE OF WHAT'S COOKING

Apples to Zucchini, Inc./Veronica Coronado
P.O. Box 25456
Dallas, TX 75225   214-521-7524

Great tasting recipes for your best health. Recipes are low in fat, cholesterol, and sodium, including ones such as Herbed Feta Cheese, Barbecued Shrimp, Pork Tenderloin with Dijon Mustard Sauce, etc. Simple preparation, easy-to-find ingredients, and great presentation.

$14.95 Retail price each book
$ 1.54 Tax for Texas residents
$ 3.75 Postage and handling each book
Make check payable to Apples to Zucchini, Inc.
ISBN 0-9649658-0-1

MORE TASTES & TALES FROM TEXAS... WITH LOVE

by Peggy E. Hein
Heinco, Inc.
101 Explorer Cove
Austin, TX 78734   512-261-6085

The first collection of *Tastes & Tales From Texas...With Love* has already become a classic addition to tens of thousands of kitchens. *More Tastes & Tales From Texas...With Love* contains 200 all-new recipes drawn from the many distinctive regions of the state—Cajun and Deep South; German and Czech; Ranch-style, and of course delicious Tex-Mex.

$12.00 Retail price
$ .88 Tax for Texas residents
$ 2.25 Postage and handling
Make check payable to Heinco, Inc.
ISBN 0-9613881-1-0

NECESSITIES AND TEMPTATIONS

Junior League of Austin
5416 Parkcrest / Suite 100
Austin, TX 78731   512-467-8982

An attractive hardbound 550-page cookbook with over 600 triple-tested recipes. It contains a comprehensive substitution chart, weights and measures information, and ingredient descriptions. Chapters on entertaining, gift-giving from the kitchen, and menu suggestions make this cookbook an invaluable addition to your collection.

$19.95 Retail price
$ 3.50 Postage and handling
Make check payable to Junior League of Austin
ISBN 0-9605906-1-7

NEW TASTES OF TEXAS

by Peggy E. Hein
Heinco, Inc.
101 Explorer Cove
Austin, TX 78734   512-261-6085

The only thing more satisfying than going back for seconds, is going back for thirds. Yes, you can still have the tastes Texans love, Tex-Mex favorites, Chicken-Fried Steak, etc. with half the fat. Each recipe shows the fat content, just in case you can't believe something could taste so good and still be so good for you.

$14.95 Retail price
$ 1.12 Tax for Texas residents
$ 2.00 Postage and handling.
Make check payable to Heinco, Inc.
ISBN 0-9613881-3-7

THE NEW TEXAS CUISINE

by Stephan Pyles
Star Canyon
3102 Oaklawn Avenue Suite 144
Dallas, TX 75219   214-520-8111

Features award-winning Chef Stephan Pyles' recipes adapted from Texas' many different cultures and historical eras. A comprehensive overview and documentation of culinary styles throughout the state's hustory. Through richly illustrated photography, the diversity of Texas' landscape is paralleled to the ethnically diverse foods. 428 pages.

$35.00 Retail price
$ 2.89 Tax for Texas residents
$ 5.00 Postage and handling
Make check payable to Star Canyon
ISBN 0-385-42336-5

THE NEW TEXAS WILD GAME COOK BOOK

by Judith and Richard Morehead
Eakin Press
P.O. Box 90159
Austin, TX 78709-0159   800-880-8642

Wildgame is more nutritious than domestic meat, higher in protein, lower in fat, higher in fiber, lower in sodium. Wild game recipes range from venison, dove, quail, pheasant, turkey, waterfowl, and imported sheep, to javelina, armadillo, and 'possum.

$12.95 Retail price
$ .81 Tax for Texas residents
$ 1.50 Postage and handling
Make check payable to Eakin Press
ISBN 0-89015-526-7

NOT JUST BACON & EGGS

Straw Hat Productions
P. O. Box 8771
Houston, TX 77249   713-692-5622

Easy-to-read cookbook offers delicious recipes for simple to fancy breakfasts and early lunches. For the beginner cook, sections on how to cook eggs and breakfast meats. Recipes for preparing the morning meal the night before. Tips for making pancakes, crepes, biscuits and more. Ideas for quick breakfasts. Full color laminated cover. 164 pages.

$ 9.95 Retail price
$ .95 Tax for Texas residents
$ 1.50 Postage and handling
Make check payable to Straw Hat Productions
ISBN 0-9619202-1-1

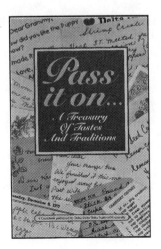

PASS IT ON...

Delta Delta Delta National Fraternity
2313 Brookhollow Plaza Drive
Arlington, TX 76006   817-633-8001

Pass It On... is a collection of 373 delectable recipes (256 pages), food memories and words of wisdom we have shared and passed from one friend to another. *Pass It On...* will inspire family, friends, novice and experienced cooks with ideas, recipes and special moments to savor.

$17.95 Retail price
$ 1.40 Tax for Texas residents
$ 3.00 Postage and handling
Make check payable to Delta Delta Delta
ISBN 0-9639957-0-7

THE PEACH TREE FAMILY COOKBOOK and THE PEACH TREE TEA ROOM COOKBOOK

by Cynthia Collins Pedregon
210 South Adams
Fredericksburg, TX 78624 210-997-9527 or 800-255-3355

These cookbooks have received raves! Practical, down-to-earth, fabulous recipes for soups, salads, quiches, breads, and remarkable desserts that are served in our Tea Room. Wonderful *handed-down* family recipes, and ones from creative friends included. 256 pages, over 200 recipes per book.

$19.95 Retail price each book
$ 1.97 Tax for Texas residents
$ 3.95 Postage and handling; two books $4.95
Make check payable to The Peach Tree Gift Gallery
ISBN 0-9627590-0-7, 0-9267590-7-4

PERFECTLY SPLENDID

ONE FAMILY'S REPASTS
McFaddin-Ward House
1906 McFaddin Avenue
Beaumont, TX 77701-1525   409-832-1906

Perfectly Splendid consists of 128 pages with 150 recipes, supplementary family history, anecdotes, and photographs of McFaddin family, friends, servants, and kitchen and dining pieces. A unique blend of family recipes once served in this Southern mansion now operated as a museum.

$ 9.95 Retail price
$ .82 Tax for Texas residents
$ 3.00 Postage and handling
Make check payable to McFaddin-Ward House
ISBN 0-9622837-1-1

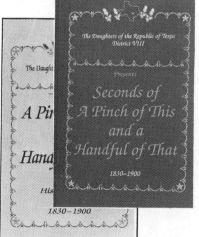

A PINCH OF THIS AND A HANDFUL OF THAT and SECONDS OF A PINCH OF THIS AND A HANDFUL OF THAT

Daughters of the Republic of Texas District VIII
Eakin Press
P.O. Box 90159
Austin, TX 78709-0159   800-880-8642

The Republic of Texas was in its infancy when some of the classic and historic recipes in these cookbooks were being used by Texas pioneers. Includes recipes, household hints, and home remedies handed down by DRT families. Some original spelling, grammar, and family names included.

$15.95 Retail price each book
$ 1.00 Tax for Texas residents
$ 1.50 Postage and handling each book
Make check payable to Eakin Press
ISBN 0-89015-649-2, 0-89015-970-X

POTLUCK ON THE PEDERNALES and POTLUCK ON THE PEDERNALES SECOND HELPING

Community Garden Club of Johnson City
P. O. Box 860
Johnson City, TX 78636   210-868-7206 or 868-7572

Potluck on the Pedernales, a regional winner in the Tabasco Community Cookbook contest, features "down-home cooking from deep in the heart of L.B.J. Country." *Second Helping* is much more and contains no duplicates!! Both books include interesting anecdotes relating to cooking and stories of how the recipes originated.

$16.95   Retail price I, $16.95 II
$ 3.00   Postage and handling, $5.00 for two books
Make check payable to Potluck on the Pedernales
ISBN 0-89015-829-0, 0-89015-090-2

RAIDER RECIPES

by David and Dawn Fleming
2629 19th Street
Lubbock, TX 79410   806-793-3330

Raider Recipes is a collection of recipes from students, alumni, faculty, and staff of Texas Tech University. *Raider Recipes* contains at least one recipe from every graduating class of Texas Tech, from the first class in 1927 to the class of 1991.

$10.95   Retail price
$ .86   Tax for Texas residents
$ 2.00   Postage and handling
Make check payable to Raider Recipes
ISBN 0-9628191-0-7

RALEIGH HOUSE COOKBOOK and RALEIGH HOUSE COOKBOOK II

by Martha R. Johnson
1431 Lois Street
Kerrville, TX 78028   210-895-2982

These cookbooks contain recipes used in Martha Johnson's restaurant, Raleigh House, in the Texas Hill Country which she operated for 34 years. Also contains favorite family recipes dating back to her Great Grandmother, recipes from friends, with some of her own. Methods and ingredients are sometimes revised for easier preparation. Both books big and full of great recipes!

$19.95   Retail price each book
$ 1.65   Tax for Texas residents
$ 2.00   Postage and handling each book
Make check payable to Raleigh House
ISBN 0-9631037-0-9, 0-9631037-1-7

SAN ANTONIO CUISINE

Two Lane Press, Inc.
4245 Walnut
Kansas City, MO 64111   816-531-3119

Karen Haram, renowned Food Editor for the *San Antonio Express News,* highlights a mouth watering assortment of over 140 recipes that include Restaurant Biga's "Sizzling Mushrooms," Anaqua Grill's "Carmel Pecan Tart," and Apple Annie's Tea Room's favorite—"Sawdust Pie." High-style, Southwest, Tex-Mex and down-home recipes.

$14.95 Retail price
$ 3.75 Postage and handling
Make check payable to Two Lane Press, Inc.
ISBN 1-878686-11-9

THE SECOND TYPICALLY TEXAS COOKBOOK

Texas Electric Cooperatives, Inc.
8140 Burnet Road
Austin, TX 78757-7799   512-454-0311 Ext. 260

These "down-home" recipes are contributed by some of the best country cooks from all across Texas. Designed as a sharing of good food just as you might exchange recipes at a social gathering, or over a backyard fence. Uses ingredients generally on your shelf. 556 pages, 1,478 recipes, ringbound hardback, illustrated, color photographs.

$13.95 Retail price
$ 1.15 Tax for Texas residents
$ 3.24 Postage and handling
Make check payable to Texas Electric Cooperatives

SMOKE & SPICE

by Cheryl Alters Jamison and Bill Jamison
Harvard Common Press
535 Albany Street
Boston, MA 02118   617-423-5803

Cheryl and Bill Jamison have let us in on all of their smoking secrets. They guide the novice and suggest brilliant new recipes to old-hands at smoke-cooked barbecue. This winner of a James Beard Award is a guide book and a cookbook with more than 300 recipes, generous tips, quirky lore, and a down-home sense of humor.

$16.95 Retail price (pb) $29.95 (hdcv)
$ 3.00 Postage and handling
Make check payable to The Harvard Common Press
ISBN 1-55832-061-X (pb) 1-55832-060-1 (hdcv)

SOME LIKE IT HOT

Junior League of McAllen
P. O. Box 2465
McAllen, TX 78502   210-682-0743

The climate, culture, and cuisine of South Texas abound in 400 kitchen-tested recipes. Seafoods, tropical fruits and vegetables, "caliente" Mexican flavors, and wild game are some of the ingredients used to create distinctly imaginative dishes. A 1993 Tabasco Community Cookbook Southwest Regional Award Recipient, it's a winner!

$16.95 Retail price
$ 3.00 Postage and handling
Make check payable to Junior League of McAllen
ISBN 0-9633359-0-1

SOUTH TEXAS MEXICAN COOKBOOK

by Lucy Garza
Eakin Press
P.O. Box 90159
Austin, TX 78709-0159   800-880-8642

This delightful cookbook is straight from the *cocina* of a South Texas traditional Mexican home. Don't expect the regular fare of restaurants specializing in "Mexican" food, but a nostalgic trip down memory lane, and tidbits to tantalize even the most avid gourmet.

$14.95 Retail price
$ .93 Tax for Texas residents
$ 1.50 Postage and handling
Make check payable to Eakin Press
ISBN 0-89015-344-2

SOUTHWEST OLÉ!

by Barbara C. Jones
1901 South Shore Drive
Bonham, TX 75418   903-583-2832

Southwest Olé! contains 115 mouth-watering recipes, always enticing, often spicy and well seasoned with bravado! Exciting foods that capture the spirit and spice of Southwestern cuisine. Zesty specialties of the Southwest!

$ 6.95 Retail price
$ .52 Tax for Texas residents
$ 1.75 Postage and handling
Make check payable to BCJ Publications

SOUTHWEST SIZZLER
by Barbara C. Jones
1901 South Shore Drive
Bonham, TX 75418   903-583-2832

Southwest Sizzler has over 100 well-tested recipes that are spicy and zesty, and above all, *good*. It is clearly presented and easy to follow for family fare or festive entertainment. Tantalizing dishes with unique flavor—a colorful taste of the Southwest.

$ 6.95 Retail price
$ .52 Tax for Texas residents
$ 1.75 Postage and handling
Make check payable to BCJ Publications

THE STAR OF TEXAS COOKBOOK
Junior League of Houston, Inc.
1811 Briar Oaks Lane
Houston, TX 77027   713-627-COOK

A real keepsake, this is The Junior League of Houston's more contemporary cookbook. It has achieved a national reputation, being named as one of the top three Southwest cuisine cookbooks by Inglenook Navalle in 1991. Offering 52 different menus for special occasions, it offers a wine selection guide, historical vignettes, and great recipes with Texas flavor and flare.

$19.95 Retail price
$ 1.64 Tax for Texas residents
$ 2.71 Postage and handling
Make check payable to The Junior League of Houston, Inc.
ISBN 0-963-242-1-1-3

The Taste of Herbs

compiled by the
Amarillo Herb Society

THE TASTE OF HERBS
Amarillo Herb Society
1400 Streit Drive
Amarillo, TX 79106   806-352-6513

The inspiration for *The Taste of Herbs* came from the many requests for a cookbook from attendees to our annual herb luncheons. Our plans for the future will be to have supplements available from our luncheons. There are 366 recipes with numerous tips and herb uses throughout the book.

$18.00 Retail price
$ 4.00 Postage and handling
Make check payable to Amarillo Herb Society

TEXAS ACCENTS

Cancer Research Foundation of North Texas
900 W. Randol Mill Road
Ste. 204
Arlington, TX 76012   817-261-7654

The recipes were submitted by some of the women that are members of the Women's Auxiliary of the Cancer Research Foundation of North Texas. The recipes are family favorites. 180 pages containing approximately 370 recipes.

$10.00 Retail price
$ 2.00 Postage and handling
Make check payable to Cancer Research Foundation of North Texas Women's Auxiliary
ISBN 0-87197-272-7

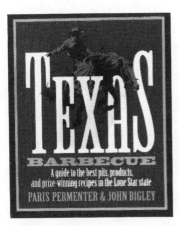

TEXAS BARBECUE

by Paris Permenter and John Bigley
Pig Out Publications, Inc.
4245 Walnut
Kansas City, MO 64111   816-531-3119

The authors journey through the smoky barbecue belt of South Central Texas sharing flavorful excursions in 40 cities and towns. Includes listings of barbecue cook-offs, festivals, mail order sources, etc. Next time you crave barbecue, grab this book to try your hand at real Texas barbecue.

$14.95 Retail price
$ 3.75 Postage and handling
Make check payable to Pig Out Publications, Inc.
ISBN 0-925175-20-X

TEXAS BORDER COOKBOOK

by W. Park Kerr and Norma Kerr
The El Paso Chile Company
909 Texas Avenue
El Paso, TX 79901   915-544-3434

The El Paso Chile Company's Texas Border Cookbook makes all the mouth-watering foods of the borderland accessible to every home cook. Here you will find over 150 recipes, 272 pages—including old favorites and innovative dishes—guaranteed to please the most hot-headed "chile heads" and everyone else who loves Tex-Mex food.

$15.00 Retail price
$ 5.00 Postage and handling (includes tax)
Make check payable to El Paso Chile Co.
ISBN 0-688-10941-1

TEXAS COOKIN' LONE STAR STYLE

Telephone Pioneers of America
Lone Star Chapter 22
One Bell Plaza, Room 315 (TC2)
Dallas, TX 75202   214-464-6115 or 817-279-0600

Texas Cookin' Lone Star Style is very user-friendly. For those following their doctors' instructions, or at least attempting to, it includes everything one could want to know about each recipe, from servings to grams to techniques. Selections range from "good old" recipes from older generations to those of today. Spiral bound for easy handling.

$10.00 Retail price
$ 2.00 Postage and handling
Make check payable to Telephone Pioneers of Am #22
ISBN 0-87197-295-6

THE TEXAS EXPERIENCE

Richardson Woman's Club
2005 North Cliffe Drive
Richardson, TX 75082   214-234-1443

The Texas Experience: Friendship and Food Texas Style contains over 800 double and triple-tested recipes in a 376-page hardback edition. Fantastic recipes, The Texas Favorites section, color photos and bits of Texas trivia combine to make a nationally recognized book in its 8th printing with over $210,000 donated back to the local community.

$16.50 Retail price
$ 1.36 Tax for Texas residents
$ 3.50 Postage and handling
Make check payable to *The Texas Experience*
ISBN 0-960941-60-6

TEXAS HOME COOKING

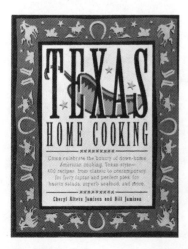

Cheryl Alters Jamison and Bill Jamison
Harvard Common Press
535 Albany Street
Boston, MA 02118   617-423-5803

Anglo, Mexican, Cajun, German, Czech, and other influences combine to make Texas cooking vibrant, colorful, and delectable. In over 400 mouth-watering recipes and with a wagon load of anecdotes and tales, Cheryl and Bill Jamison celebrate the breadth and bounty of true Texas cooking.

$16.95 Retail price (pb) $29.95 (hdcv)
$ 3.00 Postage and handling
Make check payable to The Harvard Common Press
ISBN 1-55832-059-8 (pb) 1-55832-058-X (hdcv)

TEXAS SAMPLER

Junior League of Richardson
1021 Hampshire Lane
Richardson, TX 75080 214-644-6269
Fax 214-644-0505

Texas Sampler, "Handmade-Homemade...Recipes You're Bound to Love" is an appealing touchstone of simpler times geared for present day living. The 400+ superb recipes feature dozens of freezes-well, make-ahead, holiday, time saver, and family friendly fare.

$16.95   Retail price
$ 1.40   Tax for Texas residents
$ 3.50   Postage and handling
Make check payable to Junior League of Richardson
ISBN 0-9612810-5-7

THE 30-MINUTE LIGHT GOURMET

by Lulu Grace
Taylor Publishing Company
1550 W. Mockingbird Lane
Dallas, TX 75235 800-759-8120

Prepare healthy, delicious meals in 30 minutes or less with Lulu Grace's collection of mouth-watering dishes designed to be low in saturated fats, sodium, and calories. Includes nutrition analysis of all recipes and special microwave and grilling chapters.

$18.95   Retail price
$ 1.47   Tax for Texas residents
$ 2.00   Shipping and handling
Make check payable to Taylor Publishing Company
ISBN 0-87833-671-6

TOP CHEFS IN TEXAS

by Sarah Jane English
Eakin Press
P.O. Box 90159
Austin, TX 78709-0159 800-880-8642

"Sarah Jane English...culls recipes from a corps of inventive chefs and organizes them in cleverly conceived menus, coupled with not one but two wine choices for each course. From appetizers to desserts, offerings will intrigue those in the know— and others out of it." *—Publisher's Weekly*

$15.95   Retail price
$ 1.00   Tax for Texas residents
$ 1.50   Postage and handling
Make check payable to Eakin Press
ISBN 0-89015-756-1

WHAT'S COOKING AT THE COOPER CLINIC

It's Cooking, Inc./Veronica Coronado
P.O. Box 25456
Dallas, TX 75225   214-521-7524

Recipes for heart-healthy, scrumptious dishes for your best health. Recipes are low-fat, low-cholesterol, low sodium, and delicious. Simple preparation, easy-to-find ingredients and great presentation. Meat-free meals, Mexican and Italian dishes, wholesome breads...all nutritiously delicious!

$14.95   Retail price each book
$ 1.54   Tax for Texas residents
$ 3.75   Postage and handling each book
Make check payable to It's Cooking, Inc.
ISBN 0-9633862-0-4

WILD ABOUT TEXAS

Cypress Woodlands Junior Forum
P. O. Box 90020, Dept. 242
Houston, TX 77290-0020   713-580-4970

A Bouquet of Recipes, Wildflowers, and Wines. The national Wildflower Research Center offers studies and information on preserving wildflowers. Cover artist Rosario Baxter includes 12 color botanicals of Texas wildflowers. More than 400 tested recipes and an informative section on Texas wines by Sarah Jane English. Proceeds benefit community.

$19.95   Retail price
$ 4.00   Postage and handling
Make check payable to *Wild About Texas*
ISBN 0-9622009-0-5

THE WILD WILD WEST

Junior League of Odessa, Inc.
2707 Kermit Highway
Odessa, TX 79763   915-332-0095

Wild Wild West has wonderful tastes from the West. Recipes include the amount of time it takes to make each one, a feature that is very helpful for the busy person in menu planning.

$19.95   Retail price
$ 1.56   Tax for Texas residents
$ 3.50   Postage and handling
Make check payable to Junior League of Odessa, Inc.
ISBN 0-9612508-1-X

THE QUAIL RIDGE PRESS
"BEST OF THE BEST" COOKBOOK SERIES

The cookbooks in the Quail Ridge Press "Best of the Best" series are considered the most complete survey available of a state's particular cooking style and flavor. They are compiled by searching out a comprehensive cross-section of the leading cookbooks written and published within the state, and then requesting the authors, editors, and publishers of these books to select their most popular recipes. A sampling of these recipes has been selected to create that state's "Best of the Best" edition. Each recipe included in the book is a proven favorite that conveys the state's unique cuisine.

A catalog section in each volume lists the contributing cookbooks with descriptive copy and ordering information on each book. This section is of particular interest and value to cookbook collectors. The volumes listed below have been completed as of January, 1997.

Best of the Best from Alabama 288 pages, (28-3) $14.95	**Best of the Best from Louisiana** 288 pages, (13-5) $14.95	**Best of the Best from Oklahoma** 288 pages, (65-8) $14.95
Best of the Best from Arkansas 288 pages, (43-7) $14.95	**Best of the Best from Michigan** 288 pages, (69-0) $14.95	**Best of the Best from Pennsylvania** 320 pages, (47-X) $14.95
Best of the Best from Florida 288 pages, (16-X) $14.95	**Best of the Best from Mississippi** 288 pages, (19-4) $14.95	**Best of the Best from South Carolina** 288 pages, (39-9) $14.95
Best of the Best from Georgia 336 pages, (30-5) $14.95	**Best of the Best from Missouri** 304 pages, (44-5) $14.95	**Best of the Best from Tennessee** 288 pages, (20-8) $14.95
Best of the Best from Illinois 288 Pages, (58-5) $14.95	**Best of the Best from New England** 368 pages, (50-X) $16.95	**Best of the Best from Texas I** 352 pages, (14-3) $14.95
Best of the Best from Indiana 288 pages, (57-7) $14.95	**Best of the Best from North Carolina** 288 pages, (38-0) $14.95	**Best of the Best from Texas II** 352 pages, (62-3) $16.95
Best of the Best from Kentucky 288 pages, (27-5) $14.95	**Best of the Best from Ohio** 352 pages, (68-2) $16.95	**Best of the Best from Virginia** 320 pages, (41-0) $14.95

All books comb bound, unless noted otherwise.
ISBN Prefix: 0-937552-; suffix noted in parentheses under each title.
See next page for complete listing of Quail Ridge Press cookbooks.

 QUAIL RIDGE PRESS • 1-800-343-1583

"Best of the Best" Cookbook Series:

Alabama	(28-3)	$14.95		*New England*	(50-X)	$16.95
Arkansas	(43-7)	$14.95		*North Carolina*	(38-0)	$14.95
Florida	(16-X)	$14.95		*Ohio*	(68-2)	$16.95
Georgia	(30-5)	$14.95		*Oklahoma*	(65-8)	$14.95
Illinois	(58-5)	$14.95		*Pennsylvania*	(47-X)	$14.95
Indiana	(57-7)	$14.95		*South Carolina*	(39-9)	$14.95
Kentucky	(27-5)	$14.95		*Tennessee*	(20-8)	$14.95
Louisiana	(13-5)	$14.95		*Texas I*	(14-3)	$14.95
Michigan	(69-0)	$14.95		*Texas II*	(62-3)	$16.95
Mississippi	(19-4)	$14.95		*Virginia*	(41-0)	$14.95
Missouri	(44-5)	$14.95				

Individuals may purchase the full 21-volume set for a special "Best Club" price of $225.00 (a 30% discount off the regular price of $317.95) plus $5.00 shipping. Becoming a member of the "Best Club" will entitle you to a 25% discount on future volumes. Call for information on discounts for joining the "Best of the Month Club."

The Quail Ridge Press Cookbook Series:

	ISBN SUFFIX
The Little New Orleans Cookbook (hardbound) $8.95	42-9
The Little Gumbo Book (hardbound) $8.95	17-8
The Little Bean Book (hardbound) $9.95	32-1
Gourmet Camping $9.95	45-3
Lite Up Your Life $14.95	40-2
Hors D'Oeuvres Everybody Loves $5.95	11-9
The Seven Chocolate Sins $5.95	01-1
A Salad A Day $5.95	02-X
Quickies for Singles $5.95	03-8
The Twelve Days of Christmas Cookbook $5.95	00-3
The Country Mouse Cheese Cookbook $5.95	10-0
The Complete Venison Cookbook $22.95	70-4

ISBN Prefix: 0-937552-. All books are comb bound unless noted otherwise. Prices subject to change. To order, send check/money order to:

QUAIL RIDGE PRESS
P. O. Box 123 / Brandon, MS 39043
Or call toll-free to order by VISA or MasterCard:

1-800-343-1583

Please add $2.00 postage for any amount of books sent to one address. Gift wrap with enclosed card add $1.50. Mississippi residents add 7% sales tax. All orders ship within 24 hours. Write or call for free catalog of all QRP books and cookbooks.